A GUIDE TO STATUTORY SOCIAL WORK INTERVENTIONS

A GUIDE TO STATUTORY SOCIAL WORK INTERVENTIONS

THE LIVED EXPERIENCE

MEL HUGHES

First published 2019 by
RED GLOBE PRESS

Red Globe Press in the UK is an imprint of Springer Nature Limited, registered in England, company number 785998, of 4 Crinan Street, London, N1 9XW.

Red Globe Press® is a registered trademark in the United States, the United Kingdom, Europe and other countries.

ISBN 978–1–352–00251–5 paperback

This book is printed on paper suitable for recycling and made from fully managed and sustained forest sources. Logging, pulping and manufacturing processes are expected to conform to the environmental regulations of the country of origin.

A catalogue record for this book is available from the British Library.

A catalog record for this book is available from the Library of Congress.

CONTENTS

CONTRIBUTORS

Julia Armstrong is a social worker in the Drug and Alcohol Statutory Team (DAST) for Bournemouth Borough Council.

Jennifer Bigmore is a lecturer in social work at Bournemouth University and an experienced children and family social worker.

Sophie Buckley is a University student with ataxic cerebral palsy and contributor to the chapter on being supported to live independently.

Rosslyn Dray is a lecturer in social work at Bournemouth University and an experienced social worker and Approved Mental Health Professional (AMHP).

Fay (name changed) has a history of substance use, depression, domestic abuse and eating disorders, and is a contributor to the chapter on being assessed as needing substance use treatment.

Naomi Fraser is an experienced adoption social worker currently with Aspire Adoption.

Sarah Fulton is mother to Jack and Harry and contributor to the chapter on having an s17 Child in Need assessment.

Maggie Harris is a young carers officer within the Borough of Poole children and young people's social care.

Dr Mel Hughes is Principal academic in social work and academic lead for the PIER (Public Involvement in Education and Research) Partnership at Bournemouth University.

Gareth Hunter, along with his wife, is an approved adopter and contributor to the chapter on being approved as an adopter.

Rachel Jury is a user of adult locality and hospital social work services and contributor to the chapter on being assessed under the Care Act.

Kirsty, Niki, Ant and Lee (names changed) are part of a young carers' group and contributed to the chapter on having a young carer's assessment.

Stefan Kleipoedszus is a lecturer in social work at Bournemouth University and previously the Principal Social worker for children and families for Bournemouth Borough Council.

Leanne is mother to O and contributor to the chapter on having a child taken into care.

Dr Sally Lee is a lecturer in social work at Bournemouth University and an experienced adult social worker. She completed her doctoral research exploring social work practice, physical disability and sexual well-being.

Zoe McQuade is a care leaver, newly qualified social worker and contributor to the chapter on being taken into care.

Tim Mitchell is a senior social worker with the Poole Child Health and Disability team.

Richard Murphy is a lecturer in social work at Bournemouth University, an experienced AMPH and social worker.

Margaret Parker is the dementia lead for Tricuro, a Local Authority Trading Company wholly owned by Dorset, Bournemouth and Poole Councils. Margaret is a qualified social worker and practice educator with over 30 years' experience in adult social care, including working for ten years with people living with the later stages of dementia within day services settings.

Penny Riggs is a social worker and area practice manager based at Poole General Hospital with experience as a Senior Support Worker within a mental health charity; a qualified social worker within a Community Team for Adults and her current role in the local acute hospitals supporting hospital discharges for adults.

Sue Smith describes herself as a wife, mother, daughter, a carer for her learning-disabled son and more recently her 91-year-old mother who has dementia. Before Sue retired her background was managerial administration and fundraising. Sue is contributor to the chapter on having a carer's assessment.

Emma Spicer is a social worker in adult services with Bournemouth Borough Council.

Michael Wooten is a father, husband, care leaver and newly qualified social worker. He is a contributor to the chapter on having multiple fostering placements.

Zoe is a long-term user of mental health services; active mental health campaigner and contributor to the chapter on being detained under the Mental Health Act.

INTRODUCTION

Mel Hughes

This book provides a key text for social work students and practitioners undertaking or learning about statutory social work interventions such as: being detained under the Mental Health Act; having a child removed to a place of safety; or having a carer's assessment. As a social work student in the UK, you are required to gain experience of statutory tasks involving legal interventions as part of your practice learning. This book will provide you with formal knowledge such as legislative and policy frameworks, but from the perspective of people who have experienced them first-hand. Recognising the expertise of people with a lived experience is an essential part of social work practice but this voice is often lacking within social work text books. *The Guide to Statutory Social Work Interventions: the lived experience,* shares people's experiences in an engaging and person-centred way. We consider dilemmas and difficult decisions social workers have to make and explore the impact of professional judgements and legal interventions on the lives of people we support. Each chapter is written by a service user or carer, with formal content such as broader implications, underpinning legislation, policies and research, added by a social worker. In some chapters, contributors have both areas of expertise as they identify as a service user or carer and are a registered social worker. Our approach to the book is underpinned by principles of: how we learn as adults; values and ethics of the social work profession; and the requirements to involve people with lived experience in social work education in the UK. These, along with how best to use this book to support your own learning and development, are outlined below.

How we learn

This book is underpinned by educational theory and an understanding of how we learn as adults. The leading educational theorist Malcolm Knowles argued that, for adult learning to be effective, we need to view learning as purposeful and relevant to our lives (Knowles, 1984). When encountering new information and knowledge, we draw on and relate it to previous experiences and what we already know in order to form an opinion or conclusion. For many of us, we enter the social work profession with the intention of having a positive impact and to make a difference. Having a positive impact, however, is not always how it is experienced or perceived by people in receipt of social work interventions. In Chapter 6, written by four young carers, for example, all were of the view that social workers had only made their lives worse. As an educational text book, the aim is to create a guide to statutory social work interventions by drawing on the lived experience to make this learning purposeful; to enable you as a social work student to learn about legislation in the context of how it is enacted in practice and to understand the impact it can have. The unique experiences shared within this book can be used as a catalyst, a trigger, from which to critically reflect and analyse current legislation, policy and your own practice.

Values and ethical principles

This book is also underpinned by the values and ethical principles on which social work practice and education is based. In the UK (England, Scotland, Wales and Northern Ireland), these are set out within the British Association of Social Workers' Code of Ethics for Social Work. Key principles include: promoting the right to participation; developing professional relationships; recognising diversity; and working in solidarity (BASW, 2012). The global definition of social work (revised by the International Federation for Social Work in 2014) states that:

> Social work is a practice-based profession and an academic discipline that promotes social change and development, social cohesion, and the empowerment and liberation of people. Principles of social justice, human rights, collective responsibility and respect for diversities are central to social work. Underpinned by theories of social work, social sciences, humanities and indigenous knowledge, social work engages people and structures to address life challenges and enhance wellbeing (IFSW, 2014).

In relation to valuing the lived experience, the global definition is important, particularly in the UK where social work practice is often viewed and evaluated at a personal level – where responsibility is placed with an individual or family to 'address life challenges and enhance well-being' with less emphasis on challenging the systems, structures and external factors such as poverty and oppression which can limit people's ability to do so. The aim of this book is to give a voice to people who have been in receipt of social work services to address this power balance; to enable people with lived experience to generate and inform knowledge of statutory interventions and to shape subsequent practice, interventions and outcomes for others. As recipients of services, their expertise gained from this lived experience is recognised and valued. It is essential when developing a knowledge and understanding of statutory interventions that this incorporates the experiences and perspectives of people for whom these were designed to support and protect.

Language and terminology

The term service users and carers can include a wide range of people. The British Association of Social Workers (BASW) explains how we work with a variety of people in a range of statutory and non-statutory settings including:

➢ Older people

➢ Children with disabilities

➢ Teenagers with mental health problems

➢ Young offenders

➢ Adults with learning disabilities

➢ Adults with a mental health problem

➢ Adults with a physical disability

➢ People with alcohol, drug or other substance misuse problems

➢ Refugees and asylum seekers

➢ People who are socially excluded

➢ Families where there is a risk of family breakdown

➢ Children who need to live apart from their families

➢ Foster carers and adopters

➢ People, including children, who are at risk of abuse or neglect, or have been abused and neglected

➢ Carers

(BASW, 2017)

Involving people with lived experience may not only include people who use social work and social care services but also those with relevant experience who, for whatever reason, do not access services and formal support.

It has been argued that the use of language and terminology over time reflects changes in the social work relationship (McLaughlin, 2009). Consideration of our use of language as social workers is important due to the images different words create in our minds and what this tells us about how we might view a particular person or group and our relationship with them. For example, consider this in relation to the different words used to describe older people: the elderly, geriatrics, community elder and older person are all potentially accurate terms to describe people of older age but create very different images in our minds. As such, they are likely to influence our view or treatment of that person and the power dynamic with them. One concern is that the terms fail to reflect the diversity within this wide-ranging demographic and as such are likely to lead us to see 'older people' as one homogenous group.

McLaughlin (ibid.) suggests that generalised terms such as patient, clients, customers and consumers, and experts by experience and service users are all problematic as they fail to adequately reflect the nature of the social work relationship. This is particularly so in relation to statutory social work interventions, such as those explored in this book, where the person's involvement is not always voluntary and where the choices available to them may be limited. McLaughlin argues that the term 'service user' falls short given its focus on only one aspect of a person's life, that of using a particular service, and neglects those who are not accessing services. While the term 'expert by experience' acknowledges a person's expertise, it 'fails to differentiate between the nature and types of experience' (ibid., p. 1114).

These are risks when using any generalised term to describe a group of people. The same applies to the chosen term for this book which is people with *lived experience*, not least because it is a term which applies to any and all of us. We all have lived experiences and these can be wide and varied. Specifically in relation to this book, the aim is not to generalise but to identify individuals with unique and individual experiences with regards to particular social work statutory interventions and for the reader to value the expertise and the insights the person is able to share having lived this experience. As the reader, you are encouraged to consider this experience in relation to your own practice, seek a dialogue with others you encounter to explore whether this was similar or different for them and consider the influence of diversity and equality. Consideration, for example, of the protected characteristics outlined in the Equality Act 2010 is a useful way of exploring if there is parity in social work provision and the different ways people experience statutory interventions and outcomes. For example; how might a person's age, gender, sexuality, disability, race, or religion influence a person's experience of social work interventions?

Service user involvement remains the most frequently used term in current literature, policy and practice in the UK and is also used throughout this chapter and book. Readers are encouraged to keep in mind McLaughlin's suggestion to 'develop a continuous critical dialogue concerning the language we use, deconstructing it and unearthing the assumptions behind its usage' (2009, p. 1114).

Requirement for you to learn from people with lived experience

Involving people who use social work services in social work education became a requirement in the UK in 2002. The Department of Health's 'Requirements for Social Work Training' document (which set out the requirements for the degree level qualification) stated that service users and carers must be involved in student selection, assessment of students, provision of placements, design of the degree, teaching and learning provision, learning agreements, quality assurance and preparation for practice learning. Specifically, they identified that preparation for direct practice 'must include the opportunity to develop a greater understanding of the experience of service users' (DoH, 2002, p. 3).

Involving service users and carers in social work education remains a requirement of social work education and training and is currently regulated across the UK by four councils: Health and Care Professions Council (soon to be Social Work England; Social Care Wales; the Northern Ireland Social Care Council; and Scottish Social Services Council).

The Health and Care Professions Council (HCPC) currently set out the standards by which programmes they regulate must demonstrate to be formally approved. Standard 3.7 makes explicit the requirement that 'service users and carers must be involved in the programme' and that this may include some or all of the following: admissions and selection; developing teaching approaches and materials; planning and developing the programme; teaching and learning activities; feedback and assessment; and quality assurance, monitoring and evaluation. Across all four UK regulatory councils, the focus is on maintaining and enhancing quality and standards in social work education. They emphasise the need to involve service users and carers in the design and delivery of programmes for this to be achieved.

In addition to the requirements for social work programmes to involve people in their programmes, as a social work student and practitioner, you are required to demonstrate how you are involving people in your practice and working in partnership with people to reach decisions about their lives. In England, students are currently assessed against the Professional Capabilities Framework (PCF) for social work. The PCF consists of nine interconnected domains with descriptors at nine levels from entry to qualifying programmes through to post qualifying practice at a strategic level. Throughout these, specific reference is made to service user and carer involvement. By the end of last placement, qualifying level, this includes demonstrating respectful partnership work with service users and carers (values and ethics); valuing and taking account of the expertise of service users, carers and professionals (knowledge); and identifying, distinguishing, evaluating and integrating multiple sources of knowledge and evidence, including service user and carer experience (critical reflection). Seeking the perspectives of people with lived experience therefore is intrinsic to your education and to your subsequent practice.

Co-production

The process of writing this book has been based on these principles and of the Professional Capabilities Framework (PCF) for social work. Throughout this book you will read views of service users, carers and social workers advocating the need for increased partnership working, social workers' recognition of service user expertise and the need for effective sharing of information. At the start of the book writing process, a steering group was established which consisted of academics, social workers and people with personal experience of social work interventions. The group provided direction to the editor on the content and format of the book and they reviewed chapter outlines and first drafts.

Good social work practice is tailored and adapted to the needs of the individual involved. The same applied to enabling people to share their stories and write their chapters in this book. You will see some consistency in the format of each chapter but each one takes on a distinct style and tone depending on the style and preference of the people writing it. We felt this individuality should be encouraged. Some of the lived experience contributors wrote a full first draft before sharing it with the social worker they had been linked with. Others were interviewed by the social worker and their narrative was transcribed, others met regularly and wrote it together. For the young carers' chapter, Chapter 6, I attended a young carers' group and we recorded a group discussion between four young carers. I posed questions to the young carers to enable them to share their experiences and views. They then worked with Maggie and staff at the young carers' service to transcribe the recording and create their chapter together. As you read this book, you are encouraged to think about the value of service users, carers and social workers working in partnership to reflect and share their experiences and to consider how you can incorporate similar models into your everyday practice.

How to use this book

Reading this book from beginning to end will enable you to explore different experiences and consider these in relation to your own practice. Each chapter, however, has been written to provide a stand-alone narrative to provide insight and guidance from one perspective on a particular statutory intervention and so can be used to inform your focus on different areas of social work at different times. This is an opportunity to ensure that the lived experience informs your knowledge and considerations of your own developing social work practice. The intention is not to claim that each person's experience is how it has been or will be for anyone else, these are unique stories and personal perspectives which give us insights from which to reflect on a broader context.

Overview of the book chapters

Chapter 1

In Chapter 1, we review the evidence of why we should involve people with lived experience in social work education. I draw on a range of research studies to date which have sought to evaluate the impact of involvement on your learning and development as a social worker and consider what impact this may have on your subsequent practice. The chapter presents an argument for the need to recognise people's expertise and the impact this may have on enhancing your personal and professional development and in achieving positive outcomes when undertaking statutory roles.

Chapter 2

In Chapter 2, Richard Murphy, a social work academic, Approved Mental Health Professional (AMHP) and NHS trainer, provides an overview of the legislative and policy framework for statutory social work in England.

Students are often unclear on what statutory tasks or legal interventions are, despite it being a requirement of qualifying programmes for students to gain experience of statutory tasks including legal interventions as part of their practice learning. This chapter defines these terms and provides examples of what statutory and legal interventions involve – where they might take place and by whom. Particular emphasis is placed on identifying the personal and professional roles and responsibilities of students and qualified social workers as this is an increasing area of concern and pressure for students engaging in statutory practice and legal interventions for the first time.

Chapters 3–13

In Chapters 3–13, we hand over to those who are experts by experience. Fifteen people with lived experience share not only their stories but also their views and recommendations for students and social workers undertaking statutory and legal interventions. Each contributor tells us about themselves, the statutory intervention they experienced, what happened next and their message and guidance to social workers. They not only share not only their lived experience but also the insights and expertise they gained as a result.

Text boxes have been incorporated into each chapter to provide formal knowledge of the intervention such as legislation, policy, research and wider literature in the form of quotes, statistics and explanations, to underpin the contributor's experience. For example, if mentioning that a social worker came to their home to undertake an assessment, this is supported by a text box which outlines the statutory duty to do this and what it should have addressed. In some cases, the social worker who has contributed to the chapter was the social worker involved and so has shared their own perceptions and reflections on the intervention. The chapters are loosely ordered according to age – starting with a child's view of being in foster care and moving through experiences of children's services through to adults and care in older age.

Chapter 14

In Chapter 14, we seek to give a voice to those who are at risk of being the least heard within social work practice: those who have limited communication or lack capacity. Margaret Parker, an experienced social worker who manages a specialist dementia service, reflects on how people with limited capacity can still communicate and how it is our role as social workers to consider how this may be achieved. Margaret reflects on her own experience of interpreting people's communication, behaviours, needs and wishes and of how this has been used to inform decisions made. Methods and challenges of engaging people with limited capacity to make decisions about their lives, such as those with later stages of dementia are incorporated into her discussion along with a combination of lived experience and formal knowledge in relation to statutory interventions.

Chapter 15

Having explored these different and varied experiences, I suggest ideas in Chapter 15 on how you can take this learning to develop and inform your own practice. We reflect on the themes and recommendations which have emerged from the various narratives and you will be supported to consider how reading about the different experiences has informed your own knowledge and understanding of statutory interventions and on whether this will influence your own practice. Specifically, we consider what you can do in your own practice settings to develop a culture of meaningful involvement, collaboration and consultation – to ensure the development of practice which is based on challenging structural and procedural inequalities and on developing partnership working and respectful relationships, even when in some statutory interventions, choice and control is minimal. We consider the challenges you may encounter, provide suggestions and recommendations, and incorporate testimonies from student social workers and the contributors to this book.

Conclusion

Finally the Conclusion of the book draws this learning together and makes recommendations for the future. If this is the starting point, what is the next step? The concluding chapter draws the book to a close with an overview of what the book has sought to achieve and what your learning from it might be. As throughout the book, this chapter will emphasise that each experience is unique to the person who shared it and, as the reader, you are encouraged to consider the wide range of experiences and expertise you can draw on so as not to assume that this applies to everyone.

References

British Association of Social Workers' Code of Ethics for Social Work. Available from: www.basw.co.uk/codeofethics.

British Association of Social Workers (BASW) Professional Capabilities Framework (PCF) for social work, Available from: www.basw.co.uk/pcf.

Department of Health's 'Requirements for Social Work Training' document. (2002). Available from: www.scie.org.uk/publications/guides/guide04/files/requirements-for-social-work-training.pdf.

Health and Care Professions Council (HCPC) Standards for Education and Training (SET). Available from: www.hcpc-uk.org/aboutregistration/standards/sets/

International Federation of Social Workers in 2014. Available from: www.ifsw.org/what-is-social-work/global-definition-of-social-work/

Knowles, M. (1984) *The Adult Learner: A Neglected Species*. 3rd edition. Houston: Gulf Publishing.

McLaughlin, H. (2009) What's in a Name: 'Client', 'Patient', 'Customer', 'Consumer', 'Expert by Experience', 'Service User'—What's Next? *The British Journal of Social Work*. 39: 6, 1 September 2009, pp. 1101–1117. doi.org/10.1093/bjsw/bcm155.

1

Valuing the Expertise of People with Lived Experience

Mel Hughes

This chapter will review current research and literature in relation to valuing the expertise of people with lived experience in social work education and of how this can inform your personal and professional development and improve outcomes for individuals, families, groups and communities you encounter in your subsequent practice.

The requirement set in 2002 by the Department of Health to involve service users and carers in social work education meant that all social work programmes in the UK developed strategies and activities aimed at embedding the lived experience in the social work curricula and for involving people in the design and delivery of social work programmes. Good practice was shared across programmes through published, peer reviewed research and discussion papers exploring and evaluating different ways of involving people in social work programmes. Much of this literature has focused on sharing and evaluating models of practice such as the inclusion of service users and carers in admissions interviews (Matka et al., 2010), simulation and role play activities as part of the preparation of students for practice (Duffy et al., 2013), assessment of students' work (Anka and Taylor, 2016; Skoura-Kirk et al., 2015), exploration of complex issues (Duffy, 2012), practice learning (Hughes, 2013; MacSporran, 2015; Teater and Baldwin, 2009) and, more recently, the use of social media and online tools to facilitate discussions and feedback to students from people with lived experience (Franklin et al., 2016; Quinney and Fowler, 2013; Westwood et al., 2017). As practice has evolved and programmes have developed strategies and partnerships for involvement, research and discussion has focused increasingly on identifying and evaluating the different types of involvement in social work education and the need to identify the impact on students' learning and subsequent practice, i.e. does it make a difference? It is important therefore in this chapter to consider the evidence that seeking the perspectives and insights of people with lived experience, can improve your practice and outcomes for people in receipt of social work services.

What do we mean by learning from the expertise of people with lived experience?

There are many ways that people with lived experience are involved in social work education and in influencing the personal and professional development of social work students and practitioners. People with lived experience may have been involved in the design of your qualifying programme's curriculum and the individual sessions, modules and resources within it. They may have contributed to decision-making on applications and interviews when you applied for your course. They may have been part of your preparation and assessment of your readiness for direct practice and the development of practice skills such as communication. They may have been involved in delivering lectures, facilitating groups, sharing experiences and perspectives, in simulation and role play activities, in assessing your work at different stages of your programme or in supporting elements of your learning out on placement. While much of the literature focuses on evaluating the impact of specific types and examples of involvement, the principles remain the same: the need to involve people with lived experience in the design and delivery of social work programmes and to create opportunities for students to learn from the expertise of people with first-hand, lived experience and to use this insight to critically analyse, evaluate and reflect on other areas of knowledge such as legislation, social policy, research and practice.

In addition to classroom-based contact, learning from people with lived experience can also include seeking out opportunities to gain feedback; ask questions and practise skills with a range of people you encounter in your life. As adults, we learn from the world around us and your development will be influenced by factors beyond that of your formal education. It will include your own life experiences (personal and professional) and will be influenced by your own views and values. O'Sullivan and Taylor (2004, p. 22) discuss the concept of transformative learning where education can lead to changes in how we view the world. They widen the concept of educators to include:

> Those who enable our learning – colleagues, friends, neighbours, parents, children, organisational leaders, spiritual leaders, artists, researchers, teachers, mentors – especially those who enable us to learn as we live and work and inspire us to a life of inquiry, openness and discernment.

Learning from people with lived experience is something you can approach in your everyday life as you engage in conversations, discussions and wider reading and adopt an openness to learning from a range of experiences and perspectives which may differ from your own.

Why is it important to learn from people with lived experience?

Activity

Before reading on, it is important that you first take a minute to consider this question. Why do you think it is important to learn from people with lived experience? As the introduction to this book demonstrates, there are many requirements for social work programmes to embed service user and carer involvement in social work education but why has this proven to be such a consistent requirement? In your experience of social work education, what do you feel the benefits to your learning and practice have been or will be?

There have been a number of published studies which have sought to explore this question. In our own evaluations of activities involving people with lived experience, students across a range of disciplines (nursing, physiotherapy, paramedic science, midwifery, occupational therapy and social work) identified that direct involvement enabled them to: gain different service user and carer perspectives; develop an emotional understanding of the lived experience; develop skills in communicating effectively with service users and carers; and identify how to be an effective practitioner in their chosen field (Bournemouth University Public Involvement in Education and Research (PIER) partnership evaluations). Students consistently rate the involvement of people with lived experience as one of the highlights of their programme. Robinson and Webber (2013) however, who reviewed 29 published studies on service user and carer involvement in social work education to identify what models were being used and evidence of their effectiveness, suggest there is a need for empirical evidence to show that involvement actually leads to changes or enhancements to subsequent practice.

In a study conducted with social work graduates, to explore whether they felt that service user and carer involvement in their education had impacted their subsequent practice (Hughes, 2016), graduates identified four types of impact:

➢ Enhanced awareness of the lived experience

➢ Taking on board suggestions of good practice from service users and carers

➢ Developing a more critical 'real life' understanding

➢ A culture of recognising service users and carers as experts

Is this similar to the list you identified?

Other published research studies have found similar findings. Irvine et al. (2015, p. 144) found that students from different cohorts identified that having involvement in their education had provided a 'link to the real world' which better prepared them for the realities of practice. In an evaluation of an online activity where students and service users regularly engaged in online discussion groups there was evidence of students finding common and shared values, realising different perspectives, sharing and revising views and reflecting on issues. Students reported that the online discussion involving service users challenged them to think differently (Quinney and Fowler, 2013). Tew et al. (2012, p. 327) created opportunities for social work and mental health nursing students to meet with service users and carers to engage in dialogue relating to mental health theory and practice with the majority of students taking part reporting that 'assumptions had been challenged and barriers broken down'. Common themes in our own research and wider afield appear to be the opportunity to engage in a dialogue with a range of people with lived experience and for students to be supported to explore learning and insight gained in relation to their own developing practice.

In much of the literature, it is often taken for granted that service users should be involved in social work education. Learning, however, needs to be purposeful. To ensure that involvement isn't tokenistic, it is important to think about what types of involvement might contribute to your learning and development and enhance your subsequent practice. There has been some criticism that research into service user and carer involvement in social work education has focused more on 'what' and 'how' we involve people with lived experience, with less focus on 'why' (Hatton, 2017; Levy et al., 2016; Robinson and Webber, 2013; Tanner et al., 2017). The remainder of this chapter will focus on some of the evidence as to why it is important to your development as a social work student and practitioner to seek opportunities to learn from, and value the expertise of, people with lived experience such as by reading about the experiences of those contributing to this book. This is an important process in developing a culture where you value the expertise of people with lived experience in the development of your knowledge and practice and can use this to improve the process and outcomes for those you work with, particularly in statutory settings where involvement can often be short term, at crisis point and with limited opportunity to develop relationships over a period of time.

Learning from people's lived experience can challenge how you view the world

I started this chapter with reference to transformative learning and how the development of knowledge can change how we view the world around us. Transformative learning theory was developed by Mezirow in the 1990s and was offered as an explanation of how 'adults learn to think for themselves rather than act upon the assimilated beliefs, values, feelings and judgments of others' (2003, p. 1). It involves you developing an awareness of your own values and recognising, questioning and reflecting on these. Transformative learning involves making changes to your behaviour and practice based on the resulting shifts in thinking or frames of reference. Engaging in dialogue with people with lived experience; hearing their stories and experiences and being open to different perspectives, can be a catalyst, or trigger, for this shift in thinking and can lead to tangible changes to your practice. Cabiati and Raineri (2016) suggest that 'providing students with direct exposure to stigmatized people in roles that emphasise their humanity and strengths rather than their deficits' can be an effective way of challenging preconceptions and bringing about change. Hatton (2017) argues that by developing models of involvement which are based on equality and partnership and where the personal expertise of people who use services is utilised and fully recognised, meaningful change can be achieved as service users can affect the way services are delivered.

Activity

Before reading on, you may want to give some thought to the experiences which are shared by contributors in this book. Consider each of the chapter headings. What are your immediate thoughts, preconceptions or views of who might have experienced the different statutory interventions being explored? Make a note of the images these conjure up or the stereotypes that may exist about people with this experience, for example, a child with multiple foster placements or an adult being assessed for substance use treatment. Keep this to one side so you can refer back to it later.

Learning from people's lived experience can help develop your knowledge

As well as leading to increased awareness, insight and perspective changes, there is evidence that service user and carer involvement can enhance your knowledge and understanding of a range of issues.

Gupta and Blewett (2008) report on a module which brought together service users, academics and students to explore perspectives of families living in poverty. Students were able to recognise the far-reaching effects of poverty and the impact of this on family life and how poverty was not just about a lack of money. Duffy (2012) evaluates a teaching initiative which sought to bring victims and survivors of political conflict in Northern Ireland together with students to explore the issues. Those involved in the project identified that, as a result of open discussions and dialogue, students felt more confident in discussing the needs of victims and survivors of conflict in their practice and recognised the importance of addressing rather than sidelining such issues.

For there to be an impact on your knowledge, there is a need for you to be open to different perspectives and viewpoints. Beresford and Boxall (2012) highlight the challenges involved for people with lived experience questioning dominant theories and argue the importance of doing this if lived experience is to have an impact on practice. They use the example of mental health and disability campaigners seeking to challenge the prevalence of biomedical and individualised models and theories of disability which fail to acknowledge the impact of wider societal structures. Exploring formal knowledge with people with lived experience and being open to different perspectives will enable you not only to develop a broader knowledge base and understanding but also a more critical appreciation of current legislation, social policy, theory and practice and the impact these have on people's lives. In an evaluation of a service user led unit where students worked in small groups with a service user to explore an allocated topic (Hughes, 2013), students identified that having the opportunity to observe and discuss the impact of particular policies and legislation on different individuals and organisations they had encountered had enabled them to critically reflect and analyse these and develop a better understanding of the realities for people, the implications for practice and the complexities involved.

Learning from people's lived experience can improve your practice

You may experience opportunities within your social work course to practise your skills and receive feedback from people with lived experience either in the classroom or out on placement. There is an increasing range of evidence across social work and health disciplines to show that this can have an impact on your subsequent practice. One commonly used activity in social work education is involving people with lived experience in role plays and simulation activities to enable you to practice and demonstrate skills without the immediate pressure of being out on placement (Hughes and Warren, 2018). Duffy et al. (2013) identified that students found that role plays with service users and carers made the experience more authentic and real, enabled them to learn from the service user's knowledge and experiences and showed that they could respond to different styles and emotions. While some students and staff expressed concern regarding the impact of this on those involved, the service users valued the opportunity to share their experiences and to 'use their position to support students' (Duffy et al., 2013, p. 50).

Having a range of opportunities to meet and learn from people with experiences you have not previously encountered can also break down barriers and lead to more inclusive practice. Ward et al. (2016) evaluate the involvement of Christian Raphael who has profound and multiple disabilities and works as an independent consultant including as an advisor to the Department of Health and NHS England. Raphael was commissioned to design and deliver specialist teaching to a group of social work students. In addition to the knowledge gained in relation to personalisation, person-centred planning and family experiences, students reported on the broader experience of being part of the sessions and the opportunity to learn from engaging with, and observing, someone with profound and multiple disabilities and his circle of support.

Learning from people's lived experience can help develop your emotional resilience

Perhaps sometimes overlooked within the literature and research into learning from people with lived experience is the opportunity it can provide to develop your emotional resilience. Social work is a stressful profession. You will be working with people whose experiences may be traumatic and difficult for you to hear or observe. Some of their experience may resonate with you because of events in your own life. It is essential that as a social work practitioner you develop strategies for being sensitive and responsive to people's life experiences but without this being detrimental to your own health and well-being. You may find some of the accounts shared in this book, difficult to read.

Developing emotional resilience is an area frequently identified as an outcome of involvement in our own programmes where students identify that listening to people's stories and discussing their experiences can be emotional and intense at times. Having the opportunity to explore this in a relatively safe and supportive environment, can enable students to develop strategies for managing the emotional impact. In a service user led unit which we deliver in the first year, students engage in small group work with people with lived experience to explore a particular topic. Over the years, we have increasingly focused on emotionally difficult subject areas such as adult survivors of childhood abuse and the needs of families caring for a child with a life-limiting or life-threatening condition as a way of enabling students not only to learn about specific areas relevant to social work but also to create opportunities not only to face, encounter, explore and develop strategies for managing the emotional impact.

A natural self-protection strategy can be to seek to avoid situations and experiences we are fearful of or find difficult but evidence within the literature such as Duffy's work to enable students to discuss sectarianism in Northern Ireland and Cabiati and Raineri's (2016) strategy for introducing students to stigmatised groups show that direct involvement can lead to more positive attitudes and confidence among students when working with certain individuals and groups.

Activity

Before moving on, are there particular groups of people you would find it difficult or distressing to work with? Are you able to identify why this is, i.e. is it due to your own life experiences or due to concerns you have about this group? What steps can you take to learn more about this group and to identify strategies for managing your own feelings about them? Take a moment to list any groups this may apply to and consider how you might discuss this in supervision or a tutorial.

Summary

The main purpose of this chapter has been to present the evidence base for involving people with lived experience in your social work education: in shaping the curriculum and optimising opportunities for learning from people who are experts by experience. There is increasing evidence to show that meaningful and purposeful involvement such as: learning from people's experiences; discussing what works in practice; identifying challenges, ethical dilemmas and complexities; practising your skills; and gaining feedback from people who use social work services can all be useful in enabling you to develop as a practitioner. For transformative learning to occur, where you seek to view the world differently, you need to be open to learning from people who may have views and experiences which differ from, or in some cases are similar to, your own. You can use their experiences and insight to then reflect on your own knowledge, understanding and experiences and to consider how you might incorporate this into your own practice and engagement with people who use the service in which you are based.

The remainder of this book will seek to provide some of these opportunities by giving a voice to people who have experienced social work statutory interventions and for them to share with you their unique stories, experiences, insights, knowledge and recommendations for your developing practice.

References

Anka, A. and Taylor, I. (2016) Assessment as the site of power: A Bourdieusian interrogation of service user and carer involvement in the assessment of social work students. *Social Work Education: The International Journal*. 35: 2, 172–185.

Beresford, P. and Boxall, K. (2012) Service users, social work education and knowledge for social work practice. *Social Work Education: The International Journal*. 31: 2, 155–167.

Cabiati, E. and Raineri, M. L. (2016) Learning from service users' involvement: A research about changing stigmatizing attitudes in social work students. *Social Work Education: The International Journal*. 35: 8, 982–996.

Duffy, J. (2012) Service user involvement in teaching about conflict – An exploration of the issues. *International Social Work*. 55: 5, 730–739.

Duffy, J., Das, C. and Davidson, G. (2013) Service user and carer involvement in role-plays to assess readiness for practice. *Social Work Education: The International Journal*. 32: 1, 39–54.

Franklin, P., Hossain, R. and Coren, E. (2016) Social media and young people's involvement in social work education. *Social Work Education: The International Journal*. 35: 3, 344–356.

Gupta, A. and Blewett, J. (2008) Involving service users in social work training on the reality of family poverty: A case study of a collaborative project. *Social Work Education: The International Journal*. 27: 5, 459–473.

Hatton, K. (2017) A critical examination of the knowledge contribution service user and carer involvement brings to social work education. *Social Work Education: The International Journal*. 36: 2, 154–171.

Hughes, M. (2013) Enabling learners to think for themselves: Reflections on a community placement. *Social Work Education: The International Journal*. 32: 2, 213–229.

Hughes, M. (2016) What difference does it make? Findings of an impact study of service user and carer involvement in social work students' subsequent practice. *Social Work Education: The International Journal*. 36: 2, 203–216.

Hughes, M. and Warren, A. (2018) Use of simulation as a tool for assessment and for preparing students for the realities and complexities of the workplace. Chapter in: Morley, D. (ed.) *Enhancing Employability in Higher Education Through Work Based Learning*. Basingstoke: Palgrave Macmillan.

Irvine, J., Molyneuux, J. and Gillman, M. (2015) Providing a Link with the Real World: Learning from the student experience of service user and carer involvement in social work education. *Social Work Education: The International Journal*. 3: 2.

Levy, S., Aiton, R., Doig, J., Dow, J. P. L., Brown, S., Hunter, L. and McNeil, R. (2016) Outcomes focused user involvement in social work education: Applying knowledge to practice. *Social Work Education: The International Journal*. 35: 8, 866–877.

MacSporran, J.(2015) A mentor's PATH: Evaluating how service users can be involved as mentors for social work students on observational practice placements. *Social Work and Social Sciences Review*. 17: 3, 46–60.

Matka, E., River, D., Littlechild, R. and Powell, T. (2010) Involving service users and carers in admissions for courses in social work and clinical psychology: Cross-disciplinary comparison of practices at the University of Birmingham. *British Journal of Social Work*. 40, 2137–2154.

Mezirow, J. 2003) *Epistemology of transformative learning*. Available at: learningtheories.synthasite.com/resources/Mezirow_EpistemologyTLC.pdf

O'Sullivan, E. and Taylor, M. (2004) *Learning Toward an Ecological Consciousness: Selected Transformative Practices*. New York: Palgrave Macmillan.

Quinney, L. and Fowler, P. (2013) Facilitating shared online group learning between carers, service users and social work students. *Social Work Education: The International Journal*. 32: 8, 1021–1031.

Robinson, K. and Webber, M. (2013) Models of effectiveness of service user and carer involvement in social work education: A literature review. *British Journal of Social Work*. 43, 925–944.

Skoura-Kirk, E., Backhouse, B., Bennison, G., Cecil, B., Keeler, J., Talbot, D. and Watch, L. (2015) Mark my words! Service user and carer involvement in social work academic assessment. *Social Work Education: The International Journal*. 32: 5, 560–575.

Tanner, D., Littlechild, R., Duffy, J. and Hayes, D. (2017) Making it real: Evaluating the impact of service user and carer involvement in social work education. *British Journal of Social Work (2017)*. 47, 467–486.

Teater, B. and Baldwin, M. (2009) Exploring the learning experiences of students involved in community profiling projects. *Social Work Education: The International Journal*. 28: 7, 778–791.

Tew, J., Holley, T. and Caplen, P. (2012) Dialogue and challenge: Involving service users and carers in small group learning with social work and nursing students. *Social Work Education: The International Journal*. 31: 3, 316–330.

Ward, N., Raphael, C., Clark, M. and Raphael, V. (2016) Involving people with profound and multiple learning disabilities in social work education: Building inclusive practice. *Social Work Education: The International Journal*. 35: 8, 918–932.

Westwood, J., Dill, K., Campbell, A. and Shaw, A. (2017) Making it 'APP'en: Service user feedback: Developing and implementing a service user APP: Reflections from Northern Ireland, England and Scotland. *Social Work Education: The International Journal*. 36: 8, 855–868.

2

The Law and Social Work

Richard Murphy, *Social Work Lecturer*

The aim of this chapter is to help develop your understanding of the relationship between your practice and the law, particularly in relation to undertaking the statutory and legal interventions explored in this book. Law impacts on almost everything we do as social workers. Service users and their carers will often look to us to explain the law and will be significantly affected by our legal decision-making. This can provoke a degree of anxiety for students and registered social workers.

To develop your understanding and confidence in relation to law, this chapter will walk you through some of the basic features of the legal framework and consider the implications for you and your social work practice. We look at: how duties and powers are constructed; how the role of social workers is defined; what to do when the law is unclear; and the implications of human rights and ethical practice. To support your learning, you will be asked to reflect on some key themes. Some of these are listed below.

Key themes

Before we move on, read through the themes and note your initial thoughts. You can then revisit them at the end of the chapter.

The law:

- creates a framework within which you practice social work;

- seeks to protect service users from arbitrary use of power;

- does not remove but strengthens the duty to act as a registered professional;

- can be contested and unclear;

- seeks to resolve conflicting rights and duties within a wider sociopolitical context;

- places you at the point of intersection between service users and the wider culture and structure of society.

Some basics

As a starting point when considering the law, it is important to understand the difference between *powers* and *duties*. If the law gives you a power then this is something that *can be* done. If, however, it places a duty on you then it is something that *must be* done.

In social work, if we are intervening coercively or intrusively, i.e. without a person's consent, we need to ensure we have a power or duty to do this. In addition, when on placement, for example, you will need to ensure that it is appropriate for you to carry out a particular intervention. There are only a handful of interventions for which the law stipulates that a specific person has to undertake it, for example only a professional who is an Approved Mental Health Professional (AMHP) can make an application for detention under the Mental Health Act 1983. However, organisations will have a duty to ensure that interventions are carried out by staff fit to undertake them and will most likely have policies in place to stipulate this. These policies should take account of students as developing social workers but, if in doubt, you can discuss this with your practice supervisor and practice educator.

The way in which a social worker is expected to develop in their understanding and use of law is reflected in the Professional Capability Framework for social workers (PCF). For example, a student at the end of the first placement is expected to:

➤ **Understand** the legal and policy frameworks and guidance that inform and mandate social work practice, relevant to placement setting.

Whereas by the end of the last placement, a student is expected to:

➤ **Demonstrate a critical understanding** of the legal and policy frameworks and guidance that inform and mandate social work practice, recognising the scope for professional judgement.

Finally, a social worker who has completed their Assessed and Supported Year in Employment (ASYE) is expected to:

➤ **Demonstrate knowledge and application** of appropriate legal and policy frameworks and guidance that inform and mandate social work practice. Apply legal reasoning, using professional legal expertise and advice appropriately, recognising where scope for professional judgement exists.

As can be seen, you will be expected to develop in stages from a general understanding of the law to a critical understanding that enables you to apply legal reasoning, use expert legal advice and apply professional judgement by the end of your ASYE. To develop these skills you will need to observe practice and use supervision to reflect on your use of the law.

Law and social work ethics

A key message of this chapter is that the law does not do social work for social workers but sets out some of the processes, tests to be applied and boundaries of our practice. Therefore the values that underpin our practice, the way we make ethical decisions and the way we relate to others, remain of central importance. One way to think about it is to consider yourself as mediating on the point of intersection between the service user and carer, the law and the wider society. How you carry out your intervention can enable the voice of the service user to be heard and discrimination and oppression to be challenged but it can also silence the voice of the service user and carer and re-enforce discrimination and oppression. In short, ethics is inseparable from law.

Banks (2012) discusses a number of ethical approaches to social work including 'virtue ethics' and a 'situated ethics of social justice for social work'. These provide a good starting point when looking to enact social work law.

Virtue ethics asks the question of what moral or ethical qualities make a good social worker. Reading the experiences of the contributors in this book will help you identify what people with lived experience consider this to be. According to Banks (ibid.), these include empathy, compassion, humility, honesty, a commitment to solidarity, moral courage and practice wisdom. These are qualities that require the development of skills and are about how you are with people. For example, empathy requires the skill of listening to and understanding other people's points of view. These are skills that are learnt through practice and are essential to the practice of social work law. They will make the difference between a social worker that, when undertaking an assessment, genuinely makes the attempt to engage with a service user and understand the world from their point of view or a social worker that is solely focused on the application of eligibility criteria and agency processes.

Ethical qualities can also make a significant difference when undertaking coercive interventions. For example, if a child is removed from their parents under a Children Act 1989 Care Order, these qualities can enable a social worker to carry out their duties in a way that recognises the experience of the child and family and treats them with dignity and respect. Without the development of these qualities it will be very hard for a social worker to maintain a practice that seeks to listen to the voice of service users and enables this voice to be heard.

A situated ethics of social justice for social work recognises that social work practice occurs with social groups that face social disadvantage and inequality and in contexts where there can be complex, and often contradictory, rights and duties. Good practice of social work law should recognise how service users can be disadvantaged by the law and its processes and seek to address this in practice. This can be as simple as ensuring a service user has independent advocacy, representation or advice and that they know their rights. This will be a theme that is returned to throughout this chapter.

The focus of this book is the lived experience of statutory interventions and so we now take a look at how the law constructs specific statutory interventions.

Constructing specific statutory interventions

As a social work student you are not expected to be an expert on all the areas of law but you will be expected to develop an understanding of what the law requires of your practice. You will be expected to develop your understanding, ask appropriate questions and discuss the use of law in supervision and in your assignments.

Questions to consider are:

Is this intervention undertaken under a specific statute?

The first thing you can seek to find out is whether an intervention is undertaken under a specific statute. For example, you may be carrying out an assessment of whether someone has eligible needs under the Care Act 2014. You can identify a statute because it will have the word 'Act' at the end. These are laws that have been debated in the Houses of Parliament, gone through the parliamentary process and received Royal Assent. There may be more than one statute that is relevant to your intervention. For example, you may be assessing a service user's needs under the Care Act 2014 and that person may have difficulty communicating and making decisions about their care due to the symptoms of dementia. In this example, the Equality Act 2010 s20 may require you to make reasonable adjustments to prevent the person being disadvantaged in the assessment process and the Mental Capacity Act 2005 s1(3) will require you to take all practicable steps to enable the person to make their own decision.

What are the legal tests that I have to apply in my practice?

Each of these statutes will contain 'legal tests' that you have to apply in your practice. For example, the test for eligible needs are set out in statutory regulations made under the Care Act 2014 s13 and are described in the statutory guidance, Care and Support Statutory Guidance (Department of Health and Social Care, 2017, Chapter 6).

Does the Act set out any processes or procedures which must be followed?

Once you have identified the 'legal test' for your intervention, you will need to ask if the Act also sets out any processes or procedures that must be followed in applying it. These procedures create rights for service users and carers. Their role is to ensure fairness in decision-making and they must be sufficiently robust to protect the rights to which they relate. Procedures usually set out things like who must be involved in decision-making, what information must be shared and which matters social workers need to take into consideration. For example, under the Care Act 2014 a person has a right to a needs assessment and for eligible needs to be met. In the process of that occurring they have the right, under s9(4), for it to be considered if the provision of care and support could contribute to the outcomes which the adult wishes to achieve and the impact the provision of care and support will have on their well-being. In order to ensure this right is met the social worker will need to consult the service user.

Does the Act have any corresponding codes of practice?

Generally, Acts of parliament have corresponding guidance or Codes of Practice, like the Care and Support Statutory Guidance (Department of Health and Social Care, 2017). These elaborate on the statute, give further guidance on best practice and can give examples. Although these do not contain the same legal weight as the statute, there is, in most cases, a legal duty to have regard to them and only depart from the guidance with cogent reasons. As a student, your preparation should involve you reading about the relevant statutes and associated processes for the work you are undertaking and discussing with practitioners and service users so you can understand how they are enacted and how they are experienced.

Is there any case law which clarifies the meaning of the processes or legal tests?

Once you have identified the processes you are required to follow and the legal test you are required to apply, you can ask if there is any case law which clarifies the meaning of either of these. Case law occurs when there are legal cases before the courts and disputes have arisen about what the law means; in these cases the courts have the job of interpreting the meaning of the law. If the court is senior enough then this can set a precedent and all lower courts have to follow this when they interpret the law. We have three courts in England that can set precedent. In order of seniority they are: The Supreme Court, the Court of Appeal and the High Court.

An easy way to understand what is happening is to imagine that the court is creating a dictionary for statute. For example, the courts were asked to consider what the meaning of 'deprivation of liberty' was within the Deprivation of Liberty Safeguards. The Supreme Court told us that there are three components and, when considering the objective component, the concrete circumstances of a person's situation, a deprivation of liberty occurs in situations in which they are 'not free to leave and under continuous supervision and control' *Cheshire West and Chester Council v P* [2014]. Now, whenever these words are read in the statute, this is their meaning.

Another example of the impact case law can have on practice is *Davey v Oxfordshire County Council* [2017]. Mr Davey had had his care funded partly by the Independent Living Fund (ILF) and partly by the local authority. When the ILF closed, his care was taken over entirely by the local authority. On review, his care package was cut from £1651 a week to £950 a week. Mr Davey argued that he would have to spend longer on his own, this would cause him significant distress, his care team would have to change and community access reduced. His legal team argued that the local authority had not given sufficient weight to the issues set out in the Care Act 2014 s9(4), as stated above. The argument was supported by the Equality and Human Rights Commission (EHRC) who were concerned about the impact of austerity on those living with disabilities. The local authority argued that more time alone would benefit his independence and there would be no undue negative impact on Mr Davey. The High Court held that the local authority are entitled to take the view they did. The Court of Appeal dismissed Mr Davey's appeal and agreed that the local authority had a duty to consider Mr Davey's views and the matters set out in s9(4) but they were also entitled to reach their own objective assessment of his need and how it could be met.

This case highlights the tensions a social worker faces when carrying out statutory interventions. On the one hand, there is a duty to listen to the voice of the service user, be person-centred, promote social justice, practice in an anti-discriminatory way and promote the best interest of the service user. However, on the other hand, you may be acting as a gatekeeper for a local authority with limited resources, who urge you to take a view on best interest that departs from that of the service user. You will need to reflect on how you maintain good practice in this context.

A framework for practice

So far in this chapter we have considered the expectations for you, as a social work student, in relation to your understanding of law and of the series of questions you can use to develop this understanding and guide your learning and preparation. We will now explore how the law constructs the role of social worker and what to do when faced with legal uncertainty.

The role of the social worker

Social work is a registered profession and, as such, social workers are accountable to the public through their regulatory body. The statutory role of the social worker was created through the Local Authority Social Services Act 1970 (LASSA). However, social work was not defined as such until the Care Standards Act 2000, which defines a social worker as someone 'who engages in relevant social work' (s55(2)(a)). To use the title 'Social Worker' you must, be registered with the social work regulator.

As a registered professional, social workers undertake to uphold the Standards of Proficiency: Social Workers in England (HCPC, 2017). All of the standards are relevant to making decisions in legal frameworks but for now you can focus on standards one, two and six which relate to the duty to practice safely and effectively within a social worker's scope of practice, to practice within the legal and ethical boundaries of the profession and to practice in a non-discriminatory manner. When you read them, think about what some of the key messages are. In particular, think about the need to know the limits of your capabilities to practice safely, the need to practice in order to promote the best interest of service users within the boundaries of the law and to promote social justice, equality and inclusion. Can you consider these in relation to Mr Davey's case explored above?

At the start of the chapter we outlined some key themes about the law and social work. So far we have started to explore these and have identified some key messages for you in regard to social work practice. These are summarised below:

➤ Be aware of the limits of your capability and ensure you're able to undertake the tasks you are undertaking.

➤ When qualified, be aware of the standards of proficiency and ask what they require of you in each situation.

➤ Ensure you act within the law.

➤ Ensure you consult with other professionals and be aware of substandard practice.

➤ As a social worker you are expected to implement the law in a way that takes account of the lived experience of service users, listens to their voice and promotes justice.

We will now look at what these mean in situations in which what the law requires is not immediately clear.

The duty to act lawfully and legal uncertainty

Our discussion so far reflects the reality that social workers are often carrying out a function of the state when they practice and do so in a relationship that gives them certain powers over service users, who can often be in a vulnerable situation. Therefore, there needs to be boundaries about what we as social workers must do, can and cannot do, how we make decisions and how the rights of those we work with are protected from arbitrary use of our power. A key starting point is to ensure we don't act unlawfully and that we have sufficient authority to do what we are proposing.

This can create difficulties for social workers as what the law expects of us can vary in clarity over time and in different areas of law. You can think about this in terms of how solid the legal ground is that you are standing on. In some cases, you will be making decisions on very solid ground and can be certain of how a challenge would be viewed. For example, you have agreed with your National Health Service colleague a Mental Health Act s117 aftercare plan that sets out a person's entitlement to support. You have identified providers of these services, had funding agreed and the service user agrees with and consents to this plan.

In other situations, the law can be a lot more uncertain and you would be advised to think about getting some foundations put in place to hold you. For example, when qualified, you may be working with a mother who has a learning difficulty and you are considering arrangements for the accommodation of her children under s20 of the Children Act 1983. She may be in agreement with this and you may be aware of her right to make such decisions the same as any other citizen. However, you may also be aware that it is a stressful situation for her and you may be concerned that she does not fully understand the implications of making such an agreement. This may lead you to doubt her mental capacity, at that time, to consent to the arrangements. You may also be concerned that she may feel under duress in consenting to these arrangements. In such situations you would be advised to seek further professional and legal advice. You may also wish to ensure she has independent advice. Finally, it may be decided an application to court is necessary to protect her rights. The following are examples of cases that grappled with these issues:

> *Coventry City Council v C, B, CA and CH* (sub nom Re CA (A baby)) [2012]; EWHC 2190 (Fam); *Newcastle City Council v WM & Others* [2015]; *Medway Council v M & T* [2015]

These types of situations highlight how the powers you hold in regard to service users can influence how and what they communicate to you. In order to ensure you are fully listening to service users it is important to reflect on these processes within supervision. The same principle applies when seeking to listen to children who are involved, who will also have a number of influences on the way they communicate with you.

There are some key questions that a social worker can ask to get a sense of how secure the legal ground they are standing on is:

What are my powers?
What are my duties?
What is my authority to intervene?
What guidance is there?
What is the best practice?
Am I prohibited from doing the action I propose?
Do I have sufficient skills, training and qualifications to undertake the intervention?
How urgent is the intervention and how high are the risks?

Seeking legal advice

If you need to seek legal advice, neither the law nor solicitors will take away the responsibility of the professional to make a professional decision. Their advice can clarify legal tests that have to be applied, the process that should be gone through, the safeguards for the individuals involved and how judges have viewed previous cases. What they should not do is make the decision for the social worker. In making the decision a social worker also needs to consider their values, requirements of their regulatory body, research and best practice. Perhaps most importantly, as social workers, we need to consider the way we communicate decisions and support service users and families through the legal landscape. For a further discussion on the professional responsibilities of a social worker see Carr and Goosey (2017, pp. 52–57).

So far, we have explored how statute, case law, guidance and codes construct practice, how a social worker's ethics and registration require- ments further define this and how uncertainty can be identified and managed. Finally, we will look at how a human rights approach enables good practice and further highlights the need to listen to service users in the practice of the law.

Human rights and international law

Recognising human rights is fundamental in ensuring social workers listen to the voice of service users. One way in which human rights are recognised in the law is through United Nations international conven- tions. When the United Kingdom signs these, they make a commitment to uphold the rights and principles they set out. Although this does not make them directly binding on our national law, they can be relied on in the courts to persuade judges to interpret our national law in a particular way.

There can be a gap between these principles and rights and the current circumstances within our country. For example, the tension between the commitment the United Kingdom has made in international law and the actual practice, can be seen by considering the United Nations Conven- tion on the Rights of the Child. In 2016 the UN Committee on the Rights of the Child published their *Concluding Observations on the Fifth Periodic Report of the United Kingdom of Great Britain and Northern Ireland* (UN Com- mittee on the Rights of the Child, 2016). They identified a number of concerns; one of which is of particular significance for this book:

> Many children feel that they are not listened to by their social workers, review- ing officers, paid carers, judges, personnel working with children in conflict with the law, or other professionals, in matters affecting them, including in family proceedings. (UN Committee on the Rights of the Child, 2016, paragraph 29(d))

Regarding social workers, this is in spite of the duty in the Children Act 1983 to have regard to 'the ascertainable wishes and feelings of the

child concerned (considered in the light of his age and understanding)'
(Children Act 1983, s1(3)(a)) and the statement of Baroness Hale (as was
then) in *Re: D (a child) (Abduction; Foreign Custody Rights)* (2006):

> There is a growing understanding of the importance of listening to the chil-
> dren involved in children's cases. It is the child more than anyone else who
> will have to live with what the Court decides. They are quite capable of being
> moral actors in their own right, just as the adults may have to do what the
> Courts decide whether they like it or not, so may the child. But that is no more
> a reason for failing to hear what the child has to say than it is for refusing to
> hear the parents' views. (paragraph 57)

The Committee also raised concerns about the disproportionate impact
of austerity measures on children and in particular disadvantaged children (UN Committee on the Rights of the Child, 2016, paragraph 12(d)).
Understanding these issues can make a significant difference to the way
you listen to service users. For example, do you hear a child speaking
from an experience of poverty or speaking of neglectful parents? As has
been discussed, the law places social workers in positions of power over
already disadvantaged groups. The impact of the disadvantage can be
greater during times of austerity. It is important that when you listen to
service users' experiences you can hear the impact of this and consider
how it can be addressed.

Statute also sets out the rights of service users and their carers to be listened to and involved in decision-making in different areas of practice. It
is important that you are aware of the duties these place on you and how
your practice can practically make this a reality. For example, if you were
care planning with an adult with severe learning disabilities who lacked
capacity to consent to the plan then s4 of the Mental Capacity Act 2005
would require you to identify and take into account their wishes and feelings. The question will be how you genuinely use your skills to be able
to see the world from their point of view, how you give this effect in care
planning and reach an outcome that is best for this individual.

We will now consider how the Human Rights Act 1998 may be able to
assist you.

Human Rights Act 1998

The Human Rights Act 1998 brings the European Convention of Human
Rights (ECHR) into national law. It requires that public authorities must
act in a way compliant with ECHR rights unless they are prevented from
doing so by an Act of our parliament. When working as social workers

for a government body you will be bound by this duty. However, it does not directly apply in the same way to relationships between private individuals.

The Act provides a strong value base within the framework of the law and can be used to challenge unfair or illegal practices. Braye and Preston-Shoot (2016) refer to the requirements of the ECHR throughout their book and suggest that those working in the field of social welfare need to be familiar with how the law regulates decision-making, and develop skills in challenging policies and procedures that are administratively unfair, or illegal, and which can run counter to social work values. What this means for your practice is that you need to ask what the convention rights require of you in any intervention. First, this means asking if our domestic courts or the European Court of Human Rights have considered the convention rights in a context similar or the same.

For example, convention rights have had a significant impact on children and family law and have addressed both the rights for children and parents to be heard and involved. This includes the rights of parents, under Article 8 (right to private and family life) to be involved in child protection procedures, which includes being given information of the local authorities plans, its factual reasons, being given an opportunity to respond, to be represented and to attend crucial meetings *Re G (Care; Challenge to the Local Authority's Decision)* [2003]. In *R (on the application of G) v Nottingham City Council* [2008] it was found that a removal of a child without parental consent or court order is a breach of Article 8.

The courts also recognise the rights of the child to be protected and the duty this places on the state. For example, in *Z and Others v the UK* (2001) the European Court of Human Rights found the United Kingdom to have breached its duty to prevent children experiencing inhumane or degrading treatment (Article 3). It was found that the local authority had sufficient evidence to have known that the four children concerned were experiencing neglect that amounted to inhumane and degrading treatment and should have taken steps to remove the children from their parents earlier. In supervision you will need to start to reflect on what it means to listen to the voice of the child and the parents, with both parties' rights in mind. Think about what it means to listen with a sensitivity to the impact of abuse, trauma and parental loss.

As well as reading legal judgements, another way of challenging your own practice is to read social care cases that the local ombudsmen has decided on and reflect on how you can develop your practice from lessons learned. Their decisions can be found here: https://www.lgo.org.uk/decisions. Although these do not create case law they do give practical examples of good and bad practice of social workers while practising the law.

None the less, it can also be argued that domestic courts do not always go far enough in interpreting the convention rights in the favour of vulnerable groups. For example, in *R (on the application of McDonald) v Royal Borough of Kensington and Chelsea* [2011] it was held that requiring a person's continence to be managed by continence pads overnight did not amount to inhumane and degrading treatment and did not breach her right to private and family life.

For further information on how the Human Rights Act 1998 enacts the ECHR and the implications of this see Brammer (2015), Chapter 5.

Conclusion

In this chapter we have looked at how the law constructs the role of the social worker and how that role is carried out in situations in which the legal context is clear and in situations in which it is unclear. We have explored how the practice of social work law cannot be separated from social work ethics. Throughout we have identified questions that will help you to formulate what your duties and powers are. We have also looked at some of the conflicts and tensions that are inherent in statutory social work and you have been encouraged to reflect on how you can ensure you listen to and take account of the voice of service users and carers. We have identified that all of this occurs in a social context in which there is already disadvantage and oppression and we have begun to consider what human rights law and a commitment to human rights means in that context and, in particular, how you listen to the voice of the service user.

As you read through the rest of the book you are likely to start to identify some of these issues in specific contexts. As you do so, start to think how your practice can enable the voice of service users to be heard in service delivery and planning.

References

Banks, S. (2012) *Ethics And Values In Social Work*. n.p. Basingstoke: Palgrave Macmillan.

Brammer, A. (2015) *Social Work Law*. n.p. Boston: Pearson.

Braye, S. and Preston-Shoot, M. (2016) *Practising Social Work Law*. 4th edition ed. Vol. Practical social work series. London: Palgrave Macmillan.

Carr, H. and Goosey, D. (2017) *Law for Social Workers*. Oxford: Oxford University Press.

Department of Health and Social Care (2017) Care and Support Statutory Guidance. Available from: www.gov.uk/government/publications/care-act-statutory-guidance/care-and-support-statutory-guidance, date accessed 21 January 2019.

HCPC, (2017) *Standards of Proficiency: Social Workers in England.* London: HCPC.

UN Committee on the Rights of the Child (CRC) (2016) *Concluding observations on the fifth periodic report of the United Kingdom of Great Britain and Northern Ireland* 3 June 2016, CRC/C/GBR/CO/5. Avaliable at: tbinternet.ohchr.org/_layouts/treatybodyexternal/Download.aspx?symbolno=CRC/C/GBR/CO/5&Lang=En, date accessed 21 January 2019.

Statute

Care Act 2014

Children Act 1989

Equality Act 2010

Human Rights Act 1998

Mental Capacity Act 2005

Mental Health Act 1983

International Law

Council of Europe, *European Convention for the Protection of Human Rights and Fundamental Freedoms, as amended by Protocols Nos. 11 and 14*, 4 November 1950, ETS 5.

UN General Assembly, *Convention on the Rights of the Child*, 20 November 1989, United Nations, Treaty Series, vol. 1577, p. 3.

Table of Cases

Cheshire West and Chester Council v P [2014] UKSC 19, [2014] MHLO 16

Coventry City Council v C, B, CA and CH (sub nom Re CA (A baby)) [2012] EWHC 2190; *Newcastle City Council v WM & Others* [2015] EWFC 42; *Medway Council v M & T* [2015] EWFC B164, [2015] MHLO 78

Davey v Oxfordshire County Council [2017] EWCA Civ 1308

Re: D (a child) (Abduction; Foreign Custody Rights) (2006) UK HL 51

Re G (Care; Challenge to the Local Authority's Decision) [2003] EWHC 551, [2003] 2 FLR 42

R (on the application of G) v Nottingham City Council [2008] EWHC 400 (Admin)

R (McDonald) v Royal Borough of Kensington & Chelsea [2011] UKSC 33

Z and Others v the UK (2001) 34 EHRR 3

3

I had Multiple Foster Placements

Michael Wootten

Jennifer Bigmore, *Social Worker*

At a glance

- This chapter focuses on the experience of being a looked-after child and being placed in foster care.

- Mike is a care leaver who, along with his brother had multiple foster placements. He is now about to qualify as a social worker with a job offer in a fostering team.

- Jenny is a social work lecturer and an experienced children and family social worker. Mike and Jenny have written this chapter together and provide formal knowledge underpinning the statutory interventions Mike experienced, in text boxes.

I am a care leaver and nearly a qualified social worker. I am just finishing my social work degree and already have my first qualified job. I am also a proud husband and father. I grew up for the first 12 years of my life with my mother and younger brother as my parents were not together. This is only part of my story and doesn't tell you the detail of my life before going into care. What is important for you to understand is that however hard it was, and it was hard; it was my 'normal'. It was what I was used to and I knew how to be me in that life. What happened next is what I want you to know about. These are my memories at the age of 12.

The pretend families and the one that stood out

I am going to write about what it was like as a child of 12 to enter an alleged life of 'safety and security', a complete mystery of the senses. The mystery began so unexpectedly. My mum was doing her usual thing, making us feel small and insignificant. Mum: 'I cannot go out because you boys are getting in the way, I just want to go out.' Being the ever-resilient child, this was nothing. I have been through far worse than this, seeing things that no child growing up should see. So, in this moment I am able to decipher the code my mum is throwing at me, she cannot talk or describe in a 'normal' manner. You know, the manner most mums would. I interpret this barrage of abuse to her asking approval from her eldest son that she can go out. So, I reply in a convincing and strong manner – 'Go then, we will be fine.' Well, needless to say it did not matter whether or not me and my brother would be fine. Off she went, got ready, music playing and out the door quicker than a cat running from a dog. So, begins the journey that would propel me into fear, anxiety and the unknown.

BANG-BANG-BANG, Kathy? BANG-BANG-BANG, Kathy? Whoa, what is going on? Me and my brother were home alone, it was the morning after the night before. All kinds of thoughts were going through my head. Where is my mum, why is she not answering the door? Who is this person, why are they trying to break the door down? Then suddenly I hear the banging stop, the figure that now haunts my mind is walking to the back door. *WAIT, I shout in my head.* The back door is unlocked. We left it unlocked so Mum could get in when she got back. So, in my adult, responsible head, I begin to pluck up the courage to do what every man of the house should do – defend my home. Up and towards the door I go, playing the big man, shaking unbelievably inside. Who is this person, what will I see? Then almost as quickly as my need to fight and protect kicked in, a sadness and shock hit me. For what I saw was not the sight I had expected, nor did I understand. A big police officer stood in front of me. 'What do you want?' I said in my attempted manly voice. Police officer: 'Michael and Christopher is it?'

It was at this point, without much conversation or knowledge of what was going on, I knew something had happened to my mum. She had been out partying away doing all the things her desires would ask of her and on her way back, to her two boys alone at home, she crashed into a car. Hardly surprising considering the amount of drink she had, let alone any other substances that were wracking through her body. As the police officer explained what had happened, the realisation that he had absolutely no idea what was happening next struck me. We travelled in a cop car to the station and spent the day on the front desk whizzing around the office, I have no idea what took so long to get us to a family member. I assumed they were waiting for my mum to leave hospital.

To my grandma's first, short though it lasted, to my auntie's next, then my grandma's and then my dad's. Some days here, some days there – we were the nuisance that other people were now accommodating. Then, after some time at my dad's house, he sat us down. I knew what he was going to say before he said it. Sat down on my mattress, which was on the floor in the spare bedroom looking upwards at my dad, he said, in a roundabout, tearful way: 'You are going into foster care.'

'Okay' I said, 'it's fine'. I have no idea why or how I coped with this so well, my brother was a teary mess – why was he making such a fuss? In my head, I had been through so much as a child, seen and done some silly things. Going into foster care? Easy. I had and always will, look after my brother; I knew we would be okay because I was going to make sure that was the case. I am the big man. I am the man of the house, besides, this will only be temporary while my mum is getting better, she will get better – she always does.

The statutory intervention

When we began writing this chapter, Mike had only had limited access to his files. Since then he has had the opportunity to read them and it has revealed some of the context of the intervention in his case.

Clearly at the point of Mike's mother being hospitalised it was necessary to find alternative accommodation for him and his brother, and the wider family was explored. This led to Mike being pushed from one set of relatives to another and it is clear from his memories that he perceived this as multiple rejections which would inevitably impact on his sense of identity and well-being.

When a child cannot be looked after for whatever reason by their parent or parents it is the duty of the local authority under Section 22 of the Children Act 1989 to make a decision about where the child should be accommodated. Wherever possible a child should be placed with a parent or a person who is not a parent but has legal parental responsibility, which might be under an order like a child arrangements order. If that is not possible then there is an emphasis on exploring the wider family for a kinship or connected persons placement. A connected person can be a relative, friend or any other person with a prior connection with the child or young person.

For more detailed information on this you can read the Statutory Guidance for Local Authorities. Family and Friends Care (2010) published by the Department for Education (DfE) – see references.

In Mike's case, placement with family including his father was not a sustainable option and therefore local authority foster care was the alternative option.

When working with Mike on this chapter it was not known what his legal status was during his many years in care although I suspected that it had been under Section 20 of the Children Act 1989 which relates to accommodation on a voluntary basis. Mike had no idea, although we have since found out that this was the case.

Going into foster care

And so, the first day of the rest of my childhood began; a placement had been found – whatever that means. I have no idea who makes these decisions, all I know is the sudden realism and impact of my father's decision was about to be enacted. My dad started to go through the details of how the move would work. He explained we needed to pack all our things, we would go to school and at the end of the school day he would pick us up and take us to our new home. No matter how he put this, I do not understand what all this really means. The blur of the process, the smiles being given to me, they are all cold and never give any warmth or comfort to my heart. The day at school was slow, watching the time so intensely. Each tick of the clock, each minute passing – all was adding to the apprehension of what was to come, the tick tock, the school bells, the tick tock, the school bells – it seemed to go on forever as I go from lesson to lesson. Finally, the school bell rings one last time and I stop looking at the clock. The time has come to get in the car and meet my new family. The drive felt long, the winding roads of an endless journey, it was all new – the familiar scenes that were my surroundings for my life now, just a view in the back window. A view symbolising change as I entered the new and completely foreign view which was through the front window.

The final approach as we turn into the last road. These people are posh! Their house is massive! My friends are going to be well jealous, I thought to myself. Never, I thought, this house is huge, and I am living here, and then all of a sudden, we are getting out of the car on their driveway. The fresh air smacks me across the chops. I am hot and very nervous. As my dad approaches the back door I am not only just beside him but also slightly behind him, my manly exterior was no more. The temporary life I had with my dad, soon to be a memory but, during that short time, he had become my protector, the person I could look up to. Now, as the final approach is made I can feel his protection and influence on my life slipping away. He is about to thrust me and my brother into the unknown, without him. As we get to the front door, my dad decides to ring the fancy doorbell. To make doubly sure, he also knocked.

As the door opens, I am greeted by a couple of people all smiling and happy. As we are walking the short journey into the front room, the immaculate and expensive flooring, the shiny new leather sofas fresh with the scent of new, the ornaments on the fireplace and the coffee table all began to show a picture of the lavish lifestyle this family lead – this fails to mention the massive TV they also had. This TV was the pure reflection of wealth in my eyes. This new world my dad was so readily walking us into, was so alien, so … scary. Am I allowed to walk on this carpet? Shoes on or off? I want a drink, but I am too scared to ask. I am hungry but am I allowed a snack? Does the remote have batteries in it? Can I use it? These questions, and more, I had no answers to.

As we sat down on the comfy sofas, not crowded like at home, the strange person who introduced himself as the social worker had his say, and then the others started talking about stuff. Right now, why is everyone talking and what are they saying? I sit there, not sure what is expected of me, looking across to my brother who I am sure has less of a clue than me, wondering to myself what all this is and means. The social worker is telling me about how this is short term and the aim is to go back to our mum's when she is better. The new family are telling me that me and Chris will be treated just as if we are part of their family. The social worker is filling out some paperwork and everyone is nodding and smiling, I sit there wondering and thinking about my mum and how I wish she was okay and could take us back.

Once everyone had left, this new family, 'foster carers', sat me and Chris down and started to list down rules. In my head I do not understand. Why? I have been acting like an adult for ages, keeping money safe for Mum and doing things that adults do. And now they want to write down rules, have a bedtime, this all sounds like they are very bossy.

As time goes by, I settle into the rules, understand the routine and grind of daily life. Get up, breakfast, shower, school, homework (I am not doing that!), dinner, bed and repeat. The days turned into weeks and the weeks turned into months, this short-term placement is not so short term. The social worker turned up a few times in the first few months; each time coming with a wad of paperwork with questions they wanted answering. These questions seemed structured, after an answer there would be another question. The feelings that they genuinely cared about me soon left when they kept coming with more and more paperwork. It began to feel like they only came when they needed to do more paperwork and ask more questions.

What began to become apparent was how the smells and textures that struck me to begin with, were suddenly just a general item that my conscious never took in. This short-term home was now where I lived permanently, with no sight of leaving to go live with my mum. The grind of daily life began to take its toll; the light that was so clearly present at the end of the tunnel was getting dimmer and dimmer. As the realisation began to kick in, the foster carers' attitude began to shift also. We were a part of their family, but only when it suited them. Instead of being dropped off at school, we would be dropped off by the roundabout half a mile away because it was inconvenient for the foster carer to drop us off as she needed to turn right to get to work and not left to drop us off at school. Our bedrooms became less of a safe place, being kicked out without warning to accommodate friends who had come over for a house party – we were left on the sofa. And then, to top it off, the foster carers sat us down and said they were going on a family holiday and we were not invited.

I am not invited I thought to myself, I am a part of this family, my brother is a part of this family. They lied to us, everyone is lying to us. We are forever an inconvenience for people, all I want is to go home with my mum and everyone keeps saying how we are so welcome and we are a part of the family. Yet, actions speak louder than words and people are not honest. The final straw for the foster carers was the deterioration of my behaviour. I started to become aggressive towards everyone, including the foster carers' teenage birth children. The male foster carer restrained me on several occasions, which I did not think they could do. All this did was make me angrier and angrier to the point I wanted to smash everything up. This behaviour became a regular occurrence, and it was all down to people not being honest and open, people lied to me and treated me like a fool.

One morning, nearing the end of this placement one of the foster carers said something to me, something like: 'You know you were only ever supposed to be short term, we did not expect to have you here this long.' Well, in a rage and fury I shouted at her to stop the car or I'll jump out. As soon as she stopped the car I jumped out and ran off, I was walking to school and I was not going back. I ran and ran until I could run no more, up and over the fences, through various fields along certain roads. I was retracing the 11-mile journey to my school, I knew the way and I was going to get there. Then suddenly somebody pulled up alongside me. 'What are you doing? Where is your mum?' I shouted back, 'I don't have a mum, leave me alone,' and carried on walking, but this did not stop them, they shouted, 'Where are you going? I'll take you.' Again, in my anger that had ceased to leave me, I shouted, 'Nowhere, leave me alone or I'll run off into the woods.' At which point this strange figure stated, 'Well, I have phoned the police and they are coming.' The police turned up, shortly followed by the foster carer I so readily hated. After a short discussion, I was in the police car headed to school. Although this was not the immediate end to this placement, I knew this was when the seriousness of the situation presented itself, this was when all the people in control of my life began to push through the next family home that would be 'matched' to make sure we were okay. During this short time, the foster carers said to me: 'You know why they are struggling to find you boys a home? It is because nobody wants teenage boys.' This line says everything I needed to know about that smiling, happy family that was so falsely portrayed at the start. During the process of this breakdown, there were meetings that I was not involved in and meetings I was partly invited to. Something about a disruption meeting and pathway planning which meant nothing to me, and at the point all this was happening, I really did not care.

Respite

The one positive point that came from this family going away and not inviting us was we got put into what is called a 'respite placement'. This was explained to me as being a holiday for us, but it's just not a proper holiday. I do not understand what that meant, but all I knew is that we had another family to get used to. Who were they going to be? What were they like? Where do they live? The social worker came to see me one day and said they had found a 'lovely' respite placement. They had animals; ducks, cats, dogs, goats, chickens, rabbits and guinea pigs. This was suited to me and Chris because we loved animals. The social worker believed this was going to be a lovely respite place but all I am hearing is; new family, new rules, new house, lots of animals, strange place. All of this sounds very similar to when I moved from my dad's to the new shiny big house, the fear of the unknown. Respite was never a part of this first placement for so many months, then, all of a sudden, the foster carers requested it for their holiday and then wanted it on a regular basis. Once a month was agreed behind the scenes without a question being asked to me. What I did not anticipate was this new respite family becoming more involved in my life than I could have ever thought. We turned up to this respite placement which was a last minute, emergency thing.

I was soon off; the journey there was facilitated not by my social worker but my foster carer. We turned up to this house on what must have been one of the steepest hills I had ever seen, although not as steep as the hill outside my nursery where I got expelled, that one was steeeeeeep! As we pulled up outside this tiny, end of terrace cottage it could not have felt more underwhelming compared to the big glossy house we had been pro-pelled into at the start. As we open the rusty gate, along the path to the side entrance I hear a dog barking loudly! 'Floss, shh' comes a voice from within. 'Quack, Quack, Quack' I hear from the garden, 'mehh, mehh' soon follows. What is this crazy place, I was humoured by it, but it did not fully distract me from the terrifying thought of another strange person with new house rules and new smells. So, my foster carer bangs on the flimsy wooden door, a stark contrast to the sturdy one I had become accustomed to. She tries to ring the broken doorbell too.

By this time the strange figure from the inside was approaching – apparent from the shape in the glass getting bigger and bigger as they approached. Then, as the door opened, a ginger curly-haired figure with big glasses appeared and said: 'Hi, welcome to the farm I hope you had a nice journey, come on in, come on in.' Her warmth was immediately apparent, this feeling was completely different to that of my first place, and I could tell my current foster carer felt out of place. The house was not shiny with new flashy things everywhere; there wasn't any flashy cars, big TVs or anything shouting at you 'we have lots and lots of money'. This house smelt like animals, there was animal paraphernalia everywhere and what there was, was modest in style but absolutely suited to the picture that presented itself and that I bought into this from the minute she opened the door. We sat down, were offered drinks, biscuits and a tour! The focus was not on any paperwork. Once we had been shown around, had a drink and some food, my foster carer had a chat with this new respite carer. After the chat my foster carer came into see us as we were watching TV and said she was leaving. My respite carer was visibly annoyed by something, but she did well to cover it up. I did not say anything as I was enjoying the hotel hospitality that was being presented. I later found out that she had repeated the same line to this respite carer as she did to us: 'You know why they are struggling to find these boys a home? It is because nobody wants teenage boys.' I know this has, even to this day, stuck with this respite carer and she never forgave this breach of trust.

Anyway, me and Chris were alone in this lovely but small (in comparison) house. We had got used to the surroundings amazingly fast, except the iguana – that thing was scary! 'You'll be holding him by the end of the week,' said the new lady, 'no I won't I replied'. Never did hold the thing. Anyway, after dinner had been and gone, and the night had started to approach, I was told the other respite carer would be arriving home soon. I do not know why but this sent me into an inner meltdown, maybe they did mention someone else, maybe I just forgot. Nonetheless, I coped with this sudden and fearful thought with the approach 'I am going to hide, pretend we did not come'. I am not sure what I was expecting when he arrived, I heard him open the rusty gate, the dog barking and the animals singing in turn, it was like clockwork for a person approaching. Upon hearing the gate, I ran into the front room which had become a place of solace and pleasure during my short few hours at the house. Off the light went, and behind the door I hid. To my wonder and surprise, the lady went along with my corrupted game, she played it to perfection. There she was, pottering in the kitchen and she asked him how he was, what his day had been like. Then he asked: 'Where are they?' The lady explained how we had not come and he replied, 'Oh, that is a shame.'

I immediately felt a mix of emotions. I had not seen this guy and had no idea what he looked like or what he was about, but, in that short moment, in the one line that related to me, he was disappointed that we had not arrived. This was such a contrast to everything that had happened before, I felt they were genuine, they wanted me to be there. Hell … they were even looking forward to it. So out I crept, to get a better look. But as I did, I saw he clocked me and, in an effort to not be deceived and to ensure the game was legitimate, I jumped out 'surprise'. And then began an amazing week with this family. This respite placement turned regular, they would be the rock, the person in my life that was missing. They did not have to say it. They did not have to do extravagant things. They just had to remember I was there and answer me if I called. This was what made them special, and still does to this day.

Time in care

This early time in care was such a mix of emotions, my very first placement was bursting with mistrust and deception and my respite was built on trust and a willingness to support each other that never wavered. It was this rock that would continue to be present throughout the remaining years and multiple breakdowns that were to present themselves throughout my time in care. During this time, my mum was out of hospital and we were in contact through *Facebook*, texting and in any way we could. She would say things like: 'Do you want me to fight for you.' Of course I did, but I would always reply: 'No, Mum, focus on getting better first.' Because, even though we had been through so much with my mum, I would always be looking out for her. The worst thing anyone could do, would be to doubt my desire to be with and protect my mum. My dad had two other children, the main reason as to why I ended up in care (or so I thought). When he was explaining the reasons to me, I sold it to myself that the main reason was because the house was too small with my newly born brother and my family couldn't have me.

The real reason I have found since reading my notes was that my dad's partner did not want us in the house. There wasn't a willingness to accommodate our existence as a part of the family. The council were trying to keep us with our dad. His partner would throw up walls and they would attempt to jump over them. In my notes it says something along the lines of; there were concerns about how much space was needed to raise all the children, so the council offered my dad a bigger house. He turned it down. My dad was stuck in a place that I now, as an adult, wish I never have to face. The choice between your two eldest boys and your two youngest. I guess he figured we were able to withstand the difficulties of foster care and all the turmoil that would be. He could not possibly foresee the turmoil of multiple placement breakdowns that I would go through.

Section 20 of the Children Act 1989: Voluntary accommodation

Provision of accommodation on a voluntary basis is intended to be seen as a service to support parents and children in need and it should be noted that that Section 20 (or s20) of the Children Act 1989 comes under Part III of the Act which details Local Authority Support for Children and Families.

The local authority must accommodate children in need who appear to require accommodation as a result of:

a) There being no person who has parental responsibility for him;
b) His being lost or having been abandoned; or
c) The person who has been caring for him being prevented (whether or not permanently, and for whatever reason) from providing him with suitable accommodation or care. (Children Act, 1989)

If a child is accommodated under s20, rather than being secured with a care order, the only people with parental responsibility for that child remain the parent or parents. The arrangement is voluntary and the parent should be consulted on significant decisions, particularly if there is to be a change of accommodation.

What is significant for Mike is that he now knows from reading his records that over the years he was in care, his mother asked for him and his brother to be returned to her care and this was recorded as being refused with no clear reason. Recent conversations with his father have revealed that he did not have any understanding of the arrangements under s20 and thought that he had no rights to request that his children were returned to him.

To someone on the outside of the system, fostering is depicted as being a special and amazing thing. You get to take a child and change their lives. In reality the stigma that betides a child in care is one of turmoil and disruption. It is like the system desires to be something it doesn't have the ability to be, the portrayal to foster carers of lovely, young 'fluffy' children compared to the realities of a spotty, mouthy teenager turning up at your door. Now, this is not to say that the respite carers that have been so influential had it easy, we had arguments and fell out and I ran away over stupid things – to this day I hold against her that the ducks wanted to come back in even though she said they did not, never shall I forgive her for this. But, they are still there waiting with a cup of tea and biscuits whenever I visit.

Over time, various placements were found. Sometimes we would turn up and meet them beforehand, and then move in. Other times, it was an 'emergency' and we were moved within hours. What was true for every single one of these consequential moves, was that the trust and belief that this next one would be better or different was chipped away at until it was no more. Whether or not it was a respite placement, short-term or long-term placement, it did not matter. They were all new people, new rules and new things to get used to. Every single one of these people let me down, multiple times. The paperwork, the checkboxes, the 'best interest' nonsense, in my case, achieved nothing.

What achieved something was that one foster carer (who provided respite care) was always there when I picked up the phone. If I ran off in a rage of anger, they would have a cup of tea ready for when I returned, and we would talk about it. The difference of *being there* no matter what, makes the true difference. If being a foster carer and focusing on the outcomes is paramount, foster carers and professionals will forget about the child in the room and instead focus on what can be tried next. When sitting in meetings with professionals all surrounding the table, I had so much to say but so little ability or desire to share it anymore. This was down to years of people letting me down, forgetting I exist and failing to convince me that they cared, a pay packet was achieved, and this felt like the endgame for many.

Criticism of the use of Section 20 of the Children Act (voluntary accommodation)

In recent years there has been significant criticism of the misuse of s20 accommodation and Lord Justice Munby, President of the Family Division of the High Court in England and Wales has issued new guidance. He identified four problems with the use of the arrangements:

- Failure of councils to get informed consent from the parents from the outset.

- How consent is recorded by local authorities. There is no requirement, in law, for the agreement to be in or evidenced by writing, 'but a prudent local authority will surely always wish to ensure that an alleged parental consent in such a case is properly recorded in writing and evidenced by the parents' signature,' Munby said.

- That Section 20 arrangements are allowed to continue for far too long.

- Local authorities are reluctant to return the child to the parent(s) immediately after parental consent is withdrawn.

▶

◄
Lord Justice Munby set out new guidance as follows:

- Where possible, the agreement of a parent to a Section 20 arrangement should be properly recorded in writing and evidenced by the parent's signature.

- The written document should be clear and precise and drafted in simple and straightforward language that a parent can readily understand.

- The written document should spell out that the parent can 'remove the child' from the local authority accommodation 'at any time'.

- The written document should not seek to impose any fetters of the parent's right to withdraw consent.

- Where the parent is not fluent in English, the written document should be translated into the parent's own language and the parent should sign the foreign language text, adding, in the parent's language, words to the effect that 'I have read this document and I agree to its terms'.

If this new guidance had been in existence during Mike's time in care it might have made the local authority more accountable for its decision-making. This may not have made a difference to outcomes for Mike and his brother but may have avoided drift in the care system and made discussions about permanence more explicit.

What happened next

Upon leaving care I was moved to a type of 'halfway' placement. It was a strange mix between having a foster carer but being allowed to do a lot more that did not require me to seek permission for everything I did. I had to contribute to the rent but what time I came back, when I ate and what I ate, was all down to me. There was a sudden gulf in my skill set. My previous foster carer had tried to teach me to cook, how to wash and what needed to be done. The failure here was that the social worker would turn up and we would sit down and begin to explore what my move on plan was, what my future would entail. At age 16, sitting down and thinking about this, being aged 18, felt like so many years away. I never fully understood, or cared to try and understand, the severity and importance of the task at hand. So, as the teaching and learning was progressing slower than I am sure everyone wanted, I found myself at age 17 being moved into this halfway between independence and total support. This semi-independence brought about a need to use the skills I was taught, but the problem was those skills never manifested themselves fast enough to be effective in this new environment. Then, before I knew it, I had secured my own flat through the council bidding process.

As I was leaving care and turning 18, I was able to go to Band A of the council housing list, this resulted in me getting a place so soon. So, as quickly as I had moved to this semi-independence I was gone again; into my own flat signed for on my eighteenth birthday.

There was no help from social services, other than a cash handout to partly kit my place out. I eventually got given a bin, this was about as much help as I got. Luckily for me, I survived this rush to independence not through any skill or endeavours on my own part but because I met a girl who would, before long, become my wife. She was the reason I was okay. She is the reason today that I am okay. Without her, my life could have easily taken a turn for the worse; almost ten years of the best support a person could ever ask for. The support you only get from someone you call your family, not someone who walks away and can have the nights and weekends off. She was living my life, and luckily for me, she came with the skills I lacked.

Throughout the next couple of years, I had a leaving-care worker, not a social worker. They would come and do a pathway planning form, but this meant nothing. Just like the paperwork I had done about me while in care, nothing seemed to come from it. It was more a tick box exercise that was demonstrating they were somehow, through this meaningless paperwork, supporting me. The state took a massive step at some point in my life to remove the burden of parenthood from my parents, and to permanently stick it on the local authority's shoulders. The problem with this approach is that, throughout care and beyond, the state did and does not care for me, they plonked me into a system that churns out broken children. Then, once they have left that system, the responsibility gets discharged from them and you are merely a figure of outcomes, an after-thought of the system with no further intervention or support.

My message to social workers

The thing that makes the difference is truly being there.

Social worker's perspective

The statutory framework for Mike's care experience does not capture some of the qualitative issues which are raised by his story.

Mike tells us about his lived experience and we hear the voice of a scared and vulnerable child who is trying to be brave, to protect his mother and his brother, and his perception that most of the adults he encounters are more interested in their paperwork than in him. He says that he was let down by most of the adults he encountered including social workers and foster carers. As professionals we talk repeatedly about 'hearing the voice of the child' and we have prompts on paperwork and databases to record this. My question is, are we really listening? It is not good enough to ask a child if they have any views or what their wishes and feelings are. We are not listening to the right thing. I strongly believe that a child's behaviour is their language and, when they are telling us to 'fuck off' and smashing the foster carer's things, they are telling us loud and clear that something is wrong.

Mike talks about his respite carers and what it was about them that made them so important in his life, both at the time and now. They stuck with him whatever he did. They understood that his behaviour was the language of a scared and vulnerable boy and they didn't judge him or give up on him. They were always ready with a cup of tea, warmth and acceptance. This is why they are still part of Mike's life and I know he sees them as a role model for his own life.

A recent survey was carried out by Bristol University (Selwyn & Briheim-Crookall, 2017) entitled *Our Lives Our Care: Looked after children's views of their well-being*. Sadly, many of the concerns that they raise are the same as those Mike experienced some 15 years ago:

➢ Children and young people not having a good understanding of why they are in care;

➢ Not always feeling involved in decision-making; and

➢ Not feeling safe and settled in their placements.

They talk about how coming into care is 'scary' and how professionals need to keep in mind how children are feeling and do everything they can to reduce stress. They also talk, as Mike does, about the home environment and how this makes them feel wanted or not. A key issue raised is the need for foster carers to be curious about why their foster children behave the way that they do.

As previously stated, since commencing this chapter, Mike has had the opportunity to read his case files, albeit a redacted version with lots of gaps. The files reveal some contradictions with Mike's memory of events. When we talked about this I asked him how this made him feel as I was concerned about the impact of the information on his well-being. He replied: 'I'm fine because I don't believe it.' I did not find this at all concerning because, as he explained, his memories are his truth, based on his lived experience. For me, the lesson from this is that a key part of the professional role with children and young people is to think into the future about the adults they will become and how important it is for them to understand the decisions which were made on their behalf. Ensuring that they are encouraged and enabled to participate in the decision-making process in a meaningful way – listening to their voice to ensure it is heard, however it is expressed, and taking care to ensure that the reasons for them being in care are revisited appropriately, would go some way towards improving the care experience.

Mike's memories highlight a perceived lack of 'care' and an impersonal, procedural approach from social workers, focused on form filling rather than seeing the young person in front of them and understanding his needs. I could now make all sorts of excuses as to why busy, overstretched social workers might adopt this approach. Mike would say – 'I don't care! That's not my problem,' and I think he would be right. Children and young people do not want to know about staffing issues and high caseloads and lack of resources. They want you to find the time to get to know them and chat about football or whatever else may be important to them and to make them feel valued and cared for.

Mike is soon to embark on his career as a social worker and he is passionate about using his experience to improve the lives of children and young people as well as to support foster carers to better understand the children in their care. I have every confidence that he will achieve his goals.

References

DfE (2010). Family and Friends Care: Statutory Guidance for Local Authorities Available at: assets.publishing.service.gov.uk/government/uploads/system/uploads/attachment_data/file/288483/family-and-friends-care.pdf

Lord Chief Justice (2016) The Lord Chief Justice's Report. *Judiciary of England and Wales* [online], 1–35.

Selwyn, J. and Briheim-Crookall, L. (2017) Our Lives Our Care: Looked after children's views of their well-being, School for Policy Studies, University of Bristol. Available at: www.bristol.ac.uk/media-library/sites/sps/documents/hadleydocs/our-lives-our-care-report-2017.pdf.

Statute

The Children Act 1989.

4

My Son had a Section 17 Child in Need Assessment Due to his Disability

Sarah Fulton

Tim Mitchell, *Social Worker*

At a glance

- This chapter focuses on the assessment of a child under Section 17 of the Children Act 1989 due to their disability.

- Sarah is a mother to twin boys, Harry and Jack. Harry has Duchenne Muscular Dystrophy and Autism.

- Tim is a social worker in a child health and disability team. He has worked with Sarah and her family over a number of years. He reflects on this experience throughout the chapter and provides the formal knowledge underpinning the interventions in text boxes.

In 2004 Harry and Jack came into the world. Their father, Tom, and I were very happy and enjoyed the boys for 18 months before Harry's diagnosis. Their father and I are now divorced but he is still very much involved with them.

Initially, Harry was meeting his milestones when visiting the health visitor. I first noticed an issue at around 18 months old when he wasn't crawling normally – dragging one leg along and needing support when sitting up and pulling himself up. He went along to see a physiotherapist at our local hospital to look at his hip movement. Harry had a few learning issues as well at the time and attended the Child Development Centre (CDC) for play therapy and physiotherapy to help his movement. After leaving the CDC we were given a portage worker to help alongside the nursery he started to attend. He attended the clinic to see the paediatrician who, after blood tests, diagnosed Duchenne Muscular

Dystrophy (DMD). This was after even thinking he had cerebral palsy. I almost wish that is what he had instead. We were very shocked and you never forget the day they are diagnosed.

Portage

A portage worker is primarily an education provider, working with disabled children of a pre-school age (usually until the age of five). Their role is to help parents give children the learning experiences they need in the early years before school. Social work teams working with disabled children are often based in the same offices as special educational needs teams and portage workers. Shared offices are popular with local authorities, particularly following the introduction of Education, Health and Care plans (EHC) in the Children and Families Act 2014 s37.

Section 37 of the Children and Families Act 2014 states that, where it is necessary for special educational provision to be made for a child or young person in accordance with an EHC plan, the local authority must prepare that plan and maintain it. Needs, outcomes and provision are to be specified as well as any health and any social care provision reasonably required by the learning difficulties and disabilities which result in a child having special educational needs. It also specifies, in the case of a child or a young person aged under 18, any social care provision which must be made for him or her by the local authority as a result of Section 2 of the Chronically Sick and Disabled Persons Act 1970 (as it applies by virtue of Section 28A of that Act).

There was a concern with Harry's speech and language and we had appointments to check his hearing, eventually being referred to the Ear Nose and Throat Consultant at a hospital around 40 miles away in the next county. Harry also mouth-breathed and snored a lot at night. He had an operation to remove his adenoids and to put grommets in his ears. We have had a social worker for Harry since just after his fourth birthday.

Assessment of child in need

One of the roles of a portage worker is to support pre-schools (which Sarah calls nursery) to meet the specific needs of a disabled child. Once the child is at school, portage work ceases. The portage worker, in this case, referred Harry to my team which is a child health and disability team.

▶

◀

Once my team accepted the referral, this initiated an assessment under the 'Framework for the Assessment of Children in Need and their Families' – Department of Health (2000). The framework is a document informing assessment under s17 of the Children Act 1989. Section 17 places a duty on local authorities to safeguard and promote the welfare of children within their area who are in need; and so far as is consistent with that duty, to promote the upbringing of such children by their families. A child is in need if

'he is unlikely to achieve or maintain, or to have the opportunity of achieving or maintaining, a reasonable standard of health or development without the provision for him of services by a local authority; his health or development is likely to be significantly impaired, or further impaired, without the provision for him of such services; or he is disabled'. (Children Act 1989, s17).

The child health and disability team also has eligibility criteria and so does not work with all disabled children.

A specialist assessment covers specific areas of developmental need and has a section for a carer's assessment alongside a section for parenting needs, followed by a section for environmental needs. Milestones, or the expected things children will be able to do at certain ages, can be used to gauge whether a child is 'unlikely to achieve or maintain, or to have the opportunity of achieving or maintaining, a reasonable standard of health or development without the provision for him of services by a local authority' (Children Act 1989, s17). These can help identify the areas of need such as what services are needed and which children may need local authority services to reach their potential. Assessing what support the child needs, however, cannot rely on starting from developmental milestones as these are not always true of severely disabled children, who may never reach some milestones. Expectations for the child have to be worked out within the assessment.

As developmental milestones may differ, consultation with pre-school or school, paediatricians, therapists, nurses specialising in behavioural issues and other professions involved with the family are important alongside observation and any communication possible with the child as well, of course, as the parents' views. Important, too, is an evidence base of research and knowledge additional to that which may be to the fore in social work with non-disabled children. Consultation is important in a different way from that carried out for a non-disabled child. For example, in Harry's case, his muscles have degenerated over time and at one point it was crucial to establish whether he needed to work at toilet training so he could master that skill and the developmental confidence it gave, or whether this was to expect too much of him as he was beginning to deteriorate. This was also dependent on what parenting support Sarah needed. Harry's brother Jack's psychological well-being was also important, as he became confused and frustrated over Harry's difficult-to-resolve presentations, which could vary from day to day.

Harry had febrile convulsions as a baby and toddler, which we thought he would grow out of, but it soon became apparent that he was having seizures and that these had triggers other than temperature. He had an Electroencephalogram (EEG) which found nothing. When he had another one in 2011 age seven, the EEG found he was having focal seizures. This meant he had to go on medication to prevent the seizures.

Harry was diagnosed with autism in 2016. He had hallucinations and lived in 'My Little Pony World'. He tends to repeat a lot and laughs which, for me as a single mum, is stressful on top of the physical side with the DMD. The local hospice service helps a lot giving me eight hours a month mainly at home and sometimes in the hospice. I have found Harry's behaviour worse at bedtime and when he wakes up in the morning after having a lot of bad dreams.

Social work role

As a 'child in need' Harry has reviews held every six months to make plans to support him through the next six months. As his social worker I organise and chair these. Crucially, I also monitor how well those responsible for arranging his support are doing so. Attendees have been both parents, school teachers, school therapists (it is a Special School), neuromuscular advisor around muscular dystrophy, community occupational therapist, psychologist, learning disability nurse and the hospice key-worker who has known the family longest. From these meetings, over time, have arisen requirements for investigations, behavioural strategies, practical support, care for attending clubs, advice to parents and sharing and understanding of information.

Autism

Autism is a condition and not an illness which can be cured. It is associated with a 'triad of impairments' in communication, imagination and social interaction. It is a 'spectrum' condition – at one end of the spectrum people's functioning is significantly impaired, at the other people can function well in many settings. Not all people with the condition are affected in the same ways (The National Autistic Society, 2018; Ben-Itzchak et al., 2014).

Jack and Harry have very different personalities and don't look alike. At one time Jack had become quite angry and didn't want to go to school. A boy was upsetting him and he didn't want to go. He was also dealing with Harry's deterioration as his walking had declined quite a bit a few years before. Jack had support from Child and Adolescent Mental Health Services

(CAMHS) and really doesn't like talking to anyone like that. He got through this time and I talk more about Harry's condition to him. He has good friends at school and enjoys football.

Support for siblings

Jack, Harry's brother, who is not disabled, has never been a 'child in need' in his own right. However, early help systems were employed to try and help him in his difficulties as the sibling of a disabled child. Part of the environmental factors section of the specialised Child Health and Disability Single Assessment and Intervention considers siblings' needs. Assessment is an ongoing process and, sometime after the written assessment, it became clear that Jack was having difficulties. A Team Around the Child (TAC) meeting was assembled.

A TAC is a type of meeting that arose from the Common Assessment Framework (CAF) under the then government's *Every Child Matters* policy following The Children Act 2004. The CAF aims to help early identification of need and to promote co-ordinated service provision. TAC is a model of multi-agency service provision and brings together a range of practitioners from across the children and young people's workforce to support an individual child or young person and their family. Members of the TAC develop and deliver a package of solution-focused support to meet the needs identified through the common assessment.

In Jack's case, a TAC meeting was assembled and met every six months, with professionals who knew him. This included the pastoral worker at his school, the neuromuscular advisor, who had organised a session on disability at his school, the hospice keyworker who had offered sibling days out, Jack's mother Sarah and me, Jack's social worker. We put various things in place at school and home and Jack's difficulties did resolve. The TAC ran for about two years, and some of its actions were also part of Harry's child in need plan. One great benefit was that I was able to write to the Schools Admissions team to explain Jack's needs when Sarah was appealing his secondary school placement to try and achieve a place in a smaller and, what she believed, more supportive school.

For a long time Harry and his brother have had overnight stays every weekend, one on one night, the other on the next, with their father at his mother's, their grandmother's, home. In May 2017 Harry's social worker explained to me that Harry couldn't sleep upstairs when he visited his father any more. I knew the occupational therapist had been worried about Tom, his father, helping him get up the stairs because Harry's muscles were getting weaker and he couldn't hold on. Harry's social worker explained that Tom and his mother were thinking about whether they could arrange things so Harry could sleep downstairs, and that, for now, he should only visit for the daytime. I was worried about Harry not being close to his father at night, but his social worker explained that monitors could be used and he would check with Harry's father that arrangements were safe. He also said that his team could offer some respite until arrangements for Harry staying with his father were sorted out. He suggested a children's home that was linked to Harry's school, which I was surprised about because I never thought I could get respite there and I thought it was full of children from a long way away who lived there all the time. It was a relief that he was offered respite even though it was only once a month for four months.

Harry's social worker says he remembers I was embarrassed by what happened next. I don't remember being embarrassed, but I did get rather fed up *as the process carried on*. After his social worker told me what the occupational therapist had said, I had let Tom persuade me that Harry was all right staying overnight, and Harry had stayed over for two nights. I got a letter, which was called a *Letter of Expectation*, which said what I had done wrong and what I was not to do, and explained that the local authority might consider further statutory action to protect Harry if I did not keep to the expectations.

A letter of expectation

A Letter of Expectation is part of a safeguarding process. Where a parent's action, or inaction, is putting a child at risk, and the parent has not acted on the social worker's advice for keeping a child safe, a Letter of Expectation may be sent to the parent. It sets out what the local authority's concerns are and what the local authority expects the parent to do or not do. It advises that the local authority may consider further statutory action if the expectations are not met. The further statutory action might be, for instance, a Strategy Meeting with a view to a Child Protection Conference under Section 47 of the Children Act 1989.

It was unusual for a Letter of Expectation to go to the parent who did not have care of the child when the concerns arose. In this case, however, Sarah had a strong motivation for arranging for an overnight break for herself, and there were other reasons why she had to hold additional responsibility in this situation. I do not have consent from other family members to explain these. The letters were applicable for one month each because it was important for everyone to see the potential for a process of change and because Tom, Harry's father, was encouraged to be active in thinking with Harry's grandmother about whether they could make her home suitable for Harry to stay overnight safely. There were Letters of Expectation in place for about six months.

What got me fed up was the letters turning up every month and the fact that it was difficult. This was mainly about my *separated* ex-husband and my mother-in-law, and their difficulties in sorting out the situation was having an effect on me. I knew the hospice worker had been asking Harry's social worker for respite for a long time, because I had been quite low ever since there were difficulties with Tom's overnight care. Before that, Harry's social worker had explained that he would not offer respite if Tom was able to have Harry overnight most weekends, because time with his father was more important for Harry. I agreed to this because Tom would be giving respite for me by having Harry. I'm not so sure about this though, because I still have to look after Harry's brother when Harry is with his father. He doesn't have them together. Harry's social worker has suggested sitters, friends and my parents for looking after Jack, but none of this really works.

Restrictions

I am very sympathetic to Sarah's issue here but I am not empowered to arrange breaks for her from caring for Jack as the legislation does not allow for it. The Children Act 1989 empowers local authorities to provide this sort of service for Children in Need and not others. I therefore cannot arrange for Jack to receive such a service, and it would not be fair to propose it to him. I can see that such breaks could be indirectly beneficial to Harry as Sarah could get out with friends and be refreshed as a mother and carer, but essentially this is for her to work out with her own resources. Tom is not able to care for both boys at the same time.

A month or two after this Harry came home and told me something that worried me, saying that he had fallen over when he was supposed to be in his father's care, and his father was not there. I was concerned about this, and I didn't like to say anything, but I thought I had to. I rang Harry's social worker and he said he would see Harry at school. He rang me afterwards and explained his concerns. He had also gone to see Tom.

Investigations under Section 47 of the Children Act 1989

I investigated this concern, after informing both parents I planned to do so, by asking Harry about it at school, and then by asking his father, Tom. This needed doing quickly as Harry was due to see his father at the end of that week. Although he impressed his teacher (who was present to provide support) with the quality of his communication, Harry was only able to tell me that his 'dad dropped' him, and he fell 'on the floor, not the toilet'. The picture I constructed in my mind was that Harry

▶

> ◀
>
> had been taken upstairs to the toilet against advice and then something had gone wrong. However, I spoke with Tom together with Harry's grandmother, and Tom gave an account, which the grandmother supported, which made sense of Harry's words but gave a much less alarming picture. This was that Tom had been helping with a pad change downstairs in the lounge and there had been a wobble, with Harry ending up on the floor.
>
> Tom was upset about the discrepancy between his account and my construction of Harry's account. I realised, and acknowledged, that Harry could have been telling me as best he could about the event his father described. Harry's father Tom accepted that the event was risky and a new approach was needed. This was an exploratory investigation to see whether Harry was a child at risk of significant harm as per s47 of the Children Act 1989. I assessed that he was not at risk as his father was prepared to take a different and safer approach to managing things in future. It was my view that Tom had also been taking the Letters of Expectation very seriously.

Harry's social worker asked me how long Harry could go without needing a pad change. An altered Letter of Expectation then came about Harry only being able to stay with Tom for that corresponding length of time unless Tom had a hoist he could use for helping with the pad change. Since then, Tom and his mother have found a way to have my mobile hoist with them when Harry is visiting his father.

Shared care

Eventually Tom and his mother decided they couldn't make the arrangements for Harry to stay overnight with them. I was advised that social services had a Shared Carer scheme where a carer would look after Harry in their own home overnight once a month. I initially saw the shared care social worker to complete the paperwork to find out all about Harry and to match him with the right carer. The proposed shared carer first came to meet Harry and me with the shared care social worker in our house. She saw and heard some of Harry's most distressing behaviours, but reassured me that she would cope. We then went to the carer's home after school where she got to know Harry a bit more, and Harry was much more settled. He went for tea on the last day of term, and we arranged a sleepover in the holidays. He has had three overnights now and it's going very well. Harry hasn't shown any of the behaviours he did on the first visit when the shared carer came to see him and I don't expect he will now.

Shared care support

The shared care social worker in this case, recruits, assesses and arranges training and some equipment for shared carers. She matches them with children, using introductory and initial tea visits to test compatibility. She works to the Care Planning, Placement and Case Review Regulations 2010 (since amended), the Fostering Services Regulations 2011 and the National Minimum Standards 2011.

Shared care is one of the services child health and disability social workers can refer to in order to meet an assessed need. It can support a parent to sustain the care a child needs by providing regular breaks to look forward to and to restore energy. Shared care can contribute in this way to good parenting and to the benefits a child receives by growing up in a supportive family. It also provides some of the benefits of family life during the short break, (see Framework for the Assessment of Children in need and their Families, Dimensions of Parenting Capacity, 2000, p. 21) where residential short breaks, for instance – where the child is likely to experience shift workers coming on and off duty, and an environment quite different from a family home – are less able to do so. Schedule 2.6 of the Children Act 1989 states under Provision for Disabled Children that 'every local authority shall provide services designed: (b) to give such children the opportunity to lead lives which are as normal as possible'. Disabled children are also subject to the 'right to family life' under the Human Rights Act 1998, Article 8. These considerations were behind the effort to support Harry to continue to stay with his father overnight, and the choice of shared care as a service.

I didn't understand quite how some things worked under shared care until recently. For instance, that we would get a choice of dates. The shared carer just gave me dates she could manage at first, but now she has asked me which I would like. I feel better now that I have that respite overnight. I don't want Tom to feel his role is taken away. He wasn't keen initially but I said it's helping us both. I got a feeling about the shared carer through meeting her and that helped me reassure Tom. He was worried because he felt we didn't know this person who was going to look after Harry. I also feel that I have more quality time with his twin brother Jack. It did take a while for the whole scheme to start and we could have done with it sooner.

I would like more respite, especially as it is such hard work at bedtimes. Harry's social worker has explained that respite is designed to give breaks to look forward to and to help parents manage, but it doesn't take away very much of the caring job. I've got more used to the breaks I get now and I have asked the hospice workers to come in at bedtime, which is one day a week and so that helps. I don't know why I didn't think of that before.

My message for social workers

Please let parents know earlier about services they might be using. I would like to have known about shared care a long time before it was introduced to me. I had to face a lot of worry about the difficulty of getting sitters so I could go out in the evening and have 'time off' and it was an incredible relief once I found out about shared care.

I would have liked to have known earlier that I could ask for dates I wanted.

I think if Harry's social worker had come and talked face-to-face more often about his concerns, and about what they meant for me and for Harry, I might not have got so fed up with the Letters of Expectation. From the start, if he had sat down with me and talked about the concerns, I might not have been so ready to accept Tom telling me it was okay for Harry to stay with him overnight.

Social worker's reflections

Providing information

I haven't yet introduced the shared carer to Tom (Harry and Jack's father), or given him a chance to see Harry with her. With hindsight I would have made sure I did this earlier, which could have reduced some of the worry for him and the stress for Sarah around his concerns. This intervention has made me resolve to talk through possibilities with parents even if they concern other services than ones I am responsible for. I could have suggested earlier, for example, that Sarah approach the hospice service to come to the home at bedtimes, not only to take some of the caring on for her but also perhaps to help her find new ways of doing things.

Sharing of information is also identified by Sarah in relation to shared care. The shared care social worker reflects that providing a leaflet explaining things like a parent's opportunity to ask for dates is difficult, because some shared carers are so booked up that they cannot offer choice. She thinks however that she could have explained early on that the shared carer had very little availability to start with but, as time went on, Sarah would have some options as to when she wanted the shared care. I could also have talked to Sarah earlier. It is important as social workers that we think about the stress a parent might feel having to think about solutions to a problem they might be facing soon, and not knowing what solution could be available. I am mindful, however, that I couldn't have offered shared care until it was an assessed need. As social workers, we need to think about how we provide information on services without raising expectations unfairly and without closing off the possibility of options that might be more beneficial to the child.

Another area of reflection is on the need to challenge. I challenged my team manager on the Letter of Expectation about hoisting for which I am glad. The manager wanted to make the Expectation open to being monitored by Sarah or by me making unannounced visits. Because of this, he wanted a defined time limit for Harry's visits to his father. I argued that this was not fair as Tom could take Harry out to places where there were hoists and changing facilities, so the wording Sarah refers to was only if there was no hoist available. I think this may have helped Tom and his mother's decision to use the mobile hoist in the home. This meant more satisfying time with his father and grandmother for Harry. It might have helped them move to a downstairs solution for overnights but, as it was, it didn't.

Face-to-face contact

Sarah's third message about discussing my concerns face-to-face makes me really quite ashamed. All I can remember is things being really quite hectic. There were things going on with Harry's situation which Sarah has not included here, and I felt pressured with so much to handle. This is no excuse, and she is probably right that I communicated by phone, and she may well be right that, if I had talked it through properly face-to-face, she might have understood the concern and we would not have had to have the Letters of Expectation. As a social worker, it is easy to hurry through what we need to do; or think we need to do; and not think enough about what a parent may need. It might be that actually going and seeing someone is more important if it saves them difficulty, rather than thinking of achieving a task in what seems to be, but isn't, the most efficient way for ourselves. This provides significant learning for us as social workers as achieving this balance can be difficult with the pressures of a heavy workload.

Involving both parents

There are strong messages for social workers at the moment about including parents, often fathers, who live outside of the household. This means including them in assessments and working in partnership with them.

Messages have come from Serious Case Reviews held by Local Safeguarding Children Boards and from Ofsted Inspection comments, such as the recent Inspection Report of Children's Services in my local authority, which said: 'In a small number of cases, birth fathers and other extended family members are not spoken to. As a result, their views and potential contribution to improving children's outcomes are not known or considered.'

The example explored in this chapter is nothing near a 'serious case'. Tom has always wanted to be involved in Harry's life and Sarah has always wanted him to be, but seeking to involve both parents is still good practice. We can do this by promoting both parents' involvement in meetings and in information-sharing as both parents' contribution to a child's development can be so important. In my practice experience, there have been other families where there have been difficulties supporting separated fathers to have satisfying contact with children due to the need to have adaptations and equipment at home.

The intervention Sarah has told us about highlights the careful work needed to try and fulfil the Children Act 1989 s17 duty to promote the safety and welfare of children 'and so far as is consistent with that duty, to promote the upbringing of such children by their families', particularly where a child is disabled, their condition is changing, and there is a need for changes to living arrangements.

Safeguarding

The other main learning from Sarah's account has been about safeguarding needs and the importance of engaging skills and caution alongside the need to act decisively where protection is needed. Harry's disclosure meant I needed to act. It can be difficult when working with a severely disabled child to get a clear understanding. It is important to keep an open mind, but a careful one, when talking to parents about an incident. A timely response is needed. A parent could be acting recklessly or not protectively and delaying might result in serious harm for a child. Having heard, analysed and reflected in this situation I needed both to be reasonable and firm in clarifying what needed to happen. My team serves around 100 severely disabled children and work such as that explored in this chapter is happening every week for the team. My main message is that we need to keep learning.

References

Ben-Itzchak, E., Watson, L. and Zachor, D. (2014) Cognitive ability is associated with different outcome trajectories in autism spectrum disorders. *Journal of Autism & Developmental Disorders*. 44: 9, 2221–2229.

Department of Health (2000) *Framework for the assessment of children in need and their families*. Available at: webarchive.nationalarchives. gov.uk/20130404002518/www.education.gov.uk/publications/ eOrderingDownload/Framework%20for%20the%20assessment%20of%20 children%20in%20need%20and%20their%20families.pdf.

The National Autistic Society (2018) *Autism*. Available at: www.autism.org.uk.

Statute

The Children Act 1989
Human Rights Act 1988
The Children Act 2004
The Children and Families Act 2014
Care Planning, Placement and Case Review Regulations 2010
Fostering Services Regulations 2011
National Minimum Standards 2011

5

I was Taken in to Care

Zoe McQuade

Jennifer Bigmore, *Lecturer in Social Work*

At a glance

- This chapter focuses on the statutory intervention under s47 of the Children Act 1989 of removing a child to a place of safety.

- Zoe, is a care leaver who was placed with foster carers along with her sister when she was a teenager. She has recently qualified as a social worker.

- Jenny is a social work lecturer and experienced children and families social worker and was Zoe's and her sister's allocated social worker at the time. Jenny and Zoe have written this chapter together and provide the formal framework for the legal intervention in the text boxes. Both reflect on their learning from this experience.

Zoe:

This is the story of how my sister and I came into care when I was aged 14 and my sister was 12. I have written this with Jenny who was my social worker at the time and who has come back into my life in recent years. The chapter will focus on one particular summer's day which I will never forget. This was the day that my sister and I went to a child protection conference and the day we went into care.

My name is Zoe and I was in foster care for four years until I was 18 years old. My upbringing was very different to an average person. I was born in Hong Kong and lived in South East Asia and Africa, until moving to England at ten years old. My parents worked in hospitality and my father travelled the world, opening new hotels, while my mother looked after myself and my sister. Some would say we had a very privileged life living abroad with a big house, swimming pool, maid and gardener. When I was ten years old we moved to England and we had nothing; we lived at my grandparents who only had a two-bedroom bungalow so things were very cramped. My father and mother struggled to get work and experienced years of money troubles and loss of close family members which then resulted in both my parents turning to drink.

My mother became very ill and ended up in hospital locally and in London for a year; she had a condition called Korsakoff syndrome which is influenced by alcohol, although I didn't know this at the time. When she returned home from hospital she was on medication, had to walk with a stick and her personality had changed. By this time both my parents were alcoholics and drank all day, every day. My mother mixed alcohol with medication, which meant she became violent and angry towards me and my sister. My father was not violent but did nothing to protect us. When I reflect back to my teenage years there were no boundaries as my parents were always drunk and there was lots of shouting and anger. I think at times me and my sister took advantage of these occasions, where we would have parties with drugs and alcohol at a young age. This continued for a year or so, until things got so bad we knew we couldn't carry on.

During this time my behaviour deteriorated and I was always in trouble at school: bunking off; being rude to the teachers; walking out of classes; and it was the same for my sister. Reflecting back, the school was aware of some of the problems at home but saw us, and our behaviour, as the problem. Our friends and their parents were also aware and our friends were not allowed to come around to our house and their parents did not want to get involved. My sister is two-and-a-half years younger than me and we were very close, we both decided we would live at our grandma's. Unfortunately, she was too old and we had no other family members to look after us so the only option was foster care. I remember meeting my social worker, Jenny, for the first time and she was kind, patient and showed empathy towards me and my sister. We told her everything and didn't hold back and wanted to be involved with the process of what happened next.

There are certain days that stood out for me the most in the process of going into care and the effects from speaking out about what was happening at home and these are what we are going to talk about in this chapter.

Jenny:

I was the allocated social worker for Zoe and her sister and am in the very fortunate position that they have come back into my life as adults. We have been able to share our memories of the very significant event in Zoe's life.

None of us can remember the exact details of what happened next and who finally contacted children's services but the catalyst for change was when Zoe and her sister went to their local youth club for the evening. Both girls decided they had had enough and didn't want to go home. Both of them wanted to live somewhere else. Youth workers were aware of the problems at home and the evening ended with the youth workers delivering the girls to their grandmother and the next day Children's Services were contacted.

I have found myself in a unique position in having two former looked-after children come back into my life as adults. I was the social worker for Zoe and her sister for several years prior to leaving practice to teach social work in a university, 14 years ago. Zoe contacted me when she saw my name on the university website, at a time when she was undertaking an Access course with a view to becoming a social worker. She emailed me starting, 'I don't know if you remember me….' Well, of course, I remembered her! The hardest part of leaving practice had been saying goodbye to all of my looked-after children and I often wondered how they were. From time to time I had updates on Zoe and her sister when I bumped into their former foster mother who was still part of their lives. I knew that their mother had died in very difficult circumstances.

All children and young people are special in their own way and Zoe and her sister were no exception. I remember my first meeting with them. They were a feisty pair (still are) and had made a decision that there had to be some changes to their lives. Both their parents had developed serious problems with alcohol and their home life was volatile, frightening and physically and emotionally dangerous. What made these two remarkable young people stand out for me was that they insisted that they could not remain at home and wanted to come into foster care. Other than their paternal grandmother and a godmother, they had no extended family and there were no alternatives.

Zoe has her own story to tell about what happened next. What I want to share is my story since she and her sister came back into my life and what I have learned from the unusual and privileged opportunity to reminisce and also become part of their 'present'. Shortly after Zoe began her social work degree, she invited me to her wedding in Thailand. She told me her foster mother was going too and that it was just a few of the people closest to her who would be there. My heart told me to accept the invitation immediately but I hesitated before agreeing. Would this be crossing a professional boundary? I am still a registered social worker as well as a lecturer. However, on reflection I felt that as Zoe and her sister were now adults and had initiated the contact with me it would be appropriate for me to accept. Their father was happy for me to be there. Tragically, Zoe's father passed away two days after her wedding in

Thailand and in the years since, we have become extremely close. Both Zoe and her sister have become part of my extended family. I make no apologies for this and can say that it has brought me great joy and hopefully has meant that they know they are loved and have a support network.

Working together on this book chapter has been a wonderful opportunity to share our memories and also to clarify some details which, at the time, perhaps should have been made clearer by me in terms of reasons for being in care, understanding statutory processes and, probably most importantly, explaining some of their parents' behaviour and their own responses to this.

Spending time with Zoe and her sister as adults has highlighted for me the enormous responsibility that social workers and other professionals have when they intervene in someone's life. The fact that, once involved, for however long or short a time that may be, you become part of their personal narrative, their life story and this cannot be erased. With one exception, I have known Zoe and her sister longer than anyone else living and one of the things we enjoy doing is reminiscing. Many of our conversations begin with 'Do you remember when…?' This is very similar to the conversations I have with my own family and I believe is fundamental to a sense of identity, continuity and belonging. What I have also been able to do is to answer questions about how and why things happened which may have become lost or distorted over time. Not that my memory is faultless, but I can nevertheless offer some insight into their history which I believe has helped in many ways for them both to come to terms with their past.

As Zoe has explained, her mother had a diagnosis of Korsakoff syndrome which is a chronic memory disorder, usually caused by alcohol use. One of the symptoms of this condition is severe short-term memory loss – loss of day-to-day memory. As we have looked back on events leading to Zoe and her sister coming into care, one of the things she and her sister found hardest to deal with was their mother's denial of having been violent or abusive to them. While we know that it is common for parents to deny maltreatment of their children, in this particular case, it is perfectly feasible that their mother had no memory of her behaviour. Understanding this has, I believe, helped them to work through their feelings towards their mother and enabled them to reframe their memories of what happened to them.

My involvement with Zoe began when Children's Services became aware that the girls were staying with their paternal grandmother (now deceased) because they did not feel safe at home and that she was unable to look after them on a long-term basis. I visited them at their grandmother's home and they were memorable from the start. Without wanting to evoke stereotypes, it was unusual to meet two such confident and assertive young people who had clearly made a decision that they could not continue to live with their parents because of their drinking and their mother's physical abuse of them and that they wanted to come into care. In reality, they had little understanding of what this really meant but they were adamant that they could not go home and there was no one else to look after them. Their grandmother was equally assertive and clearly a lady who was used to being listened to! When they explained what had been going on at home over a long period of time it was clear that there were serious concerns which needed to be addressed. The girls had an air of self-confidence and resilience which I believe had come from their early experience of a life of some privilege and a lifestyle which included a good education and some appropriate parenting. They certainly knew their own minds!

The statutory intervention

Given the nature of the concerns an assessment process commenced. Meeting their parents reinforced the picture of an unusual and privileged upbringing and parents who were now in denial about finding themselves under scrutiny from statutory services. Their father, in particular, was a man used to running international businesses and was affronted by the presence of statutory services in the life of his family and therefore the initial stages of working with them was challenging.

A decision was made, following a strategy meeting that the circumstances met the threshold for a Section 47 enquiry (Children Act, 1989).

Section 47 Children Act 1989

A Section 47 enquiry is initiated to decide whether, and what type of, action is needed to safeguard and promote the welfare of a child who is suspected of, or likely to be, suffering significant harm (HM Government, 2018, p. 43).

Working together to safeguard children (April 2018)

Working Together is a guide to inter-agency working to safeguard and promote the welfare of children. It is updated from time to time to reflect changes in the approach to safeguarding and, when the intervention with Zoe and her sister took place, a different version would have been in place. However, the essence of the guidance remains to manage individual cases and includes flowcharts setting out the steps

▶

◀

professionals should take when working together to assess and provide services for children who may be in need, including those suffering significant harm.

Contrary to public perception, Children's Services do not make decisions alone as to the way to proceed with cases where there is thought to be a significant risk of harm. A strategy discussion is held to discuss the action between social workers, the police and, in some cases, the National Society for the Prevention of Cruelty to Children (NSPCC). If there is an immediate risk to the life of the child, or a likelihood of serious immediate harm, local authority social workers, the police or NSPCC should use their statutory child protection powers to act immediately to secure the safety of the child.

If it is necessary to remove a child from their home, a local authority must, wherever possible and unless a child's safety is otherwise at immediate risk, apply for an Emergency Protection Order (EPO) (Children Act, 1989, p. 44). Police powers to remove a child in an emergency should be used only in exceptional circumstances where there is insufficient time to seek an EPO or for reasons relating to the immediate safety of the child (ibid., p. 31).

In the interim, the girls stayed with their grandmother with their parents' consent and then went to stay with their godmother in Brighton for a few days leading up to the Child Protection Conference. Given their parents' cooperation with this safety plan, it was not thought to be necessary at the time to secure the girls with an order at this time.

One hot summer's day...

The initial child protection conference

Child protection conferences

Child Protection Conferences were first introduced in the UK in the 1970s, following the death of Maria Colwell, as a way for professionals to share information. Since then, conferences have become an inter-agency forum for professionals and family members, including children (when appropriate), to work in partnership to plan how to safeguard and promote the welfare of children.

The purpose of the conference is to bring together and analyse, in an inter-agency setting, all relevant information and plan how best to safeguard and promote the welfare of the child. It is the responsibility of the conference to make recommendations on how agencies work together to safeguard the child in future.

▶

◀

Conference tasks include:

- appointing a lead statutory body (either local authority children's social care or NSPCC) and a lead social worker, who should be a qualified, experienced social worker and an employee of the lead statutory body;

- identifying membership of the core group of professionals and family members who will develop and implement the child protection plan;

- establishing timescales for meetings of the core group, production of a child protection plan and for child protection review meetings; and

- agreeing an outline child protection plan, with clear actions and timescales, including a clear sense of how much improvement is needed, by when, so that success can be judged clearly.

(HM Government, 2018, p. 47)

The day of the conference dawned. My report prepared for the conference had been shared with both the parents and the girls and the purpose and structure of the conference explained by the conference Chair. Both Zoe and her sister were in no doubt that they wanted to participate in the conference as it was their lives which were being discussed and they wanted to have a say in it. In my experience it is uncommon for children and young people to attend a conference and, in fact, this was my only experience of it during many years of practice. Both Zoe and her sister were fearful that their parents would deny any problems with their drinking and behaviour and that the professionals would listen to their parents rather than to them. This was part of their motivation for attending, to make sure their views were made clear.

The conference was held on a very hot summer's day and the girls were brought by their godmother from Brighton in order to attend. One of my enduring memories was the girls arriving and Zoe's sister gleefully handing me a sick bag to deal with. I know that for her there was a certain sense of excitement about the unknown. Zoe was far more hesitant.

Zoe's sister recalls:

I felt nervous on the journey to the conference. I was scared that no one would believe us and then we would have to go home with Mum and Dad and things would be worse. Our godmother reassured us that she would not let that happen. During the conference I remember feeling so angry with my parents and Dad said that I was a serial liar and always told tales. Zoe and I were so shocked by what they were saying which I think showed on our faces.

Zoe:

We arrived at the council office after travelling with my godmother from Brighton and my sister handed her sick bag to the social worker to dispose of, as she suffered from car sickness. At the meeting we sat next to our parents and there were two police officers, the head of year from school, social workers and other people we didn't know. I remember being scared of the police being at the conference. The room felt very tense and it was very hard for me and my sister to hear all the lies our parents were saying to the professionals. We were labelled liars by our father, our own role model, and we felt stupid and that no one would believe us until, at the end of the conference, the chairman put our parents in their place and it was agreed that we should go to live with foster carers.

We were involved in the child protection meeting and spoke in front of our parents. Both my sister and I felt that if the professionals didn't speak to us directly, then they would listen to my mother and father's lies. My mother never admitted physically and emotionally abusing me and my sister and I now realise this is because of her memory loss from her illness and alcohol. Fortunately, all of the professionals listened to us and could tell by our facial expressions that we didn't agree with what our parents were saying.

Hearing the child's voice – Children and young people's participation

When working with children and young people it is very important that their rights are taken into consideration and decisions take account of the articles within the United Nation's (UN) Convention on the Rights of the Child (1989) (DfE, 2010) as well as the Human Rights Act 1998.

UN Convention on the Rights of the Child (1989) – (ratified by the UK in 1991)

Article 12 - Respect for the views of the child

Every child has the right to express their views, feelings and wishes in all matters affecting them, and to have their views considered and taken seriously. This right applies at all times, for example, during immigration proceedings, housing decisions or the child's day-to-day home life.

What does this mean in practice? You should have a say in all decisions that affect you.

▶

◄

Children Act 1989

One of the central principles of the Children Act 1989 is contained in s1(3) which states that regard must be given to:

a) The ascertainable wishes and feelings of the child concerned (considered in the light of his age and understanding).

Jenny:

As the allocated social worker I remember aspects of the conference very clearly. First, there were lots of people in the room which was located in a cramped portacabin. Zoe and her sister, mother, father and grandmother, as well as all of the professionals, filled the room. I cannot remember the detail but I can remember the dynamics and emotions in the room from my own perspective as the social worker. I participated in many conferences during my years in practice which I cannot remember now but certain aspects of this one remain ingrained in my memory. Most initial child protection conferences are emotive and challenging and it is important to be aware of the power dynamics within the room. I felt a multitude of emotions including some empathy with the parents and grandmother. The issue of culture, identity and class has been raised as an issue in a recent serious case review (Kingston and Richmond LSCB, 2015) and whether class has an impact on child protection procedures. Certainly, for the adults in this family, they had never had experience of involvement with social workers and I believe this challenged them on many levels. For professionals it can be challenging in meeting not only resistance but also a level of authority in the nature of the challenges posed to them by parents.

As the conference proceeded it was very clear to the professionals attending that both Zoe and her sister were shocked by their parents' denial of their problems with alcohol and their behaviour towards their daughters. This was evident throughout in their facial expressions and body language as well as when their views were asked for. The final decision of the conference was that Zoe and her sister would be placed on the Child Protection Register and a child protection plan was drawn up. This included the decision that they could not return home and that a foster placement would be sought. (The Child Protection Register has since been replaced by a Record of Children with a Child Protection Plan).

Zoe's sister:

I wasn't scared or worried. I was just so happy that people had believed us. I remember Mum and Dad going without saying goodbye to us.

Zoe:

After the conference my sister and I sat outside the offices waiting for the social workers to find us a home. We couldn't return home as neither grandma nor my godmother could look after us, so we were left for hours waiting to hear where we would live. I remember feeling a sense of regret. Did we do the right thing to be dumped somewhere?

Jenny drove us to the placement. When we first arrived no one answered the door because it was the foster mother's birthday and there was a party in the garden so, with lots of strangers and not knowing anyone, I was so scared. Jenny and my godmother had to leave after a short period. I stayed in the room and felt frightened, upset and guilty for what had happened. I did not feel welcome in the house – like I had ruined the foster mother's birthday for turning up at short notice. That day I stayed in my room all night and called my friends in tears. My sister remembers going to play with the foster sister as I wanted to be alone, she felt angry at me for being selfish and not coping with the situation. Me and my sister had asked to go in foster care to get away from the violence and abuse, however, being placed with strangers seemed more scary at the time.

On reflection, it wasn't the ideal situation to put siblings straight from a child protection conference into a foster placement. There was a lot of waiting around and unknowns for my sister and I, we didn't have all our belongings from home as we had just stayed at my godmothers in Brighton. When we arrived the foster parents were focused on entertaining their friends rather than on us. They might have thought to give us some space but, to me, I felt I wasn't wanted and an inconvenience. It is a frightening experience entering a foster home not knowing the household rules and routines. My sister took the experience with a sense of an adventure but when the fun stopped she wasn't happy in the placement and left after a disagreement with the foster mother.

Jenny:

For reasons I cannot remember, a foster placement had not yet been identified. I suspect that, due to the shortage of foster placements, the fostering team delayed finding an appropriate placement until they had confirmation that one was needed. This meant that Zoe and her sister had to hang around the local office until one was confirmed.

Eventually, quite late in the day a placement was confirmed and I took the girls to their new foster home. I could only imagine at the time how this must have felt. I had very little knowledge myself of the foster carers so was unable to give much information on the journey there. In its favour was the fact that it was fairly close to their home and school. When we arrived there was a garden party going on for the foster mother's birthday so there was a house full of guests and general chaos. It soon became apparent that Zoe and her sister would have to share a bedroom with the foster care's daughter, which is far from ideal.

After doing the required paperwork and settling the girls as best I could, I drove away with a sick feeling in my stomach as I always did when placing a child. I could sense Zoe's distress and felt guilty that there had been no possibility of matching or time to prepare them. At moments like this you had to trust the foster carers to understand and support the child or young person and ignore the urge to scoop them up and take them home with you. Aspects of this placement would contravene current National Minimum Standards (2011).

Fostering services: National Minimum Standards (2011)

10.6: In the foster home, each child over the age of three should have their own bedroom. If this is not possible, the sharing of a bedroom is agreed by each child's responsible authority and each child has their own area within the bedroom. Before seeking agreement for the sharing of a bedroom, the fostering service provider takes into account any potential for bullying, any history of abuse or abusive behaviour, the wishes of the children concerned and all other pertinent facts. The decision-making process and outcome of the assessment are recorded in writing where bedroom sharing is agreed.

Zoe – What happened next:

When you are a child, there is some information which is not explained by adults and this is confusing for our feelings and thoughts. I was very angry at my parents and my way of coping was to block them out of my life and I did not want any contact when I first entered foster care. However, I did care for and love both my parents – I just had my own coping strategy to deal with the situation. My first contact with my parents after being put into foster care was a very strange and confusing time for me. The contact was supervised at my parents' home by my social worker. My mum and dad wanted kisses and cuddles and were apologising and upset. I still felt angry. I had so many questions but didn't want to talk to them. My main feeling was why were they sorry now? They had never apologised before and I felt it was all a bit too late for forgiveness. My world had been pulled upside down because my parents were too selfish. Were they going to change or was this another lie they made up? As a child you don't understand why adults drink and act differently, and Mum's illness was never explained to me. I wanted change from the violence and abuse but I still wasn't happy living with strangers and having to share a room with a foster sister and my own sister. I was 14 years old at the time and my friends were my life and I told them everything. However, I did fall out with friends at times and felt very lonely without a family or friends and there were some very low points in my life.

As time went on in foster care, I did start to trust and talk to my foster mother and social worker but it took time and patience from their side. My sister and I were always close at home but, once in foster care, we soon did not get on. She wanted to go home as soon as possible and sometimes grudged me about speaking up about the abuse and being in foster care. My sister was always there to protect me when the violence started at home, even though she was younger. Then, when we went into care, my sister wanted to care for Mum and Dad to become better parents and bring the family back together. In a way she was trying to please everyone and she felt responsible for them. She became very frustrated when things weren't as she wanted them to be. I was determined to stay where I was. I wanted to be settled and to do well in my GCSEs and my way of coping was to shut things out. Both my sister and I have had very different experiences and memories of being in care, where staying together wasn't always the best strategy.

My sister returned home and, on the surface, things had improved in the family home. My parents had both undertaken some rehabilitation work, although my dad had done better than my mum. Mum was being supported by adult services in relation to her illness and my dad was felt to be in a position to be a protective factor. My sister hid what was really happening. I was on a visit one day and Mum had been drinking again while ironing some clothes. Both my mother and I had a few cross words then, just as I sat in the lounge, my mother approached me with a pint glass and smashed it across my head. I was in shock, angry, upset and felt a sense of realisation that things had not improved. I then grabbed my phone called my boyfriend and foster mum and ran out of the house with my sister. My mother followed us shouting while waving her walking stick. Neighbours watched in shock. I felt so ashamed of my mother, my family and that people thought I was a troubled child. My sister was then angry at me once again for breaking up the family as she had to go back into care.

Over the years I built a strong bond with my foster parents and, when things were better at home, I still asked to stay in foster care to continue my education in a structured environment until I was 18 years old. My sister didn't like foster care and returned home as soon as my mother moved out and my father was off the alcohol.

Then when I was 26 years old I wanted a change in my career from hospitality and looked into social work. After travelling around the world I wanted to make a difference and help others. I was lucky to have a positive experience with foster care and social services and this has always stayed with me. I found out Jenny was working at my local university, while looking on their website for social work courses. I sent an email to Jenny and we made contact. It was an amazing experience to talk about my past and she was able to fill the missing gaps. I was doing an Access course in college at the time and then continued to do my social work degree, where I qualified three years later. The course has changed me as a person and my experience has helped me to qualify as a social worker and, overall, made me passionate to help others.

My message to social workers

The child protection conference

Listen to the child or young person

➢ Ask the child if they would like to be involved in the child protection meeting and give them options. It was really important to my sister and me to be there.

➢ I felt that the professionals wanted to hear my side of the story and I wanted them to know about the lies that were believed in the past with the school (things my parents told them about home). We felt that we were listened to.

➢ I wanted things to change, and they did through the child protection process and the support of my social worker.

➢ Explain to the child what a child protection meeting is and what will happen afterwards.

➢ Use different tools and imagination to explain to the child so they understand.

The first day in care

➣ The first day the child is placed in foster care will be part of their history. Be prepared for the child to cry and to be scared of the unknown.

➣ Think of the emotional and physical effects on the child in one day (for us, the conference and going into care was all in one day).

➣ If possible, make a list to make sure the child has all their most important possessions. For example, their teddy to hug when scared; their school uniform so they don't stand out from others; a picture of their pet or family.

➣ Talk to them about having to fit into a new family with different ways of doing things like going to church.

Remember that siblings are different

➣ Ages – different behaviours because of their understanding. Older siblings may get angry with other siblings.

➣ Siblings may present different behaviours and may not support each other.

➣ Sharing a room? Individual assessment is necessary to give both children choice if possible.

Relationship between me and my social worker

➣ My social worker would repeat some of my comments to make sure she fully understood what I was saying.

➣ My social worker took the time to talk and didn't rush me or pressure me into talking if it was a bad day.

➣ It is important that a social worker remembers things you have discussed and understands that some days you just want to talk about music or toys. Sometimes the purpose of a visit is just to eat chocolate cake!

➣ Think about where you have discussions. If in public, think who can overhear conversations.

➣ When discussing problems think of a hobby you can do for an hour with the child instead of sitting in a room being quizzed.

➤ Social workers need honesty, reliability, confidence, good listening skills.

➤ The child will always remember you, think how you would like to be remembered.

➤ The child may have no positive role model in their life. Social workers can be good role models to children no matter what age.

Social worker's perspective

We have focused on one very big day in Zoe's life. What this has highlighted to me is that days like this may be a regular part of your life as a social worker and part of standard policy and procedure but for the children and young people involved, this is far removed from their normal experience and, as such, the unique needs of those children and their families must be considered and prioritised because memories can never be erased. You cannot go back and do it again. You need to get it right first time.

Concluding thoughts from Zoe

I have had several conversations with my sister about our feelings and memories of our time in foster care and we both have very different accounts. One of my coping mechanisms as a child was to block out memories – like they didn't exist – to protect my feelings and worries. During this process it has been hard to unlock some of the past experiences and hard to put into words my feelings at the time. Since working with Jenny on this chapter, I have done quite a bit of reflection on my experience, feelings and thoughts. Meeting Jenny in adulthood has helped fill those missing gaps, especially when both my parents have now sadly passed away. I now look at Jenny as family and, doing this has made me realise with so much loss and trauma you become very close to the people who shared those experiences.

When becoming a social worker and working with children with past and present trauma, one person can be the role model they need and make positive changes to their life. It is important for the child to have a voice, and that is something Jenny always encouraged. As a child you don't always learn everything about child protection with the procedures and interventions, just the memories of how you were feeling. I hope sharing my experience will help future social workers think twice when working with vulnerable children. Going through the care system can be a scary, lonely experience and your social worker can be a friend as well as an advocate. As a social worker you may work with many children, you may forget all the cases you work with. However, that child will remember you forever and you will be part of their life story whether it is positive or negative.

In telling my story and reflecting on the past I want to say that, in spite of the difficulties I have written about, I know that my dad loved us and did everything he could to overcome his problems with alcohol and to enable my sister and me to return home. I probably didn't appreciate this at the time. He had to make very hard decisions in order for this to happen. He battled his alcoholism but was always there for us and in his last few years was a wonderful grandfather to my niece. He came to Thailand to give me away on my wedding day and this was a very proud moment for him. Jenny always encouraged contact with Dad and now I know why.

Undertaking my social work degree has given me an insight into my own life and I now understand that parents can let their children down but sometimes circumstances are out of their control. My parents did not choose to be alcoholics and I understand that addiction is an illness which can have long lasting consequences. As a family, we had a strong foundation of family values and traditions. I think that they helped us to reunite as a family in later years and enjoy occasions like Sunday lunches and Christmas and continue our relationships.

Jenny:

Zoe has suffered many losses and had to cope with more than her fair share of adversity in her life. However, in the past few years she has overcome these to achieve her goals of being a qualified social worker and during the course of writing this chapter, a wonderful mother. I know that Dad and Grandma, in particular, would be as proud of her achievements as I am.

References

DfE (2010) *United Nations Convention on the Rights of the Child (UNCRC): How legislation underpins implementation in England - Publications - GOV.UK.* [online] Available at: www.gov.uk/government/publications/united-nations-convention-on-the-rights-of-the-child-uncrc-how-legislation-underpins-implementation-in-england.

HM Government (2018) *Working together to safeguard children* [online].

Serious Case Review: Family A. Available at: kingstonandrichmondlscb.org.uk/
    media/upload/fck/file/SCR/Family%20A%20Serious%20Case%20Review%20
    Report%20November%202015.pdf.

Statute

The Children Act 1989
Human Rights Act 1998
The Children Act 2004
National Minimum Standards 2011

ds were Assessed Due to Being Young Carers

Kirsty, Niki, Ant and Lee,

Maggie Harris, *Young Carers Officer*

At a glance

- This chapter focuses on the statutory intervention of being assessed under the Children Act 1989, Care Act 2014 and Children and Families Act 2014 as a young carer, and the requirement of the local authority to assess if they are in need of support and if they should be considered as a child in need.

- Kirsty, Niki, Ant and Lee are all young carers who care for a parent or parents and, in some cases, their siblings too. For this chapter they were interviewed as a group and the recording used to provide their stories, views and suggestions.

- Maggie is the manager of a young carer's service. She has known Ant, Lee and Niki since they were five years old and Kirsty since she was 14. In this chapter, Maggie provides the formal knowledge underpinning statutory interventions for the young carers in the text boxes and at the end of the chapter shares her reflections and recommendations for working with young carers.

About ourselves:

I am Kirsty. I am 16. I go to college. I am doing Performing Arts. I am the youngest of two and I have a stepsister. I live with my mum. My stepsister lives in South Africa with her family and my sister lives close by with her baby. My mum suffers from Post Traumatic Stress Disorder (PTSD), anxiety, depression and high blood pressure. It's sort of for as long as I remember.

I am Niki and I am 17. I go to college; I am doing Level 3 Child Care. I am one of 11. I live with my mum and dad and I am basically the oldest in the house at the moment. I am fourth oldest but the three oldest have moved out. They have children. The youngest is three years old. I care for my mum who has back problems. She also has mental health problems and a learning disability. She has to get around either on crutches or in a wheelchair and, yep, I help my mum a lot. I help out my dad, I cook and I help out with my younger sister because she is disabled.

My name is Ant and I am 16. I've definitely not had the best life but do not see how it affects me. I am more or less happy unless I have to do paperwork. I am the eldest child of two, three, ... Jesus, forgot how many brothers I had! I am at college doing Brickwork. I live with my dad and my dog. My brothers are in care, just me and my dad at home. Mum is dead. I used to look after my mum and dad and try help out as much as I could with my brothers but we ended up in care and, eventually, Mum moved out. I came home and now I look after my dad. He has got Brugada syndrome. He has problems with the heart where it stops about 14 times a day. When it stops, I sit him down make sure he is comfy and make sure he stays alive.

I am Lee, 16, I do not know what to say really about me. Really, I ain't that interesting. How bad is that? I live with my mum and brother and am the youngest. I am at school. I care for my mum she has fibromyalgia, postural tachycardia syndrome, sleep apnoea, hypertension and asthma. So much she has.

> A young carer is defined in legislation as 'a person under 18 who provides or intends to provide care for another person' (Children Act, 1989; Children and Families Act, 2014; The Care Act, 2014). This excludes doing so as part of voluntary work. Being a young carer usually involves providing practical and emotional support and personal care to someone such as a parent who may have a disability, long-term physical or mental illness, or needs relating to substance misuse.

Life as a young carer

Lee: You worry about the person at home. You are put on emergency call list like if your mum falls over. That is why my phone is on all the time; even when I am at school. I got one the other day then I had to phone up my mum. My mum fell over; (she) taps a button on her phone and sends a message: 'I need help at this location'; tells you at what location. It goes to me, my brother and, I think, my nan. I phone her all the time even when I am at school. I got one the other day. She fell over, a message comes on my phone. I go to reception and phone. It happens at least once a week.

Ant: Being on alert your mind is never at rest. Since you first wake up you're doing stuff until last thing when you go to bed, really, and (my mind) is never at rest until I go to bed. I help out my mum; whatever she needs. My brother, he has mental health issues; I help him. Sometimes he does not want to get up and do stuff. Sometimes you don't want to get up and do stuff. It varies. Something simple like making a cup of tea to pulling him out of bed because he cannot move because his back has frozen up or his legs have frozen up. No one day is ever the same. It's always something different. Some days I might not have to wake him up at all because he is there before I am. Oh, okay, it's going to be a bit of an easier day today. Sometimes he cannot move and struggles breathing. It's pretty crap to be honest.

You have got to be on the ball. When I am at college or young carers or anything, my auntie is the first one to be told about anything and she will ring me and she will come and get me or see if I can get to her. It's been like that for quite a while.

Niki: When I wake up, I wake up a little bit before Mum to make sure she is up to get the children up for school. There is a support thing near her bed so she can get up. I help her if she cannot get up; make the bed; lay out school clothes for the children. There are a few who go to school. Let me think, there are five of them who go to school and of course my younger sister. My dad is carer to my mum as well so, he helps a lot.

Kirsty: Well my day is quite normal in the morning, cos my mum is always awake. If she can't sleep she'll turn on the TV and just watch it because she can't sleep so she either has to take sleeping pills, which make her really, really depressed or really moody or she just feels like she can't take them because she feels like she's becoming a vegetable as she has really bad anxiety. She turns everything into a constant worry. Her constant worry keeps going through her head and so she has to call me to check I am okay, so sometimes in a really, really down mood she calls me crying, about little things like if she's thinking about my dad, who is dead, or my sister being pregnant. She just can't control when she is feeling bad, cos sometimes she feels really suicidal, so if I wasn't there she would be … I don't really know where my mum would be…

I also suffer from depression, PTSD and anxiety so with my mum worrying about me and me worrying about her and because sometimes she has to have medication given and she doesn't like medication. She thinks they are poisoning her.

Thinking about what everyone has to do (as a young carer), puts it in perspective. All of us are different but all very stressed.

'A child in need' is defined under the Children Act 1989 as a child who is unlikely to achieve or maintain a reasonable level of health or development without provision of services by a local authority or whose health and development is likely to be significantly or further impaired, without provision or services, or a child who is disabled.

Section 17 of the Children Act 1989 outlines the duty of every local authority to safeguard and promote the welfare of children within their area who are 'in need' and, as is consistent with that duty, to promote the upbringing of such children by their families by providing a range and level of services appropriate to those children's needs. As part of this, s17 states that the local authority (so far is as reasonably practicable and consistent with the child's welfare) should ascertain the child's wishes and feelings regarding the provision of these services and give due consideration to such wishes and feelings.

In relation to being a young carer, s17 of the Children Act 1989 (amended by The Children and Families Act, 2014) places a duty on a local authority to assess whether a young carer in their area needs support and to identify what those needs are. An assessment should consider the impact on the child's health, well-being and education and whether it is appropriate for them to be providing the care in question. This is outlined in the Young Carers (Needs Assessments) (England) Regulations April 2015. The young carer assessment should clearly state if the local authority considers them to be a 'child in need' (legislation.gov.uk).

The Care Act 2014 also legislates the local authority's duty to consider the needs of children living in households where there is an adult who has a disability or impairment that requires help or care as part of a 'whole family assessment'. The aim is for the Care Act 2014 and Children and Families Act 2014 to work together to strengthen the rights of young carers (SCIE, n.d.).

It is important as a social worker working with children who are young carers to also consider their wider needs and any safeguarding concerns.

Contact with social workers

Ant: I've always seen the social worker as someone who's not really there to help, and to cause more trouble, that's always what it's felt like. We've had social workers for my mum and dad and social workers for me and my brothers. When I was about five years old I went into care to live with my nan and my grandad, so did both my brothers. After a couple of years, we came out, and then we ended up in care again, and just in and out of care. I ended up a few miles away for a few months. My brothers were living somewhere else together and then we all got split up. I see my youngest brother … I saw him twice last year, once at my mum's funeral and once before Christmas. I would have tried to keep me and my two brothers together because seeing your brother, who you wake up every morning to, to seeing him twice a year, it's just not right. One is living far away, the other one lives a few miles away. I see him once every two weeks. At some points (I think I was at risk at home, yes) but I thought that my mum and dad would probably end up sorting it out, but it never got to that point.

Niki: Just hearing another story I think, it's different from my story, of course, but it's what could have happened, if you know what I mean? Going into care, it didn't get that far. My dad, he just listened to the social workers, and did what they told him and now we don't have them anymore, which is good. The only social worker we have is for my sister, because she is disabled. I'm not really clear (why social workers first became involved), but I think, cos we only had a four-bedroomed house, and there was all 11 children and Mum and Dad in the same house. We were basically sharing rooms. Me, and my three sisters were staying in the same room and my brothers shared a room. And then, one of my brothers had to sleep downstairs, my sister slept in a room because she had a child, and then we had to make a room downstairs. I'm not very clear on why they got involved, but I do understand a little bit. There was…, not complaints, but the social workers said, something about our beds, and apparently we didn't have any bed covers, which was a lie, and pillows and so in the end my dad was like, 'okay'. He made me my own room, my two brothers moved out and my sister just moved out, and then two girls share a room, my brothers share a room, and my other sister has her own room. My mum and dad are downstairs with my youngest sister, and it was just little things about getting to school on time, making sure they're doing their homework, making sure they're eating the right thing, because, apparently, we were all overweight.

I was in college, and I was just in my lesson, and I got dragged out by my social worker. My tutor didn't know, I didn't know, and so we were sat there, and we were just talking. I can't remember what they said … it was quite a few months back, probably about a year ago now. They were just trying to get me to say things I didn't want to talk about. They made me cry. They just bring up my family. They keep asking me about the bedroom situation and I'm telling them the right thing and they keep asking and I tell them all the time the same thing, which is true, and they're just trying to make me…, I can't explain it but like, say stuff that they want me to say. I came out, and my dad called me saying, 'oh yeah, she was meant to see me but she only told me yesterday'. I wasn't in … I got home late from college, they were like, 'oh, you're never in when I'm here, where are you?', 'I'm at college, I'm at full-time education, where else am I?' They were just basically trying to dig into me, asking where I was, which to be honest, it's none of their business but I was definitely at college. The minute I wake up I go to college, when I come back I look after my mum, I look after the children, I do everything.

I do everything for my mum, they were never there, and they come around at stupid times, like 3 o'clock. I go to college Monday to Friday, all my weekends I'm at home, and they ask me what do I do on my weekends? I'm like, I just sit there, and I help my mum and I help out with everything. They never saw it, and they made me feel bad. I came back from class and my tutor just gave me a minute to calm down and then I rang my dad. I was crying and he was like, 'what's wrong?' I'm only young – they just don't believe what you say. You say something and they're: 'is that right?' I'm like, 'I'm telling you the truth'. I'm an emotional person, I cry, I know it's stupid, but it does get to me.

I'm happy they're actually out of my life. I understand that it is their job, but my dad hasn't done anything bad in his life. They think different, like neglecting and I'm like, we've got a house, we've got food in our cupboards, do you want to look, we've got clean clothes. Because I asked my mum where my shoes were, they thought I didn't have any shoes. I just didn't know where they were. I said, 'where's my shoes?' She said they're just in the back room as that's where we keep our shoes. I can't see them but I'll have a look and so they put that in the form saying, that I didn't have any shoes, and apparently having dirty clothes, mmm, I don't think so. They'll just lie.

Lee: I misplaced my tie for school and they came straight into my mum and said 'why haven't you got the right school uniform?' I just wanted them to go and jog right on. I've got it, I've just lost it, I'm only young.

A Children's Society report into the experiences of young carers in England analysed government commissioned data on over 15,000 pupils aged 13–14. The data clearly showed that being a young carer restricts educational achievement which in turn can affect longer term employment opportunities. Young carers were more likely to: be living in low income households; be from black or minority ethnic communities; and have a disability or special education need themselves. It states that, 1 in 12 young carers is caring for more than 15 hours per week (a number thought to be the 'tip of the iceberg') and 1 in 20 misses school because of their caring responsibilities. Despite this, there was no evidence to show that young carers were more likely than their peers to have social work contact or support despite the legal requirements already outlined.

Some local authorities commission specialist young carer services to provide this support.

Young carers support services

Ant: Young carers have always been there, if ever I've needed anything. They have always been there. We needed help with money; we've always got food vouchers from Young Carers whenever we need help. For example, fairly recently I had some trouble sleeping because the height of my bed was too small, and I mentioned it and a couple of weeks later a new bed turned up. There is always someone to talk to at Young Carers which has been really helpful.

Kirsty: If we don't want a meeting we say to the young carers worker we don't want it and the young carers worker says 'are you sure?' 'it may benefit you' and she makes sure we are calmer and not scared to do it. Like when I had a problem eating, the young carers worker said not eating can make you fat because my problem was I was scared about getting fat and she was: you know you can try this and you can try that. Now I am eating every single day and I am not being sick or being rushed into hospital after having taken medicine. The young carers worker is different to them as they don't care, but she does.

Lee: She is like Batman with trousers! It's true. All of us come to young carers and it's all run by one person. The young carers worker shouldn't be our social worker, but she is. So, if she can do it why can't they?

Views on the social worker's role

Niki: I think the social workers should be there if there's actually physical signs; things you can see, for example, child abuse or something. They should not like … I can't say it I can't think, like they can't decide….Like there's nothing to get involved in. They made my dad do out the rooms, paint it all, he spent so much money on it; they didn't help. Nothing. I don't think they helped. He got new beds, bunk beds, because we didn't have bunk beds, we had one set of bunk beds and a single bed, but my dad spent so much money. He did the back garden out once, before the bed situation and they told my dad, why are you doing the back garden, why can't you do their bedrooms? But my dad likes doing the garden. Children have got to go out there to play in the garden and it's just … I don't think they supported at all, the social workers. I was fine beforehand….My dad got really ill and he started getting this rash through all this. He went to the doctor and actually it was caused by stress.

Lee: It was when I got a hemiplegic migraine that social workers became involved. I was in and out of hospital quite a bit. I'd have these fit things caused by stress. It was home life that was stressing me out because I was doing some stuff and obviously families have disagreements like every family does. Social services see it as if you don't get along with a person in your family then that's such a bad thing. I didn't get along with my mum and brov quite a bit until I actually started to get along, and I just realised. My social worker at the time, she was trying to make you say stuff that you don't want to say. They used to come up at random times. My mum got a phone call. She rang my mum directly, which she weren't allowed to do, and was like, I'll come round yours at 3 o'clock. My mum was like, you can't cos I got hospital so she was like, oh, I'll come round still.

My mum rang up the young carers worker. She helped with everything. She has been there since I was five years old. She saw me grow up and everything and my family and stuff. She is actually the only one who knows how it is, been there, seen it and watched it happen. That's what social workers need to be like, instead of coming straight into your house and judging you there in front of you and need to actually go back and see, that's what a lot of social workers do, come in rushing into it, putting things out of perspective. Ain't on really. Social worker's supposed to be there to support you at the end of the day, to try to put support in place to help you, not to cause you more stress, 'cause if they cause you more stress, it is pointless them being in your life. They are getting paid for something different.

I've eczema so I've got it all over me, like all up my arm. As soon as my social worker seen that, they straight away: is your mum beating you? You shouldn't do that, why would you do that? That is just disrespectful. You didn't even know the woman; you don't even know my mum or anything. When they've asked that question, I feel angry 'cause they don't know my mum they don't know anything about her. My mum can't even lift her food half the time. It's like, how they have the audacity to say that to you after they are there to help you. They always presume the worse. They always assume the worse happens.

Luckily, I've got a social worker now who is doing her job. She hasn't rushed into things; she's actually taken time to get to know me and my mum. Got to know how it works with my brother. Because of his mental health issues, he is quite wary of people. She's actually taken the time to get to know him a bit so he feels comfortable around her, which my other social worker never did. She just stayed away from him, never spoke to him.

I speak to my mum quite a lot 'cause I'm obviously always with her 'cause I care for her. In a way my mum's my best friend. It's like a dog really; you are with them every day. Not like I'm going to call my mum a dog or anything but, like, a dog is by your side at the end of the day. My mum has been the only one that's been through thick and thin for me. Had a girlfriend, tried that that went wrong, out the window it goes.

The first one (social worker) wasn't doing her job properly so we made a complaint. Restart it, build from the bottom again, and start to get my family back on track. I've got a meeting tomorrow with young carers and (new social worker). She wants to see how I am doing. My other social worker did that but when I was there it was more about hammering into me and my mum about what we were doing wrong. She used to complain. There is me, my brother and my mum. My mum only gets money from me and she's got to feed me, herself and my brother and a cat with that. Cats aren't cheap these days. Now, if we get stuck for food, she (the social worker) will give us vouchers, but the young carers worker normally beats her to it. Young carers have normally got the head start on everything. I know it sounds weird, even though she's my social worker, I will still tell the young carers worker before her.

It is particularly important for social workers to make use of the child's networks. The young people in this chapter have attended the young carers' service, in some cases, since they were five years old. Social workers don't often have the opportunity to develop relationships over such a long period of time so should liaise with those that do to gain a better understanding of the child's needs. This could involve liaising with the family, school, youth workers or specialist young carer services.

Kirsty: I became a young carer 18 months, two years ago. A couple of weeks before I met the young carers worker, I met my social worker and was so frightened of her 'cause I was wondering, why is a stranger talking to me. She met me inside my school and then she dropped me home and she was badgering me for questions, like what happened to my dad, without considering how I felt. Badgering me about it like, why did he do this, why did he do that and what did he die of? Not like, how are you or are you okay about talking about this? But tell me, so I was like no, I am never going to speak about it without my mum.

She never introduced herself; was basically a stranger. She talked to me as if I was being interrogated as I'd done something wrong and my mum also knew that someone was going to speak to me and I knew someone was going to come and speak to me. When my mum didn't even know the person, she was scared and this made me scared more. After having her come to me, I had her for another couple more weeks. I switched to my other social worker, who kept talking to me as if she was friendly and nice but my mum had said I shouldn't trust this person. She was very friendly, very nice believing my mum; I didn't trust her that much. But none of them helped anything. They were just there asking the same questions. Before I was in Child and Adolescent Mental Health Services (CAMHS) for treating my PTSD, I had an eating disorder, plus depression, really bad, got anger management in school for continuously punching teachers and students and they were like, you know, what we need is someone to ask about this girl and see how her family life is. I was constantly being watched by someone. I didn't want to be watched, so I'd get mad every time I'd see someone I didn't know.

It was before I went to Uganda. She didn't want to ask me in front of my mum 'cause she knew what my mum would say so she took me away to get something to eat. She was trying to badger me. She kept telling me facts like: 2 in 4 women that go to Africa, especially Uganda, like teenagers are raped or entered into forced marriages. She kept telling me these bad facts. I have lived in Uganda since I was a kid. If that had happened, I think I would have been gone by now. She was trying to persuade me to say that I didn't want to go, that I was scared to and that I was scared of my own family. Kept badgering me – are you sure, are you sure you want to go? Question was concerning or against me going to see my family. It was kind of pushy, pushy of stuff you don't want to tell them. Like flying – flying is a nervous thing, everyone gets scared of flying but telling them one thing like I'm scared of flying can get translated into I don't want to go, I hate everyone, I don't want to go out.

Ant: I don't like it where they sit there, you walk in, introduce themselves and sit there. They've got this big, big pad, sit there and writing things, giving you bits to talk about. She's not really looking at you, not paying attention to you, it's as though she's more interested in what she is writing. It's not supposed to be what it is, you are supposed to be interested in how the kid is, how the kid is feeling; how he or she is feeling. It ain't on really, just to sit there and write stuff down. It's like, at the end of the day you could bring something up about me, with me, that you wouldn't expect would affect me, but you don't know that it would. I know what it feels like to lose something so close to you. People think I'm quite intimidating right, but you wouldn't think I'm a big softy. I have my sides. They look at you, start judging you. You don't judge the way I look or how I speak. Like the way we are 'cause the stuff we have been through; like anger issues. There is always stuff behind it. You say to a social worker, 'I keep getting angry' and they say 'oh, anger management, here you are, go to that'. I've been through anger management two times. I'm not going to go through it a third time. Some of them say, why? You have given them all you can think of and they still ask why. Oh come on, where's this all going to end. I don't want to talk about it if I've told all of it to you in one question.

As part of our duty to safeguard, social workers need to assess and respond to risk. The accounts from the young carers however demonstrate the importance of developing effective relationships based on trust and rapport, even during short encounters, to achieve this. If the young people don't feel able to be open and honest, we may miss something significant and prevent opportunities to work together on identifying and meeting need. If they don't feel safe with you then then they won't open up and you won't get an accurate assessment.

What is clear from the accounts of Lee, Ant, Kirsty and Niki is that their needs went beyond those of being a young carer. There were very few examples, however, of where they felt that social workers helped and provided support.

Our message to social work students and qualified social workers

Lee: I think the best way to go about it and before we start; ask questions about family about themselves, get to know them. Go to the cinema, talk about normal stuff that you would with your friends. Become friends with them and then ask the questions 'cause you will feel safe and you can open up to them.

Ant: when you first meet someone you don't really want to open up to them do you. You actually want to get to know them.

Niki: I understand that they have to have visits unplanned to make sure everything is okay. Just say there is a child getting abuse from either parent, I think the social worker should get to know the child first because, if that child is getting abuse from the parents, how do they know they (the social worker) are not going to abuse them. They think it is another person who is going to hurt them. I think they should get to know the child so the child feels safe around that person so they can tell what is actually happening.

Kirsty: my mum thought that she (the social worker) was trying to uncover something that wasn't there 'cause she was speaking to Mum and she was speaking to me completely different questions but worded almost similar to make us to say something we didn't want to.

Ant: I think students starting off in the job should take on board: get to know them first; don't always presume the worst over the littlest things; actually listen to what the child has to say as at the end of the day we don't all do the same thing.

Ant: (continued...): Not aggressively asking questions, because there have been some questions that I thought, well hang on a minute, that sounds like you are directly blaming me for something.

Lee: Not forcing the question at us, just easing it out, just slipping it into the conversation like: how has your day been, are you feeling alright, how is your home life? Just gently easing it in would be brilliant.

Ant: the last time I went into care, I ended up being moved from one place up the road, which is not too far away, and I got to see my mum and dad twice when I was up there and I was up there for 4–5 months. No one asked me if I wanted to go there, I was just taken there. Apparently there was nowhere around this area. I couldn't stay even though I had a friend that told me him and his two younger sisters and older brother went into the same place together. I thought; hold on a minute, how does that make sense?

It would be nice if they asked for some input, what would you ideally want and if they can't do that, then explain what they could do to make it slightly better. We can't make you live with your brother but you're only a couple of miles away from them so you can see them at a park or shop or anything. Last year I only saw him twice; once at my mum's funeral which is no circumstance to see your brother of whom you haven't seen for six months and then once before Christmas. They are worried me and my dad will take him out one day and not bring him home, even though my dad knows that would be very bad for them and for my brother and for everyone involved.

get to know the proper background from the parents' side, the child's side and what social services have on record because what social services have could be different from what the parents see and what the parents see could be different to both.

Lee: I know it sounds weird, but 'cause you've got other siblings, they should at least talk to them about how they are, like introducing themselves, like your brother and sister's social workers, 'cause obviously they will be seeing them as well and it will impact on them. I don't understand that if a social worker knows that someone is really upset like another sibling and they don't have any support put in place, I don't understand why they can't just step in and see if they are alright, even if they are not their social worker. Only 'cause you're assigned to that one case doesn't mean you've got to focus on that one person at that moment in time. If they live in your household, it could improve that person, it could improve the whole thing.

Ant: I think another thing they should do, is when they say you should be this, should be that, that you should do that, they make sure it's within the family's price range. There was stuff they told my mum and dad and my mum was disabled and my dad was disabled and they weren't getting much money and how the hell are we supposed to do that? New furniture, new beds, make sure the rooms are brand newly painted, things like that. I just thought, not being funny, a litre of paint is quite expensive. How are they going to paint the rooms if they are both disabled? You have got to do that and all. That is what they don't think of, both of their parents disabled. They haven't got enough money to afford a painter. You are going to have to do it yourself with a pot of paint! More struggle for the child. We ended up doing some of it, but we moved before we had finished it.

Kirsty: you have to do this not because you want to but because you're forced to even though you don't have the resources to do it. There is a time limit as well; got to be done by next week. How are you supposed to paint a four-bed house in a week? Layers, gloss, all that money, paint, new sheets and covers, all done by one teenager as the parents are disabled.

Lee: Get rid of the damn notepads they write things when you are sat next to them. They are writing and I notice that some turn the corners of the book if they don't want you to see what they are writing.

Ant: If it is something you are worried about, you share it with them. If it's worried you, they need to know it's worried you.

My perspective as a young carers officer

My main message to social workers is: listen, hear and act.

Even though I was there when Ant, Kirsty, Lee and Niki were going through all of this, I realise from listening and hearing the stories that have been told by these four very brave young people that we don't listen enough. It's easily done. There's a job to do and there is not enough time in the day. Whatever you do, talk to others who know the children: pastoral support at school; a teacher; or, in this case, the young carers officer.

Be flexible and creative and remember every child and young person is an individual.

References

SCIE (Social Care Institute for Excellence) Transition in the Care Act 2014 and the Children and Families Act 2014. Available at: www.scie.org.uk.

Statute

Children Act 1989
Children and Families Act 2014
The Care Act 2014

Suggested reading

NHS England Carers Toolkit. Available at: www.england.nhs.uk/carers-toolkit
Local Government Association (LGA) (2015) No wrong doors: Working together to support young carers and their families. A template for a local memorandum of understanding between adults and children's social services and No wrong doors evaluation 2017. Both available at: www.local.gov.uk.
Young Carers in Schools Programme: Building, sharing and recognising young carers support in schools. Available at: www.youngcarersinschools.com.

7

My Child was Taken into Care

Leanne

Stefan Kleipoedzsus, *Lecturer in social work*

At a glance

- This chapter focuses on the long, and often complex, process of child protection and accommodating a child under s20 of the Children Act 1989.

- Leanne is a mother whose daughter was taken into care.

- Stefan is a social work lecturer and experienced children and family social worker. He was introduced to Leanne by a work colleague who is a friend of Leanne's for the purpose of writing this chapter. Stefan, provides formal knowledge regarding the statutory interventions in text boxes throughout the chapter and shares his own reflections on his learning.

My name is Leanne and I am a nurse and the mother of two daughters. I met G when I was 23. He was 18 months older than me. We got married after three years, with opposition from his family but we got over that. We started a family about five years later and had the two girls. Everything seemed absolutely fine, we were not aware of any issues with O when she was growing up. Well, she was always a bit of a challenge. When O started primary school there were a few issues but just in terms of her behaviour and her reactions to things. When she first went into school, in the first two years no one really flagged anything. In year one there was this great teacher who just said she was picking up on friendship issues and she just didn't want it to become an issue further on. That was when we were first introduced to the Child and Adolescent Mental Health Services (CAMHS). The experience with CAMHS wasn't great that first time, communication wasn't very good. O was assessed and it was said that she was fine and that no referral for further support was necessary. These friendship problems sort of were a feature throughout primary school but she did really well academically.

95

In year six (age 10–11), her teacher was saying she was difficult, sometimes distracted but she thought this was maybe the beginning of adolescence. Nobody mentioned the possibility of autistic traits. It was secondary school that things very quickly started to become difficult. We applied for some independent schools and she was offered a place. The benefit of going to an independent school in this area is that there is lots of sport and lots of extracurricular activities so, we thought this would be a good place and she was more likely to find a peer group. I did not have any issues with any of the schools that she's been to. They all did a fantastic job. It was more what was going on for O and the influences she was exposed to – things that happened to her and her inability to cope in those environments.

In class, they would complain that she was always fiddling with things, she always had her hand in her desk or in the drawer. She always had something, was playing with something. Overall, her behaviour was deemed good enough. There were other children with more profound autism, another child with Attention Deficit Hyperactivity Disorder (ADHD). I wouldn't have put O in that group. Clearly there was something. She was very controlling, so she would come up with games and expect children to follow the rules. She wouldn't like any deviation from the way she saw the game and she would alienate other children. She had a very close friend, in fact, there were two other girls who were quite close but it was always a triangle. They were encouraged at some point to widen the friendship group and to not always play together. The other children would take that on board, but O couldn't. She kept coming back, she kept being drawn back to them and that was what the teacher was concerned about.

O had always done well in school, it was just something that she was going through that we needed help with. It was as part of the court process when a well-respected child psychiatrist gave this diagnosis of social communication disorder with autistic traits. O is very much like a chameleon. She is funny, will start conversations in unusual ways. She will not necessarily say, 'Hi, how are you? Nice to meet you', she will be like 'I've got snakes' or say something quite outlandish or talk at you for an hour about the topic that she wants to talk about. The whole thing with autism in girls is really not well understood and, when you look at what has happened to O going through her life, one can see this. She ticks every box and it's difficult because people, some people, most people would look at her and think there is nothing wrong with her. Because she speaks really well and can hold conversations, so she's really bright and articulate. You just assume there's nothing going on you know, but clearly there is.

Early help

Social work practice would be much easier with the benefit of hindsight. It is a challenge to look back and identify the point at which one could have done something to prevent a child being taken into care and promote the upbringing of children in their birth family. *Working Together to Safeguard Children* clearly puts the emphasis on early help which is seen to be 'more effective in promoting the welfare of children [and] can also prevent further problems arising' (HM Government, 2015, p. 12). Munro (2011) also highlights the efficiency of early help compared to reactive approaches. As a social worker in statutory services the focus is often on those children who experience some form of abuse and neglect and, not unlike other professionals, the lens with which the world is perceived is adjusted to this. Problems emerging in O's case were not related to abuse and neglect and so the possibility of O having autistic traits, the one thing that put what happened to O into context, can be hidden behind a blind spot.

Dean et al. (2017) highlight a male bias in the way professionals recognise autistic traits with girls being camouflaged behind behaviours compensating their social challenges by remaining close to peers and 'weaving in and out of activities' (ibid., p. 678) even though boys and girls appear to experience the same emotional and behavioural problems (Pisula et al., 2017). This camouflage effect could be even more pronounced because girls with autistic traits appear to have stronger communication skills and are less likely to score high on the used screening tools (Nichols et al., 2009).

O went to the first secondary school, a big girl's comprehensive school, in the September. Then she said, it is the wrong school, I cannot go there. There were issues and things happened that we were not fully aware of. There was some bullying, she was called names, some horrible names. She basically stopped eating. We were aware that something was going on but on the surface she seemed fine. We hoped that it was just the settling in period and that things would get better when she sort of established herself and got her friendship group. In January, her form tutor said O had approached her and she said that she thought O had an issue with food and that she might have an eating disorder and recommended CAMHS. We got referred into the eating disorders unit and, in fact, we were seen within four weeks, which is really good. She saw a couple of counsellors and a psychiatrist and we had some family sessions. They discharged us after six months. According to them it wasn't full-blown anorexia, it was more about control. At this stage O was 11 years old.

While we were doing all of that we decided to change schools and allow her a fresh start, perhaps she needed somewhere smaller. She was in trouble before she got there. She befriended this girl who apparently had access to drugs. This girl that she met, her father had been killed in an accident six months before and she was in freefall. She was in a really bad way herself and they just came together like magnets. They were getting up to stuff that we were not fully aware of, at that time. Travelling around on buses and I think O was going to estates and places that we wouldn't have ever agreed for her to go to. I was called in to the school before she'd taken up her place. They had seen social media posts that O had put out about making drug references, so their radar was up already. They wanted to help her to settle as quickly, and smoothly, as possible. It was awful, I was called in pretty much every day. She was late every day – had a full face of make-up, had earrings, had her uniform wrong, was disruptive in lessons, not doing homework, arriving late. They were strict on all of those things and they wouldn't give an inch. She wouldn't budge either. Literally, if the stairs said go up that way, she'd go down. By lunchtime they were ringing me to say come and pick her up. They said we can't sustain this, but the deputy head said: 'Look! Maybe you just need to move out of the area, you need a fresh start. There is this school that I referred somebody else to, it's a boarding school. You are fighting for your independence and this gives you a way of being independent but in a safe way.'

It was agreed that she would go in September. The summer was difficult. We allowed her to go out and told her to be back by a certain time and she would be late. She developed this kind of gang persona. And we didn't really know who she was hanging out with. She was only 12 years old at this time. There was an event where there were a few of her ex-primary school friends and she got into an argument with them and they videoed her. The parents were really shocked at her behaviour and what she was saying. That was before she went to boarding school. She arrived at boarding school and I could almost tell that it wasn't going to work because of how she was, quite defiant. The first night I think she stayed up pretty much all night. She got other girls up. She set off the fire alarm on day one and had a broken arm by day three after she initiated a play fight. So, she was home for a week and went back. It was okay until the half-term. She went back in after the half-term and they were really having a difficult time with her. They tried really hard but it was just not happening. Then she took a vegetable knife from a food tech lesson. She kept it in her dorm for a few days with the plan of self-harming. She had been doing this all the way through as well but sort of superficially and in easy to spot places, it wasn't hidden.

Self-harm

Self-harm is 'causing deliberate hurt to your own body, most commonly not only by cutting, but also by burning, abusing drugs, alcohol or other substances' (Walker, 2012, p. 10) and is often a way of dealing with difficult feelings. From a social worker's perspective, it is important to understand the purposes of self-harm which could be a way of communicating feelings, of distracting from emotional pain or of gaining control over your life. It may be a coping mechanism for someone who is struggling with feelings that threaten to be overwhelming.

In my practice, I worked with a lot of young people who were self-harming in ways not dissimilar from O. Looking back now, I would have liked to put much more emphasis on this, responding to this myself as a practitioner rather than relying mostly on mental health services. As a practitioner it is important to be open to communication and let the young person talk to you if they want to and ask them about what led to the episode of self-harm.

O was meant to be at a meeting that they had in the evening with all the kids and she wasn't there. She was in the dorm and sort of saying 'I hate this teacher, he's always on my back' and said that she was going to kill him. The other kids saying, 'you are being stupid, what are you doing you are going to get kicked out' and they took the knife off her and threw it out of the window. But other children had seen it and were really shocked. On the back of everything else, that got reported and she was out so, we picked her up and brought her home. The school reported it to the local police. She had a crime reference number which she posted on *Instagram*. It all went with her gang persona. She had a different accent, everything.

Now O was home but very isolated and we couldn't let her out. All her friends were at school all day, we did some home tutoring with a private tutor coming to the house. She did quite well with him because she picks up things really fast but, we were really only doing Maths and English. We were both working, just keeping her occupied was difficult. This was for a month. Then she was saying, 'I want to go back to school' and I said, 'right okay well we're going to have to see where there's a place'. We managed to get her into a mixed school with about a thousand children in the middle of a large urban estate. It is quite a tough school but home schooling was going to be almost impossible to maintain and she needed to socialise, she needed to be with her peer group. She went in the January and it was a disaster.

The first time social services were called was in July, during the school holidays. O was seeing this boy and she would go out but not come back on time and things like that. On this day she did not come back and we were frantic, we were looking for her and we had been calling all these numbers. One of the dads that G (O's father) called said 'I know where she will be, it will be this youth club'. She had gone to this youth club and said to them something along the lines of 'I don't want to go home because my dad is an alcoholic' so the youth workers flagged it with social services. We did get a call and they came to see us, they came to talk to her and a report was written. We said, things are really difficult but we are coping and they said, there is a risk but it is a low risk.

Youth services

Youth services play an important part in the delivery of services to children. Volunteers and staff have a responsibility in respect of safeguarding and promoting the welfare of children (HM Government, 2015). As such, staff in the youth club were required to flag what O had said with social services and social services would have to make a decision about the type of response required. Local authorities have to determine whether or not a child needs immediate protection, is at risk of significant harm or requires an assessment. In O's case it appears there was no assessment at this stage even though it seems the family already was in crisis.

In my practice there was often a debate about the threshold for intervention. Early help services (like the youth club) would often argue that the threshold for a statutory intervention is too high and children services would say a case has not yet reached the threshold for intervention and that early help services are better placed to respond to these types of incidents. The importance of early help has most recently been emphasised by the Children's Commissioner who called for a renewed focus on early intervention and early identification of special educational needs. Quite often, the underlying difficulty is that social services respond to the individual incident and, unless the family is known to them, they do not have all the relevant information to make a decision taking the full context into account.

The period between January and March the following year, when O was 13, was fraught. O was withdrawing large sums of cash from her bank account without any explanation for where the money had gone. She was buying vapes and various things that she could get her hands on and was selling them at school. G was really mad that she'd taken out all this money and couldn't account for it. He was cross at the bank that she was able to withdraw such a large amount of cash. They had gone into the bank and she was refusing to come in and she called him 'Prick', or something. He sort of manhandled her, grabbed her and shoved her down into a chair in the bank. People were shocked by it. She had gone into school and had said this had happened and they reported that to social services. We got this guy who came to see us. I think he visited us about that incident and we just said, she is barely in school and it has been a nightmare.

We already had a police officer from the Gang Unit involved at that point because O would call the police in the middle of the night after an argument and say things to them like 'Oh, I get my drugs for free because I'm pretty.' That rang alarm bills and they said we need to refer her to the Gang Unit.

Child sexual exploitation

Since the scandal in Rotherham (see Jay, 2014), where children were systematically sexually exploited by a group of men, Child Sexual Exploitation (CSE) has led to a distinctive shift in the way professionals in all agencies working with children and young people respond to this type of child abuse. CSE happens when someone is encouraging a child to participate in sexual activity in exchange for something like presents, money, alcohol or emotional attention. Language and practice has changed significantly. Even though language blaming the victim like '[she was] placing herself at risk of sexual exploitation and danger' (ibid., p. 39) can still be read in current assessments, there is a much stronger realisation of the potential for the oppressive use of language (Thompson, 2012). In his great book on writing assessments, Dyke (2016) shows how the simple sentence 'Steve beats Amy' can evolve into 'Amy is a beaten woman' with the effect that perpetrator does not exist anymore and it is Amy, the victim, who needs to stop being a beaten women.

The police officer we worked with was brilliant. O went missing on a night in March after having an argument with me in the afternoon. I rang the police and they said call it in and report her as missing. She was picked up at about 9.30 at night on an estate with a 15-year-old, a 17-year-old and a 20-year-old. They scattered when the police car came around. The police recognised her from the description, and said we need to talk to you. She just ignored them. They took her down, they put her in a car and they took her into the police station. She said, 'I'm not going home, home is hell'. She conceded, by eight o'clock in the morning, that she would come home but only on the understanding that she would be going out that afternoon. They brought her home and she sat upstairs with me and she said, 'I'm really sorry, Mum, I won't do that again'. She got up at 12.00, she spent hours getting ready. At 3 o'clock she said, 'right, I'm going out now'. And I said 'No you are not'. We had a big drama and argument. Friends helped me out and she went to stay with her friend around the corner.

The following Monday the social worker met with her because she had been missing on a Saturday night. He had spoken to her and then we were in the kitchen and he wanted to talk to me. In that moment she ran out of the house and went missing overnight. She approached four lads who were smoking dope and went to one of their houses. They kicked her out at about 2 o'clock in the morning. I know she was then on a bus possibly still with one them. She was using their phone to message other children. Police were at local schools interviewing children and they tried to encourage her to become somewhat visible. They picked her up at about 3 o'clock in the afternoon. She was a mess.

The police officers thought that O needed to be sectioned and we agreed because we just needed help. She was taken by ambulance to the local psychiatric hospital and we met her there. She was then seen by a psychiatrist, a paediatrician who said she needs residential care. We thought, that's it, great we can get some help. I was there until about 2 o'clock in the morning and they said just go home, once we have established where she's going we will call you and she will be transferred.

Mental Health Act 1983/2007

Any child can be detained under the Mental Health Act but this step should be the exception. All alternatives should be explored. Local authorities have the duty to consider whether any children in need, or looked-after children, especially those in foster care or in a residential placement, are subject to restrictions amounting to a deprivation of liberty (see Chapters 12 and 14 for more detail). Given that depriving a child of their liberties should be the exception, it is most likely that the local authority would explore possible alternatives like fostering or residential child care before agreeing to accommodate a child in a psychiatric unit.

At nine o'clock in the morning, O rang to ask for someone to come and take her home because she was told that she would be sent home. We don't know exactly what had happened but we were told social services were going to go and pick her up and take her back to the town hall and put her into foster care. There was absolutely no way that this was going to happen because she needed a psychiatric unit as she was out of control. We brought her back and just sat on her. G stayed on the phone to children's services and petitioned for O. The plan was to send her to the north of England to a unit that specialised in CSE. By that time she had been sexually assaulted more than once. We just thought, there's no way we would be able to maintain contact, it is a five-hour journey one way at least and, she needs us. We could let her go, we'd said fine. We would understand if it had to be that sort of specialist provision but surely there must be somewhere within three hours of home.

Placing children

Ofsted (2014) published the results of a thematic inspection of the way local authorities discharge their responsibilities to looked-after children living away from home, highlighting some important points to consider when social workers are placing a child away from home.

In practice, finding a placement is a challenge and often, there is a lack of choice. This is true especially for children like O where the complexity of her needs and the behaviours she is presenting require a more specialist response that is most likely only available in specialist residential children's homes. According to Ofsted (ibid.) children living in children's homes are three times more likely to be living away from their home area than children living in foster care. When placing a child at a distance, the following questions have to be considered:

- How can the contact to family and friends be maintained?
- How can the social worker monitor the quality and care provided?
- How can we ensure there are no delays in providing timely support to promote the child's emotional well-being and education?

As a social worker, supporting a child at a distance comes with significant demands on managing time and planning visits appropriately. It is not easy to quickly visit a child when a crisis emerges or just visit to see how they are doing. Yet, often, the simple lack of choice of available placements in the area makes any other option unattainable.

Then they came up with a children's home on the south coast. G spoke to the manager of the care home and just had great faith in her. The plan was that we would send her there on Monday, but it was quite obvious we were not even going to be able to hold on for that long. We didn't tell her, we lied to her and we said that she was going to visit family. I was already there and he walked her in. They all knew her name and then the penny dropped for her. The alternative would have been being collected by social services and taken into the placement.

Care planning

Planning a placement is key in social work practice and does not only require the immediate response to a situation but also should always focus on the long-term plan to meet the needs of a child (DfE, 2015). Principles of care planning include that parents should be as closely involved as is consistent with the child's welfare and that the continuity of relationships and attachments is important. Planning also involves the transition from home into the out-of-home care setting.

There is a great disparity between the professional's experience, who has been through this process potentially a number of times and approaches this with some routine, and the experience of the family for whom this event is most likely a once in a lifetime, traumatic event. For the latter this event will have repercussions for a long time after a child has 'settled' in the placement and after the child has returned home. This will also most likely be an event that is the end point of a long history of preceding incidents, situations and 'odd moments' that are culminating in the moment when the child is being told, or realises that, they are going to live away from home.

In my experience, this was hardly ever straightforward and there always was the feeling that the families involved were hurting. Children may feel their parents are abandoning them or they may be happy to leave (especially in cases where there has been long-standing abuse). Regardless of this planning, the transition is important to safeguard relationships and attachments and reduce the negative impact of severing the tie to the home, which is the cornerstone of our universe (Bachelard, 1994). I once removed a young girl of a similar age to O from her parents against her, and her parents', will. It was meticulously planned with police going into the family home and a secure escort service waiting outside to take the girl to a residential unit about 100 miles away. Because the girl was threatening to harm herself, the police could physically remove her and put her in the van waiting outside. The staff from the escort service transported her safely to the unit. While in principle, a success, I still wonder about the damage this caused to the child and her parents.

O was taken into care in March. She was 13 years old. Last year, April 2017 the local authority said that she needs to be looked after under Section 31, they were sort of implying that there would be more funding and it would be easier to access the type of care that she needed if she was looked-after child under s31. They basically said, we are going to court. We had six months in court, which took us up to December 2017. The first hearing, the judge said, you don't even know what you're dealing with, you haven't got a diagnosis on this child. That was when a psychiatrist was appointed. O saw her, and she interviewed us. They brought in an independent social worker to do an assessment about our parenting. He was very insightful and he had a specialist interest in autism. He said he was a bit embarrassed being here doing it but, it was probably for the best. We didn't mind having a parenting assessment done. We just thought, do whatever you need to do. We also felt confident in our parenting, it was just something that she was going through that we needed help with.

Accommodating a child under the Children Act 1989

In social work practice moving a child into out-of-home care is a rare event and in most cases, when statutory services intervene, this most intrusive intervention does not even have to be considered. Yet over the years the number of children taken into care has increased from 68,820 children in 2014 to 72,670 in 2017 (DfE, 2017). The number of care order applications has increased from 11,159 to 14,207 in the same time period (CAFCASS, 2018). This increase in numbers has created a crisis for social work practice (Justice, 2016) but, looking behind these numbers, it has to be emphasised that a child being taken into care is, in any case, unique.

According to Section 17 of the Children Act 1989, local authorities have to 'safeguard and promote the welfare of children' and must make every reasonable effort to 'promote the upbringing of such children by their families'. Even when birth parents are unable or not willing to care for their children, every effort must be made to enable their children to be brought up by their extended family (HM Government, 2015). As such, accommodating a child under s20 of the Children Act 1989, or through care arrangements, should always be the last resort.

In 2015, Lord Justice Munby identified some key problems in the way s20 of the Children Act 1989, which outlines the local authority's duty to provide accommodation, is used by social workers. There has been a significant shift in social work practice in which local authorities appear to be preferring to use a care order (s31 of the Children Act, 1989) to avoid using voluntary arrangements in which the local authority share parental responsibility. In O's case this seems to run against the 'no order' principle which basically outlines that any arrangements that do not require a court order should be prioritised.

My message to social workers

Social workers are extremely busy and under a lot of pressure and I fully understand the financial constraints children's services are experiencing. Yet, if you are on the receiving end of services, the expectation is that social workers are communicating with you and that they are proactive in doing so. This whole experience was a constant battle with social services and it did not have to be. There have been some brilliant workers who were very good in keeping us up to date and who were interested in how O was doing. Unfortunately, there have been so many changes of social workers which makes it difficult to maintain a good relationship and this is most important.

Social worker's reflections

I had the privilege to meet Leanne, G and, most importantly, O during the process of writing this chapter. O did talk to me about snakes, showed me her pet snake and talked to me about the family dog. She is a most remarkable teenager. She is very articulate, interested and funny. She seems to be a person who cares deeply about the people around her and about what is going on in the world. When I was taken back to the train station she told me how she collected about £1,000 for charity by cutting off her hair. Taking all this together, and having listened to the story, I can't help but wonder how I would have reacted to O if I had been the allocated social worker. It would have been hard to see or to imagine what difficulties this whole family might experience. On reflection this tells me that, as social workers in general, we need to be much more open to all kinds of possibilities and trust the judgement of those who are the true experts in their own lives far more. No assessment, court report or care plan, regardless of the professionalism and expertise of the author, could ever capture what goes on in a family's life. Even after listening to their story and seeing how positive Leanne, G and O relate to each other, it is difficult to understand what happened for this family to get to where they are now. I am not sure if I, as a social worker, would have seen the emerging problems without the benefit of hindsight given the strengths this family has.

References

Bachelard, G. (1994) *The Poetics of Space*. [online] Boston: Beacon Press.

CAFCASS (2018) *Public Law Data*.

Dean, M., Harwood, R. and Kasari, C. (2017) The art of camouflage: Gender differences in the social behaviors of girls and boys with autism spectrum disorder. *Autism*. 21: 6, 678–689.

DfE (2015) The Children Act 1989: Guidance and regulations. Volume 2: Care planning, placement and case review, 2 (June), 1–184.

DfE (2017) *Children Looked after in England Year Ending 31 March 2017*. [online], (March), 1–12.

Dyke, C. (2016) *Writing Analytical Assessments in Social Work*. online. Northwich: Critical Publishing.

Government (2015) *Working Together to Safeguard Children* [online].

Jay, A. (2014) *The Independent Inquiry into Child Sexual Exploitation in Rotherham(1997–2013).* Available at: www.rotherham.gov.uk/downloads/file/1407/independent_inquiry_cse_in_rotherham.

Justice, L. C. (2016) The lord chief justice's report. *Judiciary of England and Wales* [online], 1–35.

Munro, E. (2011) *The Munro Review of Child Protection: Final Report – A Child-Centred System.* [online].

Nichols, S., Tetenbaum, S. P. and Moravcik, G. M. (2009) *Girls Growing Up on the Autism Spectrum: What Parents and Professionals Should Know about the Pre-Teen and Teenage Years* [online]. London: Jessica Kingsley Publishers.

Ofsted (2014) *From a distance. Looked after children living away from their home area.*

Pisula, E., Pudło, M., Słowińska, M., Kawa, R., Strząska, M., Banasiak, A. and Wolańczyk, T. (2017) Behavioral and emotional problems in high-functioning girls and boys with autism spectrum disorders: Parents' reports and adolescents' self-reports. *Autism.* 21: 6, 738–748.

Thompson, N. (2012) *Anti-Discriminatory Practice.* 5th edition Basingstoke: Palgrave Macmillan.

Walker, S. (2012) *Responding to Self-Harm in Children and Adolescents: A Professional's Guide to Identification, Intervention and Support* [online]. London: Jessica Kingsley Publishers.

Statute

Children Act 1989

Mental Health Act 1983/2007

8

I was Approved as an Adopter

Gareth Hunter

Naomi Fraser, *Adoption Social Worker*

At a glance

- This chapter focuses on the process for being approved as an adopter under the Adoption and Children Act 2002.

- Gareth, and his wife Tasha, are approved adopters and have adopted two children.

- Naomi is a social worker in an adoption service and was part of the approval process for Gareth and Tasha when adopting their second child. Naomi provides formal knowledge underpinning this statutory intervention in the text boxes throughout the chapter and, at the end of the chapter, shares her reflections on the adoption process from a social work perspective.

About myself

My name is Gareth and I have, with my wife Tasha, been approved for adoption twice.

About us, our situation and why we chose to adopt

Tasha and I began dating in mid-2006 and started trying for a baby in early 2007. We were always aware that the prospect of starting a family would be potentially challenging. This was due to Tasha's long-term suffering from endometriosis, for which she had a number of serious operations. After a period of no success we approached our GP for advice and were referred to NHS fertility services.

Unfortunately, Tasha's endometriosis consultant said he would take on our fertility treatment which led to us gaining a very poor service. Tests had shown Tasha to not be ovulating reliably so she was prescribed a course of Clomid to stimulate ovulation and sent on her way. This course lasted 12 months and was completely unmonitored medically – we later found out that it should have been monitored monthly and should have not lasted 12 months for safety reasons.

At this point we asked to be moved to a proper fertility consultant instead and, after further testing, Tasha was prescribed a course of injections to stimulate ovulation. All treatments so far failing, we were recommended for NHS funded In Vitro Fertilisation (IVF) treatment at a private clinic. We felt optimistic and proceeded with the treatment. Tragically, the day before egg harvest, the follicles collapsed ending our treatment entitlement on the NHS. Tests during IVF treatment had shown Tasha to have a very low egg reserve so, moving forward using our own funds and Tasha's eggs was not recommended. We joined the waiting list for donor eggs, more through desperation and the timescales involved in getting to the top of the list, than through any kind of considered decision.

It was at this point, that we started discussing the possibility of adoption. I can remember thinking that my overwhelming gut feeling was that I wanted my own flesh and blood children, I didn't want to adopt. In my mind I thought adoption was a wonderful thing, just not for me. Tasha had a different perspective and had always thought on some level that she would one day adopt, so was very open to the idea.

The adoption conversation did not develop very far, when another option presented itself. Tasha's cousin, a single mother of two, offered to donate eggs to our cause. Despite the potentially difficult emotional complications of this scenario, we gratefully accepted her generous offer and embarked up on the next leg of our journey towards parenting. This round of IVF produced seven eggs but just three healthy embryos. Despite our high hopes and almost £10,000 invested, implantation of two embryos the first time and the final embryo on the second, were ultimately unsuccessful.

This brings us to end of 2011. We discussed how to proceed, with Tasha leaning towards another try with donor eggs from elsewhere, but I felt enough was enough. After five years of fertility treatment, we were exhausted emotionally. Tasha had suffered far longer than this with the severe symptoms of her endometriosis and this, with the fertility treatment, had taken a huge toll on her physically. Anyone who has been down the fertility treatment road knows how all-consuming it is. We needed a break and time to heal emotionally, and recover financially, before deciding what to do next.

In the first half of 2013, having discussed our options at length and ruling out further fertility treatment, we decided to again explore the prospect of adoption. Neither of us being securely wedded to the idea, we just decided to take one step at a time. So one step turned into many and, in early 2014, we became approved adopters with our local authority's adoption service.

Our first match, a little boy, was found quickly but this turned out to be quite an unsettling experience. Rather unusually, we were granted the opportunity to meet him at an open day event, where children with placement orders and prospective adopters can interact. We found the day to be quite strange and surreal and the little boy's social worker behaved extremely unprofessionally, saying things such as: 'there's your little son' and would also make eye contact across the room and then point at him and put her thumbs up, or flutter her eyelids with a hand on her heart.

Unfortunately, there was a huge difference between the profile we had been sold and the reality of the child's needs, which were significant and beyond what we felt comfortable taking on. Also, we did not feel any connection with him at all and this is unusual for both of us with children we meet. In reality, we had no idea if there was going to be a connection when the right child came along, how would we know when we had found the child for us? It was a difficult experience compounded by the behaviour of our social worker after the event, when she found out we did not want to proceed. We were made to feel very bad about this decision by our social worker and were quite shaken after this experience. Our social worker said things like: 'I've never had a failed match' and 'this will probably affect your representation at matching meetings.' Clearly, this was not at all what we wanted to hear and made us feel quite angry at the lack of support – how are we supposed to make good decisions regarding our future child if we don't feel supported by our social worker? Going forward, we felt a bit disempowered to make our own decisions about future matches and very anxious that we would not even be considered in the first place. Our anxiety for next time was also increased when we considered that, had we not attended this event, we would likely have moved forward with the match. How far would we progress before we realised it was not a good match for us: panel, introductions day, when they move home? Who can say, maybe it is all down to fate.

A slight curveball on the day was when we met a seven-year-old who was just so sweet. He was obviously struggling to be placed due to his age (children become harder to place after about five years old) but we really hit it off. It was heart breaking when we overheard him asking his social worker if she thought a family would like him today, we just wanted to shout 'YES, WE DO'. It called into question everything we thought we were aiming for in terms of our target age group (zero to two) and we were seriously considering exploring the match. However, when we mentioned this to our social worker, our hopes were quashed when she claimed he was outside of our approved age group, a fact we later found out to be false. Maybe it would have affected her numbers, hopefully the little boy has now found happiness with a new forever family. With all this in mind, and the new reality of the profiles selling the children's development points short, it made it all the harder when our next match came up. We were, nevertheless, matched sometime later with a little girl and, in late July of 2014 following successful introductions, we brought home our beautiful 17-month-old daughter. We had done it, we were parents.

The matching process

The matching process is outlined in adoption statutory guidance (DfE, July 2013) and underpinned by the Adoption and Children Act 2002. Prospective adopters are 'matched' with a child through attending an adoption panel for a recommendation of suitability to inform the Agency Decision Maker (ADM) who ultimately makes the decision on behalf of the local authority. Tasha and Gareth's first 'match' through a different authority did not progress to panel but they felt emotionally invested and ready to be matched. Social workers hold a lot of power in the knowledge and information they have about a child and the process and need to equip prospective adopters with accurate information to make the right decision, while not overwhelming them.

Adoption activity days are organised events which give approved prospective adopters the opportunity to interact with children needing adoptive families. They were run in the UK for a while in the 1970s and, after becoming successful with modern family finding in the USA, were reintroduced in 2011 and are run by the Coram British Association for Adoption and Fostering (Coram BAAF) in partnership with local authority adoption services. They seek to find families for children who are regarded as 'harder to place', due to their age, cultural background or additional needs by enabling prospective adopters to make an emotional connection with a child and see beyond their factual needs. Coram BAAF report statistics that cite the events as frequently successful, with families such as Tasha and Gareth connecting with a child they would not normally have considered.

If they have been deemed a good match for the seven-year-old then they should have been put forward for him as prospective adopters as suggested child age groups are a guide only. It is surprising that they felt their social worker did not take a more considered approach to offering Tasha and Gareth space to decide if the child they were linked to was appropriate or promoting an open dialogue and supportive environment to discuss any anxieties they may have. One of the most crucial roles as the social worker for prospective adopters is to ensure they feel able to talk openly and frankly if they struggle to attach to, or meet the needs of, a child being placed with them. If not, there is an increased chance of adopters not speaking up until after the child is placed and they are struggling, sometimes leading to the placement breaking down, causing significant hurt to the children involved, adopters and the wider family.

▶

A placement breakdown can often lead to prospective adopters not feeling able to consider another placement and can increase a child's chances of an attachment disorder and a related lack of trust or increased emotional behaviour that can make it very difficult for them to gain permanency through adoption.

Over the months following our daughter moving home, we progressed through the assessment period without any issues and made our application to the courts to adopt her permanently. A court date was set and at the time, we were told that the birth mother was able to apply to appeal no less than six weeks prior to the court date. This day came and went and so we started to relax and await the hearings arrival. With six days' notice, we were contacted out of the blue by our daughter's social worker who told us that the birth mother was appealing and that we had to find legal representation, (and sorry, we can't recommend anyone). This was an extremely stressful moment and we could not believe that we had to deal with this crisis on our own. We simply had no idea where to find this kind of help. I decided that the best way forward would be to lean on our daughter's social worker a little which provided us with a company name. By that evening a solicitor had been instructed and we had five more days to nervously await the outcome. Having spoken to the solicitor, who was excellent, we felt a bit more confident about the outcome. Although we were told by the social worker that the birth mother was appealing, in fact, she was seeking *leave* to appeal which would need to be granted before an appeal could be launched. We were also told that the evidence against this decision being granted was very substantial and unlikely to occur. On reflection, it would have been really helpful to have accurate information about what was happening and what the implications of this might be. Ultimately, the court day arrived and the birth mother did not attend the hearing – this was a requirement of being granted leave to appeal. The relief felt by us following this decision was enormous. All doubt was removed about her permanent status and our ability to parent exactly how we wanted, without oversight, was finally realised. We could finally relax and get on with our lives.

Legal advice

Typically, when the child is placed by a local authority with their approved prospective adopter(s), the child's social worker and their supporting legal team will manage ongoing court issues. It is only normally within private adoption cases that the prospective adopters would be required to instruct their own independent legal advisor.

Details of the assessment (second time round)

> Adoption services exist to serve children that can't remain with their birth families. They, therefore, adapt their prospective adopter recruitment according to the needs and types of children they are seeking families for and the number of prospective adopters they have already approved (as underpinned by Adoption and Children Act 2002). Agencies may decline potential families based upon certain factors, for example, the area where they live or the type of child(ren) they feel they have the capacity to adopt. They would be offered advice as to which other adoption agencies they should approach instead.

Fast forward to early 2016 and our family of three are doing really well. Our little girl is settled and thriving at home and nursery and is developing at a fantastic rate. We felt the time was right to investigate the possibility of adopting for a second time. We returned to the local authority's adoption service but were quickly rejected on grounds of our demographic being outside of their current requirements.

So, we wrote to all the adoption services from the surrounding counties and were greeted with enthusiasm by Bournemouth Adoption Services. A telephone interview was conducted and we were soon visited by a social worker to conduct an initial assessment of our suitability to adopt. We found this initial visit to be a positive experience, however, it seemed like such a waste of effort that nearly all the questions asked in this session had already been covered over the phone.

> ## Repetition
>
> I was unaware of how repetitive the early part of the process is, perhaps because it is not overseen by one person at this stage and because, under workload pressures, workers have not always reviewed information already gained before undertaking the initial visit. This is a reminder of how such 'shortcuts' can impact upon the client. I am, however, also aware that sometimes probing questions asked over the phone need re-asking when face-to-face as people tend to feel more comfortable disclosing difficult information when speaking to someone in person.

After a fairly short amount of time, we were deemed suitable to continue with our application and were allocated a social worker. From an adopter's perspective, it seems very strange to begin building a relationship with a social worker on the initial visit and divulging highly personal information during that session, only to be allocated someone completely new to carry out the assessment process. Our social worker arranged to visit us for the first time and we were sent some forms to fill out. So, for the third time (and not for the last), we began filling out all the same information that had already been gathered on the phone and in person during our initial visit. We felt that our first visit went well and that our social worker was someone who we felt comfortable to share our life story with and who we could trust to advocate for us during the adoption process. This, we feel, was crucial and had we not connected with our social worker, we would probably have had to ask for someone different.

The process and timeline for our assessment was mapped out early on by our social worker, who was fantastic at planning and worked backwards from our panel date to devise an assessment schedule. We therefore knew exactly how long the process would take and the steps that would be required, which was really great for managing our expectations. The assessment process for first-time adopters comes effectively in two stages. Since we had already adopted before, our files from the previous adoption service were requested and we were able to skip most of the first stage, with our social worker asking for information to fill in the gaps, where necessary. We found the process to be quite straightforward. There was lots of paperwork, much of the time re-recording what was already written elsewhere, but the forms are all for a different purpose. If ever a process desperately needed to be captured in an IT workflow system, it is adoption. With adopters being able to view the status of their case and work through all the paperwork online, co-authoring where necessary, the process would be so much easier and less repetitive. Alas, this is not the case.

Timescales

The statutory timescales are also set out in the adoption statuary guidance (DfE, July 2013), limiting the assessment timescale to six months, or four months if for a second-time adopter. The tight timescales are due to a national government drive to promote greater use of adoption and improve the performance of adoption services. In particular, this was following plans set out in a white paper in December 2000 to increase children being found a permanent family through adoption by 40 per cent and hopefully reduce the number of children growing up in foster care. Foster care not being life-permanent and often involving family moves and related instability and attachment problems. It divides the process into two stages: stage one is two months

▶

◄

long, for completing prescribed checks and references; and stage two is four months long, to undertake and write up a detailed assessment, take to adoption panel for an approval recommendation and gain approval from the ADM. Agencies can choose not to proceed with a family from stage one to stage two, similarly, prospective adopters can choose to change agencies at this point or take a break of up to six months.

For second-time adopters like Gareth and Tasha, they re-start the process at stage two but have statutory checks undertaken alongside. Due to the timescales, careful planning is required, the planning ahead also enabling prospective adopters to fit appointments around their other commitments. At the end of the assessment a Prospective Adopters Report (PAR) is produced, a lengthy document of two parts, each 20 to 30 pages long. The majority is available to prospective adopters to read and is an account and analysis of the information they have provided about themselves and their adoption hopes. Information gained from referees remains confidential and not available for them to read.

Our social worker was very efficient in moving the process along and issuing tasks to be achieved by the next session. As before, the process was incredibly intrusive into every aspect of our lives. Fortunately, we are very open people and do not struggle to talk honestly about our pasts and about our feelings towards different issues such as the breakup of my first marriage or Tasha's difficult upbringing during her teen years. The nature of this process would potentially make it very traumatic and invasive for adopters who are more private by nature. We felt that our case was dealt with sensitively, only probing enough to satisfy the process. One part of the process we found particularly bizarre was when our, then, three-year-old daughter, had to be interviewed on her own. We found this to be quite uncomfortable since we cannot think of any other situation where we would allow our daughter to be questioned without us being present. We had to trust that our social worker would not accidentally say something which would upset our daughter or somehow confuse her. We really didn't see the value in this part of the process since she was too young to understand any of the questions and basically gave nonsensical answers. We also felt the risk of her becoming confused, or upset in some way, was not justified by the contribution she was able to make. We had prepared our daughter over the weeks preceding the interview, talking openly about adoption and how our social worker was going to help us find her a brother or sister. Overall, we are happy that the interview was well handled and had no ill effects, but we feel that undertaking this part of the assessment, if necessary, must be conducted with the utmost care and sensitivity.

Wider family

When assessing prospective adopters, it is important to seek the views of their wider family, particularly if they reside within the home. In particular, you are checking that they too support the plan for adoption, understand what this entails and how it will affect them and that they raise no concerns as to the prospective adopter(s) being suitable to adopt. While their daughter was pre-school age, my experience as a children's social worker has highlighted not to underestimate the competence of a young child to express their views in conversation, play or drawing, all of which were used in this 'interview'. I am aware that the statements provided by children as young as five have led to successful court convictions. I was careful to find a balance during this interaction between steering the discussion and being child led, reducing the pressure 'to talk' upon their daughter.

Once all the paperwork was complete and the PAR was written, our social worker visited our families and friends who had been offered as referees. Our referees felt quite anxious about the pending visits, mainly because they didn't want to say anything which may hinder our application in some way. We just advised them to be honest, not having anything to hide, our whole lives having been keenly documented already anyway. Our referees all felt that their meetings had gone well and that our social worker was friendly and professional, setting them at ease.

One concept which was new since the last time we adopted was the idea of fostering for adoption or 'early permanency'. The aim of this pathway is to seek to place children who are currently in care, but highly likely to secure placement orders with a family who will ultimately adopt them. We felt that this, in theory, sounded like a good idea with the benefit of the child settling in to their new home at a younger age, so they can begin their healing and development process sooner. In practice, the authorities have effectively taken the concept of fostering and the concept of adoption and lumped them together to create a third category complete with the rules and legislation of each. Unfortunately, people who wish to adopt, are looking for a child to call their own and attach to and love. This is absolutely not what fostering is about. Expecting adopters to adhere to the rules and restrictions of fostering is a lot to expect in our opinion and was not something we would likely be able to partake in. Additionally, there is an enormous amount of risk involved in taking on an early placement. The child could be given back if the court fails to grant a placement order, dealing with this loss is a lot to expect of adopters; especially if, like us, they have an existing child to consider. We did however agree to apply for approval for both fostering for adoption and adoption, purely to mitigate the risk of being overlooked in the matching process.

A **Care Order** (Children Act, 1989) gives the local authority legal responsibility for the child, the parent(s) parental responsibility being limited by the local authority. A **Placement Order** (Adoption and Children Act, 2002) legally authorises the local authority to place the child for adoption, parental responsibility transferring to the local authority on the granting of the order.

The Children and Families Act 2014 placed duties upon courts to complete court proceedings within 26 weeks. However, for a baby, this is still a long time, spanning crucial attachment and development months, while 'waiting' in foster care for a permanent home, especially if appeals take care proceedings outside of this timescale. Early permanency seeks to resolve this, temporarily approving prospective adopters as foster carers for the child they are matched with so the child can move into their care before the legal process is completed. This reduces the harm of delay upon children and offers prospective adopters the opportunity to experience as many 'firsts' in the child's life as possible.

Fostering for Adoption is the most common form of early permanency used whereby the local authorities feel satisfied that they have assessed all other care options as not viable. However, there remains a risk that another option for care by a family member has been missed or that the court rules differently to what the local authority expects, possibly requiring the child to move out of the prospective adopters' care. Although, even with a placement order there is some risk to a child's placement with prospective adopters as birth parents can appeal for the child to be returned to them if they can evidence they have made significant positive changes, as Gareth and Tasha experienced with their first adoption placement. They can do this up until 21 days after the adoption order is granted.

By far one of the most difficult and unsettling components which occurs at the end of the application process, is the defining of what exactly we are prepared to take on in an adoptive child. It comes in the form of a tick list which details all the possible aspects of a child, including illnesses, ailments and potential conditions such as Foetal Alcohol Syndrome (FAS). It is a process which requires you to be brutally honest and realistic about what you are able to take on in a child. It is, of course, necessary to ensure good and successful matches but makes you, as an adopter, feel like a really terrible person.

We were delighted that this time around, we would not be required to undertake work experience to prove our abilities to look after children. It is a bizarre and fairly insulting concept that authorities consider that, since we are unable to conceive children naturally, it cannot be assumed that we have the ability to meet one's needs either. Despite our experience being uncles, aunts and godparents in current and previous relationships, despite the fact I was a scout leader for many years and Tasha a teaching assistant and despite lots of referees attesting to our ability to look after their children, we still had to undertake three months of work experience at what turned out to be our children's future nursery, in order to gain a reference to be evidenced in our application.

Thankfully, we were able to bypass this necessity second time around but we know of other current parents who were not so lucky in their adoption process. We understand the need for authorities to vet candidates thoroughly but, in normal life, parenting is learned on the fly and with our previous evidenced experience with children, it seemed excessive to also require a professional reference as well.

Prior experience

Within the prospective adopter report there is a section to report upon 'what experiences of caring for children have prepared the applicant to become and adopter? In what ways are those experiences indicative of how they might parent an adoptive child?' (Coram BAAF, 2016). The assessing social worker needs to feel satisfied they can answer these questions positively and can encourage prospective adopters to gain additional experience. Often this experience is not necessary but may increase the prospective adopter's chance of being selected as a suitable match for a child as it is easier to 'evidence' their level of likely childcare knowledge and ability.

Approval

After a fairly short wait our panel day arrived and, in November of 2016, we once again became approved for adoption and fostering for adoption. We felt well prepared for the panel both from our previous experience and by our social worker who was thorough in detailing what to expect. The panel interview did not reveal any surprises; we were asked a few questions by several of the panel members and, after about ten minutes, it was over. The panel agreed unanimously, with the medical professional noting that I could lose a bit of weight, possibly a bit discriminatory in this day and age. Following the panel meeting, there is a wait of around a week while the ADM signs off the panel's decision and it becomes official.

Family finding

Within days of approval, we had seen a couple of potential matches in the form of sibling pairs. We were open to the idea of adopting two children but ultimately, in these cases, their medical needs were beyond what we felt comfortable taking on. There was then a hiatus of several months where we did not see any further profiles. In early 2017, we were given access to the regional adoption website where you can search for children that may be of interest. This, again, is one of the most bizarre and slightly uncomfortable experiences of this process. It is quite emotional reading about all these neglected children who you desperately want to help out. Then your eye inevitably falls on their medical history and out comes the terrible person again, as you click the back button on the web browser and move onto the next profile. We did enquire about a number of children in the profiles, however, we did not hear back from any so can only assume that they either were not available, or their social workers were not interested in us. This, again, is quite an unsettling process since, by the time you make an enquiry, there is already a level of emotional attachment to the profile which is impossible to prevent. The key is not to let yourself think about it, beyond clicking the send button, until you hear something positive back. We also felt that that the profiles displayed on this website were, in general, fairly sugar-coated and were mainly children who have proved harder to place already, due to their higher level of needs.

The DfE 2013 statutory guidance seeks to empower prospective adopters by encouraging the family finding process to be adopter led. While this seems beneficial in theory, the reality of the emotional stress this can place upon them to select certain children over others is immense. The children's social worker needs to offer key facts to support prospective adopters to make decisions, without creating too much anxiety about possible additional needs or compromising the confidentiality of the child's information.

Specially designed websites are established for basic profiles of children and adopters to be shared but the sites can feel uncomfortable to use as they can seem to trivialise the emotions behind the searches and seek to put children's needs, and adopters' skills, into search engine tick boxes. Also, for infants with limited additional needs, as Gareth and Tasha were seeking, there is often an overwhelming response to a child's profile making it difficult for social workers to respond back to each personally with reasons as to why other families were shortlisted over them. This sense of rejection can be highly stressful.

In May of 2017, we were finally contacted by our social worker regarding a relinquished new-born baby boy, which at this point was a fostering for adoption placement. We were informed that we were one of two couples being considered for this placement so we tentatively agreed to move forward with the enquiry. Our main reservation was the child's legal status and how long that would take to resolve – during which time we would effectively be foster carers, not really something we wanted to do.

Memories of us turning down a match in our previous adoption resurfaced a little, but we were open with our social worker about our slight anxiety, who was very reassuring and supportive. We met with the child's social worker, a meeting which went very well and we were honest about our concerns over the child's legal status. The other couple were chosen over us due to their being more comfortable with a fostering for adoption placement. This was disappointing, but we quickly felt relieved that the decision had been taken away from us, deep down this was not how we wanted to adopt. Apart from the emotional trauma we would suffer if the placement fell through, we were not really prepared to risk putting our daughter through such a confusing and upsetting worst-case scenario. Fatefully, the child's social worker was also trying to place a six-month-old baby girl and was very interested in us for the placement. This match, we felt, was a better fit for us and we were eager to move forward. We were presented with the child's profile a short time later, after which we were very excited. We felt certain that this was the match we had been waiting for.

A match

As the matching process progresses, increasing information is shared until all information about the child is shared. Tasha and Gareth received a full report about the child, a chance to look at several photos and consultations with the foster carer and agency medical advisor. For older children, they may have also seen a DVD of the child, had consultations with the agency's clinical psychologist and with other professions who know the child, such as the health visitor of pre-school keyworker. Sometimes it can also involve a sighting of the child from a distance or a low-key 'play date', depending upon the needs and understanding of the child.

A matching panel was booked a few weeks later which we had to attend once again. The format was similar to the adoption approval panel and, in fact, contained basically the same set of people. We had something of a shock upon reaching the panel, however, when we found out that our social worker was away sick. She was replaced by her manager who was not well prepared to represent us and, in fact, made us feel extremely uneasy prior to entering the panel room – saying things like, this shouldn't be about your status as adopters (if we didn't think it was, we did now!!) and various other unhelpful comments. Luckily, we were confident in our own abilities and represented ourselves just fine. As before, following the panel we had to await the ADM decision which passed with no issues and we were ready to start introductions.

This highlights the power of having a relationship with someone and how it can inform whether advice could be reassuring or anxiety provoking.

Placement

Introductions were scheduled to begin in late June of 2017, by which time our future daughter was eight months old. The ADM decision from our matching panel was actually granted while we were on a cottage holiday. At this point we began talking to the foster carer of our little girl-to-be and receiving daily updates and photographs. This was actually a wonderful way for us to start feeling involved in her life and for the three of us to begin attaching to her. We, in turn, sent photos and some videos which she was able to watch, apparently with considerable enthusiasm – she particularly liked a video of us singing her favourite nursery rhyme.

Introductions began on the Tuesday following our return from holiday. We arrived at the foster carer's house, where the three of us were greeted by a smiling baby girl. Our main objective was to ensure that our elder daughter felt fully involved in the introductions, so we focused on her meeting her new sister as much as possible. Our foster carer had been amazing in buying her a wonderful gift from her new sister, which she was really pleased with. It's fair to say there were a few concealed tears on the doorstep as we entered the house and were immediately handed our new, very smiley daughter. The four of us spent some time playing and getting to know each other and before we knew it, the first couple of hours was over and it was time for us to leave. We were then required to attend a planning meeting where we would discuss and confirm our plan for the week which if successful, would culminate in our new addition moving home with us on the Friday.

Court proceedings

During court proceedings for this child, birth parents conceded to the plan for adoption, recognising they could not care for their child themselves. They requested, at this point, that the local authority sought to place their child with adopters who would agree to having a one-off meeting with them and were committed to writing to them once a year about how their daughter was doing (called a 'letter box exchange'). The child's social worker was keen to honour this request and Gareth and Tasha were their first choice of a match because they had demonstrated an ability to consistently maintain letter box contact with the birth family members of their already adopted child.

▶

In this case, there probably was a lot of pressure to meet with the birth parents, something they had agreed to during pre-matching discussions. It is, however, generally recommended that these one-off meetings take place as it will equip the prospective adopters with additional information about the birth parents and their family which they can share with their child. It also offers birth parents a sense of closure to their loss and establishes a relationship for positive letter box exchanges, encouraging birth parents to annually write back with birth family information.

On the Wednesday morning we were scheduled to meet our new daughter's birth parents. We were a little apprehensive about the pending encounter but were encouraged to partake. Overall, we already felt that it was important to have first-hand experiences to tell our daughter in the future and also to provide some reassurance and closure for the birth parents, who were suffering a horrific loss in their lives. Once you reach this stage in the adoption process, you are deeply familiar with the lives of the birth parents and reading about it is enough to bring you to tears. In many cases these are not bad people, they have had horrendous upbringings themselves and have suffered their own neglect, abuses and bad parenting. They are unable to parent sufficiently well because they had no frame of reference from which to learn. On reflection, we felt that the meeting went well and we were able to reassure the birth parents that their daughter was going to be well cared for and loved. Although we were keen to partake in this meeting anyway, it was clear that the authorities were strongly in favour of the meeting taking place. Social workers should be mindful that some adopters may not cope well with this scenario, so should be sensitive and not too forceful when proposing the meeting.

The remainder of the introductions week went extremely well and we were incredibly lucky to have such an accommodating foster carer to make us feel welcome in her home. The introductions process is incredibly intense and emotional and requires you to virtually live in a stranger's home, while meeting your new child to be. As an adopter, you feel constantly under the microscope for every little thing that you do with the new child. This is not a reflection on our foster carer but a symptom of the fact you are being assessed. Even as experienced parents, you start to second guess your own abilities while being under scrutiny, so the whole period is extremely draining. It is hard to imagine how difficult it would be if adopters were unable to kindle a good relationship with the foster carer. On the Friday of introductions week at nine a.m., we said our goodbyes to the foster carer and headed home with our new baby daughter, we had done it again.

In the coming weeks we had regular visits from our and our daughter's social worker, which is all part of the process of settling the child in to their new home and addressing any issues that may arise. This included two visits from an independent assessor. Following the second visit, all being well, we are cleared to apply to the court to officially adopt our daughter. This is a difficult period to work through for adopters since the legal parental responsibility is still shared with the authority and the birth parents. There is a tabulated tick list of things you can and can't do without first gaining permission from the authority which is not easy for parents to deal with, for example, if our parents were going to babysit for more than 24 hours they would need to be Disclosure and Barring Service (DBS) checked. You are also constantly worried that the child may have a little toddler's accident and that may, in some way, reflect badly on our adoption process. This period of scrutiny is probably one of the worst parts of the process overall and social workers should be mindful of how difficult this is for adopters to live with.

Social work visits

Due to the high risk of placement breakdowns during the first few weeks, the 2013 statutory guidance advises a minimum of weekly visits for the first four weeks leading up to a formal review of the placement undertaken by an independent reviewing officer. The frequency of visits is then reviewed and a further review meeting set for up to three months later. Typically, at the second review, all parties decide whether the prospective adopters and the child are in the right position for an Adoption Order to be applied for. Once a child is placed the local authority delegates many of its day-to-day parental responsibility roles to the prospective adopters but retains power over key decisions, hence a tick list to help prospective adopters understand the differing legal duties and powers. This is an uncomfortable time in the process for prospective adopters as they have the much-desired child in their care and hopefully feel strongly attached to them, keen to celebrate being a family, but they are not yet the child's parents. The fear of losing the child they have longed and fought for becomes quite significant.

Of course, with a court application comes more paperwork, so we set to the task of filling out some more forms and providing more evidence. This was, in turn, transformed into a report by our and our daughter's social worker and finally submitted to the court in November of 2017, by which time our daughter was 13 months old. Over Christmas we received a letter scheduling our hearing for 31 January 2018, on which day we legally became the proud parents of another beautiful daughter who was now 15 months old. All that was left to do was wait a further 21 days for the appeals period to expire and we could breathe easy and get on with our lives as a family.

Where we are at now

In February 2018, the appeals period passed without incident and we are now the proud parents of two beautiful little girls. It is nice to be at a point that we can now move forward with our lives as a normal family with no more assessments and no more scrutiny. It is definitely nice to not be waiting for a match to be found, or the next significant date on the road to adoption to arrive. We can concentrate on enjoying family life with our girls, with the power to make all the ordinary parenting decisions ourselves, something taken for granted by the thousands of lucky parents who conceive naturally.

We have agreed that contact with the birth parents will occur on a yearly basis via letter. This arrangement has also been maintained on a twice-yearly basis with our older daughter's birth parents. We feel that writing these letters has been beneficial to us as a record of how they have developed and what we have been up to as a family. More importantly, our daughters will have a complete picture of their upbringing going forward which will help them embrace their adopted status. Additionally, the birth parents who have suffered trauma of their own will be reassured that their lost children are being well cared for.

We are extremely pleased to have maintained an ongoing relationship with both of our children's foster carers. During the intense period that is introductions, we forged quite special bonds in both cases and we are pleased to still be in touch, trading the occasional text message or email and meeting up two or three times per year for lunch and a catch up. It is early days for our younger daughter but has been extremely beneficial for our older one who, at the age of five, is aware when we visit that this is where she used to live as a baby and where she first met us as parents. We have photographs to back these stories up, it is part of her life, they are facts that she knows and therefore will hopefully never have any hang-ups or worries about her adoptive roots.

Our overall reflections

Is adoption worth it? The answer is, yes definitely. Despite the deeply intrusive, emotional and paperwork-intensive rollercoaster that is the adoption process, you not only gain a child to love and raise as your own, but also the opportunity to offer a great life to a child who would otherwise have been far worse off. It is definitely not an easy process to undertake and you are thrust into situations that you simply would not encounter anywhere else in normal life. The process is stressful and frustrating and, with the level of scrutiny and probing, it is probably not for everyone. But when the process is over and your child is thriving in their new home as part of your family, everything you have been through pales into insignificance.

One question an adoptive parent may worry about in lieu of adopting is, how do I know that I love this child the same as my own flesh and blood? The answer, I guess, is that you don't for sure. However, what we can say is that we can't imagine how we could love a child more than we do our daughters. What we can also say without hesitation is that if we one day met Rumpelstiltskin who offered us our own flesh and blood children in exchange for not adopting our daughters, the answer would be 'over our dead bodies!' The answer to the above question, therefore, feels like yes with a high level of certainty. Would we adopt a third time? It depends what day you ask,, but never say never!

We found that during our first adoption process, the expectations regarding one of us giving up work to look after the child is quite unrealistic. We were told that we should be taking a 12- to 18-month maternity leave and ideally giving up work or working as few days as possible. There was a lot of pressure in this regard from our social worker as well, when it is frankly unrealistic financially for most households to lose an entire wage. Second time round Tasha's current three-day per week working pattern was deemed to be fine, which shows the difference in rules and approaches between social workers and the authorities they work for. There is no doubt at all that building strong attachments early are essential for adoptive children, but expectations must be realistic and balanced against a household's ability to survive financially. Clearly those children with a greater level of need will require a higher level of parental attention. This feeds into the decision-making process with the dreaded 'tick sheet' where we determine what we can realistically take on in an adoptive child. In our case, both our children have had fairly minimal adoptive needs and we found that a standard six months of maternity and dropping to a three-day working week for Tasha, has been a perfect balance in our case. In fact, we feel that it has been hugely beneficial for our children to spend a day with each set of grandparents and a day at nursery as part of their standard routine and they have learned to build strong attachments with the significant members of our family, while also gaining the benefits of independence and educational development at nursery.

One thing we learned from the adoption process is how our perception of birth parents changed. It is easy to frown upon people who are unable to parent their children from a position of a stable upbringing. Having read the profiles of many birth parents, much of the time they are the saddest of stories, where they were abused and neglected themselves, never inheriting the essential blueprint for parenting that the rest of us take for granted, with our stable home environments.

Our final reflection on the adoption process is the fact that until writing this story, we never once took the time (or found the time) to reflect on our experiences. From the time you decide to start a family, through fertility treatment and on to adoption, you spend all of your time either focusing on the next step in your process or trying to heal from the emotional trauma that you have experienced. By the time your adoption process is complete, you have a child which immediately and without break, takes on all of the attention that was previously focused elsewhere. Writing about our journey has proven to be an emotional and reflective experience and one that we have found beneficial to understanding what we went through and how it affected us.

Our message for social workers

Probably the single most important factor in the adopter/social worker relationship is communication. It is really important for both parties to be open and honest and for the social worker to keep adopters up to date with the current developments and accurate information pertaining to their case. Waiting is one of the most prevalent aspects of the process and just touching base regularly helps immensely with the anxiety surrounding this. Having had experience with different styles of social worker, it's clear that some can be so task oriented with getting the next bit of information, or addressing the next difficult issue, that they forget they are dealing with people's lives. Many adopters, like ourselves, have spent years trying to become parents naturally and ultimately failing. In particular, with the first adoption attempt, we felt that was our last chance to become parents so the level of anxiety and stress that something may go wrong, was quite high. It is vital that social workers are receptive to this fact and deal with these matters with sensitivity and compassion. It is also very important that we, as adopters, trust our social worker to be a strong advocate for us since we will, in many cases, not be representing our own cause in activities such as matching meetings. Overall it is important to spend time building a good relationship with your adopters so we don't feel like just another number. In all of this, we felt very well looked after when adopting through the Bournemouth adoption service. If in doubt, take time to consider how you may feel in their position.

Social worker's reflections

I approached Gareth to write his account for this book as I believed we had established an honest relationship that would enable him to openly share his account. I also believe the adoption process the couple went through with us second time around was fairly typical for most adopters.

When I first started working with Gareth and his wife Tasha, they were quite anxious that the process should feel as much of a partnership as possible and that communication was open. This was, in part, influenced by their experiences of their first adoption. To reduce anxieties, at our first meeting, we established expectations around this and agreed a clear plan of how we could work together. Other adopters may prefer a more relationship-building/person-centred, less process driven, approach. I stressed the importance to Gareth and Tasha of them being honest with me about what was or wasn't working from the outset and how open discussion is something to be valued within the assessment and not something they should fear negatively affecting our relationship and my perceptions of them. I believe they had the confidence to accept this more than most, due to having adopted previously, while I was, of course, aware of the huge power I held over them and this anxiety was still present, particularly with Tasha. I was always mindful of this, being the potential barrier to their dream to parent that, for many, is so closely linked to their sense of worth and success in life. Yet, as an adoption social worker, you are first and foremost a children's services social worker and need to remain child focused and not be 'swayed' by prospective adopters' emotional pull to become parents if they are not in the right position to parent through adoption. I believe their anxiety around me seeking their current child's views was closely linked to this as it was a discussion they neither had control over nor were even party to, as well as three-year-olds being unpredictable in their perception of things.

The assessment of this couple was quite straightforward, to timescale and no concerns were raised during it. The process is intrusive – prospective adopters being expected to lay themselves bare, having their values and essence of who they are examined and judged and reflected back to them. Observing ourselves in such detail is generally painful, let alone when there's limited time to build a trusting relationship. Ultimately, due to the detailed assessment, you may know more details about them and their lives than anyone else and the honour of being entrusted with that information, I believe, should be respected by ensuring you evidence that you understand them as people with their complexity of roles, identities, potentials and emotions.

The assessment time is also for educating prospective adopters about the differences of parenting a birth child to that of parenting an adopted child who has experienced loss of attachment figure(s) and possible abuse. This can create tensions in the relationship as you are supporting prospective adopters to reframe their dream of family life, while encouraging them to openly talk in detail about their thoughts, feelings and beliefs. Within this case this tension was not as present, Gareth and Tasha having mostly undertaken this work first time around.

Finding the right child for the couple also seemed fairly quick and straightforward compared to many, yet the waiting was still a highly anxious time for them. The closest analogy is telling someone they are pregnant but the gestation time frame is an unknown. There is still the potential for significant loss in the process, occasionally prospective adopters being emotionally connected to a child and then, for some reason, the match does not proceed. While Tasha and Gareth did not experience this beyond their self-directed family finding on websites, they were put in an awkward dynamic of considering whether to proceed with a child they felt uncomfortable about the legal status of until this decision was taken from them. Prospective adopters may then fear, when turning a child down, they may be unwittingly letting go of their best possible match, as well as feeling guilty of potentially leaving a child without a family. I regard my role as finding a balance between empowering adopters to make an independent decision with knowing when to step in and take difficult decisions out of their hands. With Gareth and Tasha, like most, I did not advise them of children whom I only had early stage discussions about to protect them from a sense of multiple losses and the associated emotional rollercoaster. I also felt unable to advise them of the second child the visiting social worker was family finding for, despite believing they were a better match, partially because the child's social worker and her manager were making the shortlisting decisions and partially because I feared that offering the couple an 'either-or' decision would be too emotionally stressful for them.

Once the child was placed with Gareth and Tasha, it was clear it was a good match and, from the outset, they presented as having fully claimed her as theirs and she seemed to readily accept them. This is not always the case, some adoptive families need much longer to believe and accept they are a new unit and occasionally the child exhibits new challenging behaviours or needs that can really test the placement's stability. When such challenges arise, it can often take great courage on behalf of the prospective adopters to speak openly and honestly about them to social workers due to the fears of losing the child. It is particularly wonderful and satisfying to hear how Gareth has reflected upon both their adopted children being completely right for them and that they would not have exchanged them, and the process to get them, for anything else. I find it such a privilege and delight to support a child and hoped-for parents find each other, and through this, the sense of family and belonging they have hoped for. It is particularly reassuring to hear that Gareth deeply understands that parenting via adoption is very different to parenting a birth child, no better or worse, just different and equally as rewarding and wonderful.

References

Coram BAAF 2016) Statistics England Looked after children, adoption and fostering statistics for England. Available at: www.corambaaf.org.uk.

Adoption: Statutory guidance. Statutory guidance for local authorities and adoption agencies. Published 18 July 2013, Department for Education. Available at: www.gov.uk.

Statute

Adoption and Children Act 2002
Children and Families Act 2014

Suggested websites

Coram BAAF Adoption and Fostering Academy www.corambaaf.org.uk.

9

I was Assessed under the Care Act to Enable Me to Live Independently

Sophie Buckley

Sally Lee, *Social Worker and lecturer in social work*

At a glance

- This chapter focuses on the statutory intervention of having an assessment under the Care Act 2014.

- Sophie is a university student with ataxic cerebral palsy who has worked closely with social workers throughout her life to enable her to live independently.

- Sally is a social work lecturer with experience in adult social work services. Sally was introduced to Sophie as part of the process of writing this chapter and provides formal knowledge underpinning this statutory intervention in the text boxes throughout the chapter and, at the end of the chapter, reflects on her learning from Sophie.

About myself

My name is Sophie. I am 29 years old and I have always aspired to being included in society and being active; I want to look back on what I have done and say I have had a good quality of life. I am an ambitious person and always have personal goals in mind such as getting my degree, writing this chapter and competing in boccia. I love to travel with friends, as well as on my own with support, and I love collecting photos and key rings that remind me of what I have done and who with.

I am currently in my final year of university, studying Early Childhood Studies. I have loved the chance to study with people, be included in debates and conduct research. One day I hope to be a lecturer or a teacher, but my main passion is sport, and anything goes. Now, I play boccia and powerchair football and help with other sports, including children's boccia and the Special Olympics.

I happen to have ataxic cerebral palsy. This means I am a wheelchair user when I am outdoors or need to sit for a long time. But I do walk around the house and short distances. I have poor hand control and can find skills such as eating myself difficult and tiring. There is a fine line between what I can do and what I need support with. My disability impacts on my energy levels, which is a little-known side effect of cerebral palsy. My care must be factored around this, and sometimes I need to be reminded of this as I am keen to get going.

I wanted to be involved in this book as I know social workers are 'normal'; I have trained to be a social worker and got to know them as friends and colleagues. However, as soon as it was 'my social worker' I felt anxiety about someone judging me, asking me questions that are hard to answer and having to explain my situation in ways that a person who doesn't know me would understand. Although some of my story is unique to me, I hope that this chapter supports social workers to understand life from the perspective of a person who has always needed support to achieve their goals.

My big secret is I went to Conductive Education in Birmingham when I was 18 months old, where I learnt to walk and talk.

Conductive education

Conductive education was founded in the 1940s by Professor András Petö and focused on children with neurological and mobility impairments. The education programme is task orientated with the aim of building on a child's natural abilities and their developing strategies which can be used in different environments, rather than corrective, modified or adapted environments. For more information see references.

My education seemed to be more like social work and physio mixed together rather than traditional teaching. I left full-time Conductive Education at seven, and part-time at 11. Each block of sessions had to be funded alongside attending mainstream school but, at that age, you don't understand about the funding and waiting. I was not part of this as the decisions were made by my parents, teachers and the education authority.

I moved to mainstream education as we were told that I had reached my optimum level of ability. In mainstream education I was supported by a 1:1 assistant, which was very strange because at Conductive Education you don't have 1:1 – and apparently, 'Sophie didn't like 1:1!' I went from being one of the most capable students, physically and mentally, to literally the bottom. So, although I was mentally at the same level as the other pupils, I couldn't keep up with sport and activities. Mainstream education was a shock and, apparently, I was an eye-opener for the other children too. I was walking at that time, but they had to not bump into me – they had to remember that I could fall over with a gust of wind.

Just like for other people, my education has set my life up. I have never been one to let others do things for me that I can do myself. Some people find that accepting help makes them uneasy, but it is natural for me as I have had to do it all my life. However, balancing the need for support with the drive to do things myself, and the feeling that I am responsible for providing work for the carer, can be difficult.

We moved to the South West when I was 13. I thought we were coming on holiday permanently – it never occurred to us children that we would have to go to school! But it took my parents no time to realise that there was no suitable education provision for me in our area. Schools had to do what they could to include me, but no one seemed to have specific knowledge about how to support me. It wasn't easy in Birmingham, but there were services that could offer advice or clubs that could give me meaning outside of school. I developed my love for sport and competing while at Conductive Education, which is based on keeping yourself fit and supple, as well as learning to work with your body. I learnt how to avoid pain through exercise and keeping mobile and this impacts on what I can do for myself. I play boccia and wheelchair football and that gives me my competitiveness and makes me a whole person.

I was born competitive; at two years old I got this annoying little person called my brother, and I thought 'game on!!!!' I've been blessed with two brothers and I'm not allowed to publicise how much I love them, otherwise I will never live it down! I was very competitive with my brother because I hit milestones with him, so when he walked, I walked; he talked, I talked.

I also do voluntary work. My main work is at a school and I do a lot of sports both for myself and to help others. I play boccia with the children and for my own enjoyment. I volunteer with the Brownies and the Special Olympics, which involves adults with learning disabilities; it's awesome. I get so much enjoyment out of volunteering, it's like going to work but at your pace and on your own terms.

After school, I had the chance to attend a specialist college for young people with disabilities. College gave me the best idea of independence and prepared me for adult life. This was at no expense to my education as we were able to study at the local sixth form college to get my A levels. But the most important thing I gained from college is the friendships that has seen me through; my friends understand the daily struggle of aspiring to have a good quality of life. I still prefer to mix with people who understand disabilities from experience rather than able-bodied people because there is an unspoken understanding.

Strengths-based approaches to assessment

During an assessment a social worker may focus on an individual's needs to justify the provision of care and support. However, this approach can feel disempowering for both the individual and social worker. The Care Act 2014 requires practitioners to take a strengths-based approach, exploring different factors that help or enable the individual to manage challenges, meet their needs and achieve their desired outcomes. These factors include:

- their personal resources, abilities, skills, knowledge, potential, etc.
- their social network and its resources, abilities, skills, etc.
- community resources, also known as 'social capital' and/or 'universal resources' (adapted from SCIE, 2018).

For further information go to https://www.scie.org.uk/care-act-2014/ assessment-and-eligibility/strengths-based-approach/.

My family and I have worked so hard to gain the ability I have today, and sometimes it is a struggle to keep it going and be pain free. So, when an assessment focuses on what you cannot do and there is no acknowledgement of what you can do, it can affect your self-confidence.

The first social worker I had was the transitions worker, and she wrote a letter endorsing my choice of college where I wanted to go, but I don't remember the social workers at that time, I was not really involved in the decision-making. I didn't like the mainstream school as they had never had someone as disabled as myself and the 1:1 support was focused on my safety rather than developing relationships with my peers. This made me feel different and my peers began to see me as the one who needed looking after. The attitude to me was: 'she is disabled so she needs looking after'; even the teachers had a dull view of me, thinking I would end up in a care home. But they did not think in terms of the care home where I live today. I suppose their view was of a traditional care home that has carers but not much else going on. So, it wasn't said in a positive way, instead it was said in a negative way because I needed help.

My life was sport, but I was told that I could not make a living from that, so I had to find something else. This showed that to some extent that I would follow the same path as my peers and get myself a job. But now, if I was to advise myself, I would say do something you enjoy and that you have a passion for.

The Conductive Education workers were my role models but knew I could not do the same work because of my physical disability. I knew I wanted to help others and use my brain instead of my body, so I chose to study social work. I first went to university when I was 19. The social worker had originally said: 'we will get you a budget set up when you get home from college, so you have the summer to get used to sorting yourself out before going to university.' But two weeks before I went to university I still hadn't had confirmation that I was going to get a direct payment for uni!!! Then your only option is a care agency because you can't employ anyone with two weeks' notice.

The notion of a personal budget is fantastic when it works the way it should: when it works it is like 'why am I here, let's get me out'. But the reality is a lot of work, which you don't mind as it is to give you a better quality of life. Direct payments have enabled me to go on holiday, keep in touch with my friends, and be able to do things I value. But at other times I missed out as I needed to arrange cover at short notice and constantly interviewing new staff involving, what felt like, life-changing decisions about whether the person would suit me.

Information about direct payments

A direct payment is provided by social services departments to individuals who have been assessed as having eligible care and support needs to purchase services to meet these needs (for further information see references)

Four conditions apply before a direct payment can be arranged:

- Mental Capacity: the individual must have capacity, or there must be a suitable person to manage the payment.

- Prohibitions: various criminal justice provisions apply, such as the individual being on licence.

- Ability to manage: the local authority must be satisfied that the individual, or their nominated person, can manage the payment either themselves or with assistance.

- Appropriateness: the local authority must be satisfied that the direct payment is an appropriate means of meeting the need and can only be used to meet the specified need.

Currently direct payments cannot be used to fund residential care other than for short breaks (Adapted from Mandelstam, 2017, p. 131).

I completed more than two years of the social work degree course but was informed that, although I might finish and get the degree, I might not get the fitness to practice approval. I was told that the Health and Care Professionals Council (HCPC) may judge that, if I was struggling to meet university deadlines, I may not meet deadlines in practice. This was ironic as the reason I needed extensions for my assignments was because of the placement work I had to do. Being on a full-time placement did not leave me much energy for the academic work.

I found the recruitment of personal assistants (PAs) and relationships with care agencies disempowering. There were some excellent staff who accepted me for who I am, and these PAs and carers supported and knew me, and then my life changed: I went away here and abroad and wasn't worried about how they would behave in front of others; it was stress free. But even PAs move on and, at the same time as my studies were going down-hill, my full-time PA left. I understood, as an employer, I had to replace her but there was so much to do. I managed to recruit another PA, but she only worked three days as the work did not suit her, even though we got on well. At this point I went home to my parents as I was so stressed and exhausted. Arguing with the university to stay on the course, while also organising care was exhausting. I felt that it was not worth my fighting to continue the course if the HCPC would say that I am not fit for practice. Because my family value having a degree they wanted me to stay, so I had to decide on my own whether to send the letter to the university saying, 'thanks for all your support but this isn't going to work'. I wasn't sure, but felt I had to make a decision – it was very difficult as I had so many things to consider.

When I chose to return to academic study nearly two years ago and top-up the credits I had already achieved to a full degree, it was on my own terms, without the expectations of others influencing my decision. Through this I have gained life skills and self-confidence. Living in residential care means I don't have to organise care juggling recruitment, rotas, sickness and all the other responsibilities of self-directing care. Instead, I can concentrate on studying.

Deciding to study again came at a time when I was waiting for support to be arranged. Social workers had wanted me to move from my parents' home into the community, and I was caught up in the argument of where would be suitable. I felt I was existing rather than living, even though it was better than before, doing things to keep busy rather than getting pleasure.

I resolved the situation by arguing that I could wait for the right support to come along or I could try something new and come up with solutions as problems arose. I felt nervous about studying again but felt that it was worth trying, even if it failed. I also realised that I could do the course part-time.

I am excited about lots of things like getting my degree in five months and the potential of moving out of residential care and starting a new chapter in my life. I think I am now more realistic about myself, although my previous experience causes me to be hesitant. I know I can manage without care for a day, I can plan and I have learnt that I can eat independently by using my hands rather than a knife and fork. I never want my life to only be about the support I need.

I think I have rigid thinking and, when I see what is written in the support plan, I take this as set in stone. Flexibility is needed when dealing with care agencies and I struggle with this. I do my own risk assessments in my head and calculate how to make my money go further. I do not put myself at risk.

Different interpretations of risk by service users and social workers

Some groups of people are labelled as particularly at risk, including disabled people (Hollomotz, 2010). Hoong Sin et al. (2011) identify two forms of risk commonly associated with disabled people, both of which lead to oppression:

First, there are risks to disabled people as a result of their disability. This is intimately related to the portrayal of disabled people as vulnerable due to their disability, and hence in need of protection. Second, disabled people are portrayed as risks to themselves and to others. This depicts a disability as a 'defect' that has the potential to cause disabled people to bring harm upon themselves, or to have an impaired ability to avoid harm (Hoong Sin et al., 2011, p. 64).

But it is not the disability that increases risk rather, society's response: the culture of risk avoidance sends the message that disabled people cannot and should not expect to lead full lives (ibid.). The focus of public services has moved towards safeguarding people deemed to be at risk, meaning social work concentrates on risk avoidance rather than the enablement of rights (de Than, 2015). Practitioners need to be alert to agency statements about empowerment, choice and control while policies demonstrate organisational risk avoidance (Furedi, 2011).

The relationship between risk management and risk enablement is core to social work practice as social workers have to make challenging judgements while being careful not to over risk manage, effectively limiting the social inclusion and life chances of people (de Than, 2015). Services which do not acknowledge peoples' full potential neglect opportunities to empower, leaving people vulnerable to abuse and disadvantage due to lack of self-esteem, confidence or knowledge (Furedi, 2011). This means respecting people's independence while also using authority to protect responsibly.

The statutory intervention – Supporting the move into residential care

Assessment of an individual's care and support needs is made under Section 9 of the Care Act 2014. A local authority has a duty to assess whether the individual has current need for care and support and what those needs are, irrespective of the level of care needs, the financial resources of the individual or what type of service they might require (Mandelstam, 2017).

Assessments must consider the impact of care and support needs on the individual and any carers' well-being, desired outcomes and whether support will aid these.

Eligibility is determined by three factors:

1. Needs resulting from physical or mental impairment of illness.

2. Those needs meaning the individual cannot achieve two or more of the following outcomes:

   a) managing and maintaining nutrition;
   b) maintaining personal hygiene;
   c) managing toilet needs;
   d) being appropriately clothed;
   e) maintaining a habitable home environment;
   f) being able to make use of the home safely;
   g) developing and maintaining family or other personal relationships;
   h) accessing and engaging in work, training, education or volunteering;
   i) making use of necessary facilities or services in the local community including public transport and recreational facilities or services;
   j) carrying out any caring responsibilities the adult has for a child. Managing and maintaining nutrition.

3. The individual's well-being is negatively impacted. Well-being in the Care Act 2014 refers to the following domains:

   a) personal dignity (including treatment of the individual with respect);
   b) physical and mental health and emotional well-being;
   c) protection from abuse and neglect;
   d) control by the individual over day-to-day life (including over care and support provided and the way it is provided)
   e) participation in work, education, training or recreation;
   f) social and economic well-being;
   g) domestic, family and personal relationships;
   h) suitability of living accommodation;
   i) the individual's contribution to society.

(Department of Health and Social Care, 2018)

The local authority does not necessarily have to meet all the needs but must ensure that any provision is appropriate and reliable (Mandelstam, 2017).

How needs are met can be a negotiation between the individual and local authority, and Sophie's experience demonstrates the potential conflict occurring when opinions differ.

People think care and care homes are just for older people, that the whole social care industry is for old people or children – but they can't forget about me!!!

It was my idea to move into residential care, and I had to fight for it for over two years. I was living with my parents after dropping out of university and could not recruit PAs because of the rural location. I was trying to recruit for a year and that left me using a care agency. But the agency was often short of staff, so my parents would end up providing care which none of us wanted. It was very stressful for everyone and I became very distressed about not being the person I wanted to be or being able to do what I wanted. This badly affected the family dynamics.

Respite care provides unpaid carers with a break through the provision of replacement care, either in the person's home or in a residential setting. Although the service is provided to the person with care and support needs, respite is a carers' service (Mandelstam, 2017).

I suggested residential care to my family and the social workers after I researched what was available. The social workers questioned why I wanted to move into residential care saying care homes are not for people 'like me'. But I argued that it was an option worth trying and a month of respite was eventually agreed.

By the third week of respite I was very anxious again as I did not know what was going to happen. We asked for 18 months respite to give me time to clear my head and make future plans. This was eventually agreed but it was a huge battle trying to justify to the social workers why I wanted to move into residential care.

The social worker came every six weeks to chase me out of residential care. During the agreed 18 months period I completed all the processes they wanted me to do to find other accommodation including registering with housing, looking into private accommodation, house shares and shared Lives.

Shared Lives is a nationwide scheme offering a unique form of social care with personalised services to people who need some help and support. Trained carers share their home and provide care and support in a variety of ways including:

- Long-term accommodation and support.
- Short breaks.
- Daytime support.
- Rehabilitative or intermediate support.
- Kinship support where the carer acts as 'extended family'.

(For further information go to: https://sharedlivesplus.org.uk/faq/about-shared-lives)

I found all this very stressful and, when I am stressed, I experience a strong flight response as I cannot fight physically or verbally; when I am stressed I cannot get my words out, so sometimes I would take flight and go to stay with my parents to calm down.

Personalised approaches to care underpin current social work with adults (Department of Health and Social Care, 2018) and require social workers to enable people to have a more direct role in the design and control of their support packages (Lishman et al., 2017). This means social workers take on a partnership role, transferring power to the individual who is viewed as the expert in their own lives (Thompson, 2015). However, despite the introduction of personalisation the power differentials within social work relationships remain and must be recognised to avoid disempowerment. Social workers retain their gatekeeping role with the assessment process being the method of accessing services and resources. Sophie's experience of being assessed for residential care, and having to argue for the service to meet her needs, illustrates the conflict between promoting the views of the service user as expert of their own needs and the views of social workers.

Later I was assigned a new social worker and had to go through the process of applying to housing and finding alternative accommodation all over again. It was like she did not believe that I had already done it. Since then the social worker has visited twice and the placement is permanent until an appropriate alternative is found. I have an annual review each February and always get worried as I don't know what is going to happen.

What happened next?

When I moved into residential care three years ago I needed much more support than I do now. If I was a 19-year-old now moving out of home I think it would be much worse now because of austerity: I would be given meals and showers, but I wouldn't be offered the support to build a life. I need help with things that wouldn't be eligible for help now, like filling out forms to get volunteer jobs and volunteering, as sometimes I can feel I am only there as a token. I think that is why I like being a student as I can study alongside other people and own my own work. The other things I need support with is being shown a route, so I can then do it by myself, I need to make sure that I can not only get there but also know where all the ramps are and where the nearest toilet is … I need to know my wheelchair is charged and I can get back again … it's not just going out and coming back, it's about thinking ahead.

I've also changed, at 19 I wouldn't have seen it like a plan I had to make, I would say that my cerebral palsy shouldn't be a problem, I should be able to do things the same way as everyone else, with no consideration for my disability. I did not want to make a big deal about it not only to others but also to myself. I didn't want to think about what time I had to get back for carers. I think it's about maturity and acceptance of you as you are, and at 19 I was an angry teenager and my disability was something I didn't want to have to think about or accommodate.

Now I have the maturity to plan and realistic expectations. This is not because I was lazy, but that maturity has deepened my self-understanding – something that cannot be taught. That's why I can go out and spend the weekend totally independently, which makes me think that I could live independently one day; not as an able-bodied person but, accepting me as I am and planning the next stage in terms of what do I really need and want to do. That's what residential care has given me. I don't have to do things on my own, I can if I choose them, but I don't have to do it.

I have a pot of energy every day and what I spend that pot on, I can negotiate with care staff. One of the major benefits of residential care is that staff can create an atmosphere that works for me. Staff have learnt that being direct isn't the best way with me, but if they let me know and explain how and why things are happening then it's easier for all of us. It has been a learning curve for everyone. My needs are variable so one day I can be completely able, well as able as I can be, and another day I can be stuck in bed wanting help to do the stuff I could do yesterday. I have learnt that I can't do a seven-day week even though I was trying so much to do so. Living in residential care has given me the chance to play with my energy levels and lie in bed and watch TV all day if I need to. It is very instructive for me to know how much energy I've got and how I can use it. I needed the chance to learn about myself. I already knew how to do stuff, I just needed a chance to put it into practice. I also think there is a difference in how I need care when I am in residential care because I know whatever time I get back I can get the support I need, even if the trains are late. Whereas when I had a set budget the person would only be there for set period and if I was late, I would miss out altogether. I think this is always on my mind when deciding to move.

I have established a network of social and work support which I would take with me when I move. Living at a residential care home, and my personal maturing, has led me to find out what I want and what is worth fighting for. I have learnt that when things don't go right I can take my time because I have a network of support and have learnt about distraction to stop me fixating on a problem. My support network is mutual, so people also depend on me, and this builds my self-esteem and grounds me in life.

On reflection, I can see why moving to university was … well, failed, because I was being asked to live independently almost instantly, and I couldn't do that. And then you put all the work of staffing and budgeting in, and then doing the degree on top of that. A degree is not an easy thing to do by itself, let alone with all the rest.

It's about the labour of disability – it's the hard, physical labour of managing my needs, the hard, intellectual labour of gaining insight into myself, my needs and skills. It's like trying to employ carers and manage payments and then to try to live a life on top of that and justifying that to not only social workers but also managers who may not even know you. That's several full-time jobs rolled into one. I didn't see it like that at the time. I just wanted to live a standard life, but I was spending so much time on care rotas, and even then, you get let down by carers after doing all the work.

There are people who have done so much for us and we are living off what they did for us, but it is our time and we are going to be affected by everything and that is part of the reason why I would love my own place and why I am working towards it.

My message to social workers

➢ Residential care is not a 'dead end' – the support offered in residential care can be flexible and appropriate enabling a good quality of life.

➢ Social care addresses the needs of a diverse population, not just children and older people.

> Social workers need to promote the view that service users are the experts of their own care needs.

> Social workers need to enable people to talk openly and honestly about their care needs. Part of doing this is social workers being open and honest themselves.

> Social workers need to be aware of the impact of the power the profession holds, and the influence this has, on relationships with service users.

> Social workers need to be aware of and respect the struggles disabled people and their families have faced throughout their lives.

> Social workers should not underestimate the importance of personal development. People need space and time to mature and this may impact on the support they require during different life stages.

> The experience of living in residential care and being at college has exposed me to lots of people with different experiences of disability. This has broadened my mind – learning from others is very empowering and opportunities for peer support are very important to self-esteem and personal growth.

> It can be hard for social workers and carers to work with someone headstrong like myself. This means care needs to be flexible, to do things *with* me sometimes and sometimes *for* me – but the choice needs to be mine. I need carers who are able to negotiate with me and recognise my self-determination.

> I want to be open and honest about my needs, but I fear services will be removed. In some situations, I can manage without support for a time, like when I am staying with friends because they accept me as I am. But, at other times, I need help.

> My ambition is to look back on my life and see what I have achieved rather than just living.

Social worker's perspective

Understanding 'independence'

Writing this chapter with Sophie has been an enormous pleasure. The insights into her life, articulated through her writing, provide a story of living with disability which is seldom heard. Sophie's experience is a lived example of the challenges facing social work practice where the goals of independent living, empowerment, choice and control conflict with the realities of modern practice characterised by limited resources, workforce demands and the pursuit of specific notions of what independence means. I recognise from my own social work practice the dilemma Sophie's situation creates where residential care is considered the last option rather than a positive choice. Austerity measures mean that 'best value' is primarily a monetary calculation instead of looking at the whole person, their aspirations, and work, education or social opportunities. Residential care can be an expensive option and practitioners have to balance the outcomes for individuals with the principles of social justice, including resource distribution to ensure services are fairly allocated. This is extremely challenging when resources are limited.

Sophie pursued the option of residential care to meet her needs in the absence of alternative community-based options, however, the conflict she experienced highlights the dominance of financial concerns and prescribed notions of dependency and independence. For social workers seeking to advocate for Sophie's independence her choice of residential care may seem counter-intuitive, however, for Sophie independence at this time involves residential care because it is in this setting that she can access the flexible support she requires to live well and achieve the goals she desires.

Independence conceptualised in terms of self-sufficiency (Leece and Leece, 2011; Roulstone, 2012; Secker et al., 2003; Swain et al., 2003) is rooted in the idea of autonomous, self-actualising individuals (Shildrick, 2007). Such a view of independence denies the reality of human existence which is characterised by both interdependence (e.g. social networks giving personal validation) and dependence (e.g. on public services or childhood dependence and the physical support needed due to the illness, impairment or age which most us will experience during our lives).

An alternative understanding of independence considers the lived experience of dependence/independence where living independently is 'not about disabled people living in "splendid isolation" but supporting people to live their lives as equal citizens' (Parker and Clements, 2008, p. 510). Having self-determination and control over life is a significant factor in the lived experience of independence (Swain et al., 2003). This sense of control is possible even in the presence of total care needs if the provision of support is organised in a person-centred, self-directed way which balances self-direction with avoidance of undue risk (Secker et al., 2003). Sophie's situation is a lived example of this alternative notion of independence. While her care needs are significant, she nevertheless controls how and when the care is provided, the flexibility of the residential care setting enabling a responsive support service. Sophie's reciprocal relationships with family, friends, her carers and colleagues demonstrate the interdependency of human life.

Theoretically, the Care Act 2014 promotes the alternative view of independence and independent living. The Act reflects the aims of campaigns by disabled people and disability organisations promoting social justice for, and social inclusion of, disabled people; outcomes which are aligned to social work values. However, within social care policy the need for support is also presented as dependence, something to prevent, delay and avoid:

> Care must again be about reinforcing personal and community resilience, reciprocity and responsibility, to prevent and postpone dependency and promote greater independence and choice (Department of Health, 2010, p. 5).

The perception of welfare and care systems creating a negatively conceptualised form of dependency continues to be a widely held narrative within political and media debates and has been used to justify reductions in welfare spending (Briant et al., 2013). Reducing state intervention impacts on disabled people leading to isolation and poverty (Beresford, 2013; Quarmby, 2011). Research reveals the reality:

> The official figures show 3.1 million disabled people are in poverty (26%), but JRF research shows the true figure is at least one million higher (Joseph Rowntree Foundation, 2016).

The dominance of a limiting conception of independence as self-sufficiency (Secker et al., 2003) means social workers need to be alert not only to perpetuating the status quo – where loneliness and isolation have been identified as equally damaging to health as smoking, say, 15 cigarettes a day (Handley et al., 2015; Markey et al., 2007) – but also to avoiding the importance of developing mutually supportive social structures which create well-being, build resilience and reduce the potential for hate crime (Ferguson and Lavalette, 2013; Quarmby, 2011).

Oliver (1990, p. 94) argued: 'Dependency is created among disabled people, not because of the effects of functional limitations on their capacities for self-care, but because their lives are shaped by a variety of economic, political and social forces which produce it.' The example of public services such as education and transport illustrates Oliver's point: these services are provided to non-disabled people to assist in participation in the public world, and are perceived as a right of citizenship rather than a marker of dependence. Whereas disabled people are seen as needing 'help' or specialist provision to participate (e.g. adapted transport), rather than having an entitlement (Wendell, 1996).

Sophie's personal narrative and this discussion about dependence and independence illustrates the value-laden nature of notions underpinning social policy and the impacts on the lives of people using social care services. Sophie's experience of resistance illustrates the conflict arising when dominant notions of independence conflict with those who control access to resources. Part of the social work role is being critically alert to potentially oppressive policies and practices, to challenge attitudes towards disabled people which result in inequality and discrimination, attitudes which are often unconsciously built on hierarchies of power. Article 19 of the UN Convention on the Rights of Persons with Disabilities (2006), entitled *Living Independently and Being Included in the Community*, requires governments to take action to facilitate disabled people's 'full enjoyment' of this right and their 'full inclusion and participation in the community' (Parker and Clements, 2008, p. 509). Social workers can use this to inform practice as it provides a clear agenda for social work with physically disabled people and gives substantial scope for advocacy (ibid.). This means promoting disabled people's control over day-to-day life and participation in society in ways which are meaningful to them – for Sophie this has included enabling her to live in an environment through which she has found the support to grow and flourish.

References

Beresford, P. (2013) *Personalisation.* Bristol: Policy Press.

Briant, E., Watson, N. and Philo, G. (2013) Reporting disability in the age of austerity: The changing face of media representation of disability and disabled people in the United Kingdom and the creation of new 'folk devils'. *Disability & Society.* 28: 6, 874–889.

Department of Health (2010) *A Vision for Adult Social Care: Capable Communities and Active Citizens.* London: HMSO.

de Than, C. (2015) Sex, disability and human rights. in T. Owens (ed). *Supporting Disabled People with Their Sexual Lives.* London: Jessica Kingsley, 86–103.

Ferguson, I. and Lavalette, M. (2013) *Adult Social Care.* Bristol: Policy Press.

Furedi, F. (2011) *Changing Societal Attitudes and Regulatory Responses to Risk Taking in Adult Care [online].* York: Joseph Rowntree Foundation.

Handley, S., Joy, I., Hestbaek, C. and Marjoribanks, D. (2015) *The Best Medicine? The Importance of Relationships for Health and Well-Being.* Doncaster: Relate and New Philanthropy Capital.

Hollomotz, A. (2010) 'Sexual "vulnerability" of people with learning difficulties: A self-fulfilling prophecy'. in R. Shuttleworth and T. Sanders (eds) *Sex & Disability: Politics, Identity and Access.* Leeds: The Disability Press. pp. 21–40.

Hoong Sin, C., Hedges, A., Cook, C., Mguni, N. and Comber, N. (2011) Adult protection and effective action in tackling violence and hostility against disabled people: Some tensions and challenges. *The Journal of Adult Protection*. 13: 2, 63–74.

Joseph Rowntree Foundation (2016) *Chancellor's budget giveaways failed to support an all-out assault on poverty* [online]. Available at: www.jrf.org.uk/press.

Leece, J. and Leece, D. (2011) Personalisation: Perceptions of the role of social work in a world of brokers and budgets. *British Journal of Social Work*. 41, 204–223.

Lishman, J., Yuill, C., Brannan, J. and Gibson, A. (2017) *Social Work: An Introduction*. London: Sage.

Mandelstam, M. (2017) *Care Act 2014: An A-Z of Law and Practice*. London: Jessica Kingsley Publishing.

Markey, C., Markey, P. and Fishman Gray, H. (2007) Romantic relationships and health: An examination of individuals' perceptions of their romantic partners' influences on their health. *Sex Roles*. 57, 435–445.

Oliver, M. (1990) *The Politics of Disablement*. Basingstoke: Palgrave Macmillan.

Parker, C. and Clements, L. (2008) The UN convention on the rights of persons with disabilities: A new right to independent living? *European Human Rights Law Review*. 4, 508–524.

Quarmby, C. (2011) *Scapegoat: Why We are Failing Disabled People*. London: Portobello Books.

Roulstone, A. (2012) 'Stuck in the middle with you': Towards enabling social work with disabled people. *Social Work Education*. 31: 2, 142–154.

Secker, J., Hill, R., Villeneau, L. and Parkman, S. (2003) Promoting independence: But promoting what and how? *Ageing and Society*. 23, 375–391.

Shildrick, M. (2007) Contested pleasures: The socio-political economy of disability and sexuality. *Sexuality Research & Social Policy Journal of NSRC*. 4: 1, 53–66.

Swain, J., French, S. and Cameron, C. (2003) *Controversial Issues in a Disabling Society*. Buckingham: Open University Press.

Thompson, N. (2015) *Understanding Social Work: Preparing for Practice*. 4th edition. Houndsmill: Palgrave Macmillan.

Wendell, S. (1996) *The Rejected Body*. London: Routledge.

Statute

Care Act 2014.

Suggested reading

Department of Health and Social Care (updated 2018) *Care and Support Statutory Guidance Issued under the Care Act 2014* [online]. Available at: www.gov.uk/guidance/care-and-support-statutory-guidance.

www.scie.org.uk/publications/guides/guide10/questions/question01.asp

www.cerebralpalsy.org/about-cerebral-palsy/treatment/therapy/conductive-education.

10

I was Assessed under the Care Act and Received Direct Payments

Rachel Jury

Penny Riggs, *Social Worker*

At a glance

- This chapter focuses on the statutory intervention of having an assessment under the Care Act 2014 and of having direct payments so a person can personalise their care using an assessed Personal Budget.

- Rachel has a long-term health condition and has worked with both community-based and hospital social workers and direct payment advisors.

- Penny is a social worker for a hospital social work team and was introduced to Rachel as part of writing this chapter. Penny provides formal knowledge underpinning this statutory intervention in the text boxes throughout the chapter and, at the end of the chapter, reflects on her learning from Rachel.

I never imagined at 31 I would have to admit that I have a carer or Personal Assistant (PA) that comes in every day during the week to help me with mundane things. Ten years ago this wasn't the future I had planned and I never thought I would have to have carer and social worker involvement at this age. When direct payments were first suggested to me a few feelings came up: anger towards my body; feeling like a failure, a burden; why was this happening to me; and self-pity. To me, it was a reflection and proof that I was actually ill and had a myriad of tasks that I cannot complete. Now after two years of having a PA, who is really more like a carer, my feelings have changed. I can see that I need this support and she helps me take some accountability for my illness as well as all the jobs I can't do involving lifting or changing bed sheets. I need these physical jobs to be done and I have found the biggest help has been having somebody come in every day that can help encourage me. Whether this is to do small things around the flat or a gentle nudge if I need to go to hospital. I live on my own and I like my independence so having this means I can continue to still have that aspect of my life. My story is very complicated and my consultants say I have never fitted into a 'box'. In this chapter I will try to explain my medical history, talk about my social worker involvement, care plans and direct payments.

It all started ten years ago when I was on placement studying Radiotherapy and Oncology to become a Therapy Radiographer. I contracted campylobacter from cooked chicken which made me very poorly and I was hospitalised for ten days. Little did I know this would be the start of many admissions! It wasn't long before I noticed that, at first, my bladder had lots of urinary infections and, eventually, would not empty at all. Trying to work in a busy Bristol hospital during this time was difficult and a juggling act. I had to self-catheterise at first which didn't work, then I had a urethral catheter which eventually turned into a Suprapubic Catheter (SPC). At this point, I had to give up the career I loved.

At the same time, my bowel failed to function normally which led to me weighing less than seven stone with severe malnutrition. I eventually had to have an ileostomy which is where a stoma is created by bringing the end or loop of small intestine out onto the surface of the skin and a pouch collects the output. This did help me put on weight but, at first, I struggled to accept this new way of going to the toilet. Eventually, after five years, I got referred to a specialist neurology centre in London and I was diagnosed with Autonomic Neuropathy – pure autonomic failure where my bladder and bowel failed to function as normal due to the autonomic nerves being damaged. Having a diagnosis was a relief but, due to the rarity of my disease, not many health professionals had heard of it. Then, in 2015, I had a routine cystoscopy and it was revealed that my bladder was extremely small and damaged and biopsy results confirmed the cells had mutated so, within two weeks I had my bladder removed and another stoma, called a urostomy, formed for urine (an ileal conduit).

At 28 I had two stomas but, after a horrific recovery from the surgery, I realised what a blessing this new stoma was compared to the catheter. Just before surgery, I was on a lot of pain relief to help with the horrific bladder spasms but, I used this as a crutch. After the surgery, I realised I had been taking more than prescribed and, when I challenged this behaviour, my life got better. I felt alone for years so I started a blog to talk about my story and help raise urostomy awareness called

Rocking2Stomas. This gave me a purpose and I found an online community which is amazing. Now my stomas have even found me love and my partner also has an ileostomy. I have worked through tough times and done a lot of self-development to now come out the other end and see my stomas as a miracle and a second chance at life. I have had other complications, including a prolapsed ileostomy, which have involved more than eight full abdominal surgeries within a year and a half which was why I had a care plan from the hospital, social worker involvement and now, direct payments.

Social work intervention

At the start of my journey I had no social worker involvement. It was only when I moved area and my health decreased rapidly that I had access to this. I remember asking my GP one time about a social worker and he said I coped too well and I was too articulate. This was during a really tough time where many departments were involved, and they were not communicating with each other. I felt my life spiralling and I had no control. I needed help and support. I only had just enough energy to get through the day let alone have enough energy to call the departments and get them to talk to each other. I never did get any help at that time. I often thought if I didn't cope as well or looked like I had it 'together' I would have had better access to my care and support.

GP involvement

As a social worker that has worked within community teams I feel that this could have been an ideal opportunity, with consent from the individual, that the GP could have discussed Rachel's needs in a multidisciplinary setting. Monthly meetings at the surgery are often held where professionals from the social care teams are involved. It may well have been at this point that there were no eligible needs under the Care Act 2014, however, everyone is entitled to an 'assessment of anyone who appears to require care and support, regardless of their likely eligibility' (Care Act 2014, Section 9) and, if at this point, no needs were apparent then part of our role is to look at preventative services and signposting individuals for appropriate support providing advice and information to them (ibid., Section 4). There is also the opportunity for the individual to have their needs assessed through the self-supported assessment where the person can lead their own assessment and fill out the assessment form. It is important that the social worker still remains involved to ensure that the outcomes and needs are identified. If someone has a primary healthcare need and is eligible for continuing healthcare, then a Personal Health Budget (PHB) can be provided so they have they are able to organise a care package to meet their needs themselves.

The first time I met a social worker was in 2015 when my bladder was removed after seven years of a long-term catheter resulted in the cells mutating. I was in the hospital for three months and had multiple complications that made me very ill. Before the end of my admission, I was introduced to a social worker. My parents live in Wales and, although they come to where I live for my operations, they could not look after me long-term and they have their own life in Wales. Since I moved out of my ex's, I have been very precious around my independence which was extremely important to me to remain accountable.

Person-centred assessment

It is essential as a social worker that we support individuals to have a person-centred assessment, after all, they are the experts in their lives. This enables them to be empowered and to have as much control over their lives as possible. The Care Act Assessment should focus on the individual's strengths and what they can do as well as looking at how the person's needs impact on their well-being and their desired outcomes (Care Act Guidance, 2014, 6.64). It is also crucial that the person is involved in the discussions after the assessment so that they are fully involved in their own support planning. Part of this should also include a contingency plan for any crisis situations that could arise. To prevent a person being delayed in hospital the Care Act 2014 (Schedule 3) replaced the Delayed Discharge Act of 2003. This ensures that people are assessed in a timely manner to prevent their admission being longer than it needs to be. The social work teams within acute hospital settings receive an 'assessment notice' and a 'discharge notice' to prevent a delayed transfer of care. This is sometimes referred to as Delayed Transfer of Care (DTOC). Each delay, and reason for this, has to be reported to NHS England. This is to ensure that assessments and support planning are completed in a timely manner and ensure that someone is not in a hospital bed when they do not need to be. At times, it may not be straightforward to ascertain the 'reason' for delay, i.e. is it attributable to the local authority or the NHS. I currently work in an Integrated Discharge Bureau and I feel this has helped to improve relationships between professionals and are we are able to communicate effectively to agree the reasons for delays. It is really important that, for the individual, there is effective communication between the multidisciplinary team working with them to ensure each professional is completing the work they should to be to prevent delays which would impact on the length of stay in hospital if when this does not happen.

After this surgery I think I had every complication including sepsis, kidney failure, catching c-difficile off a patient and ended up in isolation for three months. The complications took so much out of me that I do not remember much of this admission only that I couldn't eat and was fed through my arm (Total Parenteral Nutrition). This time was very tough for my family and friends and I would say it was harder for them to see me this ill. Being stuck in that room not able to leave for that long was very difficult, everybody had to be gloved and gowned-up which made me feel more 'dirty' than I already felt.

In hospital assessment

At this point it would be good practice that if the individual consents to a referral and/or an assessment under the Care Act 2014 that the wards liaise with the in-house hospital social care team, so that a discharge plan can start to be considered. Often, within the acute hospitals, the ward professionals practice is very much underpinned by the medical model and I feel that there should have been some consideration to the emotional well-being of the person. At this stage, for Rachel, there has been huge trauma and loss around a new diagnosis, very invasive treatments and then to be isolated as well can be very oppressive and cause a high level of anxiety. It may have been beneficial for a social worker to come and meet Rachel and her family to offer some support and guidance at this point. Although it may have been too early to start discharge planning, it could have offered reassurance and perhaps signposting to a counselling service if in agreement, and deemed appropriate. A challenge to this is the pressures of resources and social workers having the capacity to complete this work so early on. Unfortunately, with high caseloads and pressures of DTOCs from hospital settings, this level of early support is not always possible, although desirable.

I was extremely worried about going home and how I would cope so, after speaking to the lovely sister on the ward, a social worker came to see me about a care package for when I left hospital. This was put in a while before I left so, luckily, I didn't have to wait and meant I wasn't bed blocking.

A quick and safe discharge is ideal for the individual as people recover much better in their own environment. It also reduces the risk of picking up further infections which can compromise a person's health, as has already occurred for Rachel. A government health agency report published that one in sixteen patients fall ill with an infection in NHS hospitals. The National Institute for Health and Care Excellence (NICE, 2014) state that 'the rate of infections, which are a very real threat to patients' lives, was unacceptably high'.

I can't remember much about that first encounter with the social worker but I know I had home care when I came out for ten minutes in the morning to help me dress and clean up any accidents from my stoma bags. This lasted for a month until I went back in for another operation because my ileostomy was too tight and did not empty. I do believe it was on this admission that direct payments were discussed with me. My consultant knew I would need more operations to fix my prolapsed ileostomy (in total they added up to eight and they have all failed). Together the consultant and social worker helped nudge me to think about direct payments. I was passed to another social worker who started this ball moving. Now, when I first heard about direct payments it sounded like a minefield and confusing. I am not financially savvy and being the 'employer' did scare me. Not only this, but I also felt I had failed. At 28 I had to have a carer/PA but, while I lay in that hospital bed, I realised I would have to do this to keep a 'slice' of my independence that I cherished so dearly.

> **Direct Payments** are a great way for people to personalise their care using their assessed PHB and have control over their lives as much as possible. It is not as regimented as a commissioned package of care where often timings of visits are limited and there aren't always consistent carers despite best efforts by the agencies to provide this service. Direct payments allow the individual to interview and employ their own PAs that they can work with and have a much more flexible and person-centred support plan. It also enables a good rapport to build with the carers and the individual due to consistency of carers. If you have been assessed as being eligible for services under the Care Act 2014 and have capital less than £23,250 you may get help towards this, you can receive your allocated PHB direct to yourself rather than the social care team finding care or setting up your support package for you (Care Act 2014, Section 31). This means that you can purchase and choose the services you need yourself including, as in this case, employing your chosen PA. This can allow the person to have greater control and choice over the care and services they receive.
>
> It is always essential that direct payments are explained clearly and, if needed, a referral to a support agency to go through all the employment legislation, payroll process and liability insurances to ensure it is set up properly from the beginning to prevent anxiety for the individual and ensure that the direct payment does not breakdown.

The first social worker I met outside of the hospital was very helpful, but it wasn't long before she left. This has been a theme throughout my social worker involvement and, since then, I have hardly had any contact with my social workers.

> ### Change in social worker
>
> Unfortunately, this is often the case as social workers move between teams and there is a lack of consistency with workers. This makes it very hard for a relationship to be built between the worker and the individual. It can be very difficult for the individual as
>
> ▶

◀

often they have to go over their 'story' again which can be distressing whereas if they have someone that knows them well this can be prevented.

Limited contact may be due to constraints within the social care team's resources. Often direct payments that appear to be going well will not be reviewed by a social worker unless there is a crisis. Unfortunately, this does not always support good rapport building between the social worker and individual and preventative working with them. It is vital that communication is kept between the individual and the social care team, i.e. to advise the person if they are going to be put on a list awaiting review and that they are given a contact number if they have any issues prior to this.

There was one person throughout my 'direct payments' journey' who has always been there and has felt more like my social worker. This guy is a budget officer and has gone above and beyond his role to help me. I have a lot of gratitude for this man, he has been the only stable one that contacts me regularly and has helped me so many times. Without him, I wouldn't have understood how direct payments work without his guidance and keeping in contact with me. I am not great with money anyway and he helped talk this through with me and pointed me in the right direction to help get this looked at. He helped set up my account and organised for me and my carer/PA to go on a course to learn more about this. He suggested at the beginning to ask my cleaner if she would step into this role because we got on well, and she accepted. I find it hard directing people and struggle with the aspect of being an employer but, with his guidance, this has gone smoothly.

Support for managing direct payments

As this highlights, direct payments can be a very complex process and it is essential that it is set up correctly and the individual is given clear guidance on how to set up and manage them. However, when being discharged from hospital, ensuring a timely discharge may mean that some of this work must be completed after the person has been discharged and back within the community.

It is important that all areas are covered to prevent a breakdown in a service for the individual receiving the direct payment. At this point, it may have been useful for the budget officer to have support from the social care team to highlight some of the issues that were coming up for the individual. At this point, a good model for the social worker would have been to work in a task-centred way to break down each goal that Rachel wanted or needed to achieve.

I must say that I have felt some frustration from my social workers because they change without letting me know and the new social worker doesn't introduce themselves unless I ask the budget officer to find out who my new social worker is (which isn't really his job). Again, I am not sure if this is because I seem to cope okay and they feel I don't need that quick chat or to introduce themselves. Every time you have to explain your story to a new social worker or healthcare professional, it takes something out of you and I think: what's the point in explaining when they will be leaving soon? Maybe, because I have the budget officer, I have not chased this up as much as I should, but then again, is it really my job if a social worker leaves for me to introduce myself to the new social worker?

Repetition

This is a very difficult situation for the individual to be in having to repeat their story, this could be very disempowering, and the focus should be able to be on the strengths of the individual, looking at what has been achieved and what they are managing to do independently rather than reliving the past – that can be very difficult emotionally. It is best practice to always advise the person you are working with as their social worker if your involvement is going to end at any point for whatever reason, i.e. starting a new role or you have finished the work required with them. Although it may not always be possible due to constraints in the team for them to have an allocated worker, it is good to inform them of a contact's details if required should they need support before they are allocated to a new social worker. Good communication is integral to the social work role with people.

I pay a contribution of £42 towards my care a week. However, a downside to direct payments is in the summer. My budget officer and a lady who was a care manager came to my home to inform me that I owed a lot of money because, for a year, my contribution hadn't gone out. I set it up but, when the accounts changed, there was some issues and lots of us owed money which we have to pay back on top of our contributions. At the time I was extremely distraught about this but, with my budget officer's help, we sorted it out and he helped calm me down.

A financial assessment is required for all individuals that are eligible under the Care Act 2014 to determine the contribution that they are required to pay towards their care package and, for a direct payment, the individual needs to ensure that this is paid. Again it is very important that this is all explained and strategies are looked at as to how this will be paid and that ongoing monitoring to support the individual may be required. Luckily, in this situation, Rachel had support and reassurance through a distressing and worrying time. During this time, a good intervention to use would be a crisis approach to support the individual through this new situation.

While writing this chapter my contributions were going to be increased to £61 a week, which I cannot afford since my income is the same. Therefore, I regretfully had no option but to stop my direct payments and not have this support. I must now rely on friends to help take bins out and try to find a way around this. Unfortunately, with the change in regulations and cutbacks, this is the reality of direct payments. However, I am still grateful to everybody who has been involved and to my new social worker who has tried her hardest to get around it but, in the end, I could not find a way to afford it.

Alternative support

Other options can be considered in this scenario such as requesting an occupational therapist see if there are any equipment options that could support where there is no longer a PA. Also, ongoing monitoring through other professionals such as a GP, district nurse or voluntary agencies could be appropriate to ensure that there is some level of support still available. A review of any risks will need to be completed and, if necessary, a risk management plan completed with the individual involved throughout. At this point, or possibly earlier, an advocate referral could be made to advise throughout the process which can be very confusing at times for individuals that are also trying to manage complex conditions impacting on their well-being and daily lives. The Care Act 2014 'imposes a duty on local authorities to arrange for an independent advocate to be available to represent and support certain persons for the purpose of facilitating those persons' involvement in the exercise of functions by local authorities'.

My message to social workers

My message to social workers would be that, if you leave an area or your clients, please can you inform them that you are leaving even if this is a quick call or an email. It helps us feel like we are in the loop and to pass the details of our case on to the new social worker who at the start of the job could call everybody up on their caseload to introduce themselves. This will stop us from feeling like we are forgotten about or that we are not as important as somebody else. My care is extensive although mentally I cope quite well, however, this does not mean I don't need a social worker to touch base with me once in a while or to feel updated. You do an amazing job and I realise resources are stretched and you cannot stay with the same client throughout their care but involving them in this transition will help.

My other message would be not to judge somebody on age. I have had multiple cases where, because I am young, I am deemed that I can 'cope' and have family support. Although my family are brilliant, they live in Wales and cannot be here all the time so, ultimately, I live on my own and rely on friends. When you have a chronic illness this can affect you physiologically, physically, emotionally, mentally and physically and it is a journey. Communication is key and maybe it is good practice to try and put yourself in our situation and why we may need a quick update which can stop days of worrying.

I just wanted to end by saying thank you to all social workers. This is not an easy career to go into, to care to the best of your ability with all the cutbacks. However, your job is super important to so many people to help all of us maintain a level of independence in life regardless of our age.

The social worker's perspective

It is essential that all social workers working with individuals do not discriminate on any grounds such as age, as in this case. We must be able to empathise and show understanding to the individuals we work with and challenge, when needed, using legislation such as the Human Rights Act 1998.

As a professional it can be difficult to hear the struggles that individuals you are working with are going through when you are working under pressure, with limited resources and high caseloads and genuinely want the best outcomes. After listening to Rachel's experience while receiving services it has reinforced to me just how important good communication and building a professional rapport with the person is. Hearing Rachel's difficulties within the system has really made me think about just how daunting and complex the process is for individuals who are struggling with long-term conditions, disabilities and significant health issues already. We have a duty of care to ensure that services are provided when a person is deemed eligible under the Care Act 2014 but it goes further than this to ensure that this is provided in a person-centred way with best practice from social workers. Even if there are things on a wider level that, as social workers, we cannot control, i.e. limited resources, individually we can be honest, approachable and keep individuals up to date so this could make their experiences less daunting and hopefully less frustrating.

References

NICE (2014) Infection prevention and control. Guidance and guidelines. Available at: www.nice.org.uk/guidance.

Statute

The Care Act 2014
Human Rights Act 1998

Suggested reading

Carers UK Direct Payments. Available at: www.carersuk.org.
Health and Safety Executive (2015) Local authority duties towards people in receipt of direct payments. Available at: www.hse.gov.uk.

11

I was Assessed as Needing Drug Treatment

Fay

Julia Armstrong, *Social Worker*

At a glance

- This chapter focuses on the statutory intervention of being assessed under the Care Act 2014 when there is an adult safeguarding concern.

- Fay has a history of substance use, depression, domestic abuse and eating disorders.

- Julia is a social worker for a statutory drug and alcohol team. She has worked with Fay over a number of years. Julia provides formal knowledge underpinning the statutory intervention in the text boxes through the chapter and shares her reflections on her learning from Fay and the broader issues affecting social work in this field.

About myelf:

My name is Fay and I am 35 years old. My addiction and life aren't typical. When I was young, all I remember was being poor, there wasn't much food and it was always cold. I lived with my mum and brother. My mum showed me so much love but it wasn't enough to stop the bullies – taunting, hitting and pushing because of our clothes with holes in. My father left just before I was born as he had another family on the go. My mum was broken by what he did but it didn't stop her loving us. I hated this man for breaking the only people that loved me. I grew up tough and I became tougher – I moved out at a young age and wanted to prove I could make a good, wealthy, happy life on my own. I always had part-time jobs as well as studying. By the time I was 18 I was a qualified chef, working while travelling and seeing Europe. I always liked a drink but when I started working as a chef it became 'normal' to drink – in a hot kitchen and long hours. At 20 I met my first real boyfriend and decided to set up home. I thought: buy a house, have a family, calm down, but I had to earn the cash to buy one.

I managed to get a good job; it was very physical, but after three years of a hundred plus hours a week, I got promoted, first to manager then as a warranty engineer. This involved me flying all over the world. While I was working away to pay for the house, bills, mortgage, car and my boyfriend's higher education, he was educating himself in other women. When I found out he was cheating, the whole existence I had planned just died very quickly; I threw him out but only after he took half of everything I had. I still loved him. I dedicated myself to my work and career, unfortunately, you can only keep going for seven days a week for a certain amount of years before you collapse. I had also been being abused and harassed the whole time I was at work – I was a woman in a man's world and they were going to let me know they didn't like me being around. I had started relying on alcohol a few years prior when the threats started but, as the abuse got worse, so did my alcohol use. Around this time, at about age 25, I got into a relationship with John and was just about to start on a horrendous court case due to the abuse and harassment at work. The threats of violence started to be a reality from co-workers. I had bricks put through my window and there was spray graffiti on my house, calling me all the names under the sun and accusing me of sleeping my way to the top. I was the only female out of 3,000 men and they hated that I was good at my job. After months of daily abuse, they broke me and I couldn't take any more, so, I began court proceedings that would start to define who I became.

Two years before that something happened I had never prepared for. I was very tired and stressed out. I'd come back from a three-month stint working away and an old friend called and said she was in town so we should catch up. I got ready – dress and heels on and ready to go out for the first time in ages. I set off and that's when I got jumped. I was so unlucky, it was a lit main road with people around. They caught me off guard. They took it in turns to beat me, bash me and rape me. I woke up, blood all over me. I had to go and get examined and checked over. I had five fractures, two broken bones, my pelvis was damaged and my kneecap detached. The first thing I did was grab a bottle of vodka. The physical pain was bad but nothing compared to the shame, humiliation and the disgust I felt. I spent days, months, locking myself away. I couldn't bear the world to see what I had become; a broken washed-up loser, drinking to numb the pain, drinking to hide the fact that I was terrified. Terrified of trusting. If I left the house I was sure it would happen again. I shut myself off. I tried getting sober but it had taken over. I was no longer in control of it.

One day I woke up and I was aged 33 and four and a half stone. I'd literally wasted away and I didn't even realise. I wouldn't eat, by this time, I couldn't eat; my body couldn't process any food other than liquid. As all addicts, I made excuses for why I should have a drink – 'calories.' It was my addict talking not the real me. I was also now suffering from seizures from when I got attacked and from the alcohol consumption and, at times, withdrawal. I was in an awful relationship with John; I suppose I was looking for someone just to love me and not screw me over, but it didn't happen. It was violent, abusive and I was scared 24 hours a day. I couldn't get out of it. I was too poorly by now to safely end it. I knew it was too dangerous to stay, but it was my house, my life, I couldn't run. I was severely underweight and scared, despite years of violence I was trapped. He would follow me everywhere and track my phone and, if I said anything out of sorts, I would get a fist to the face or broken ribs as a reminder to keep quiet. The more I got hurt, the more I drank. Every black eye meant I should drink, it helped. It didn't. It drove me into more despair and I didn't want to live any more.

The life which I planned, to be happy, comfortable and successful, had turned into barely existing; a very ill girl, running on vodka fumes. I somehow managed enough courage to seek help. I managed, through my GP, to get in contact with the local drug and alcohol team. I was constantly in hospital from seizures or beatings. I was living in a painful revolving circle of life that I didn't want; I was still trapped, in fear in my own home and worrying, if I did go out, what I'd get when I walked back through the door. My friends were all gone, they'd all been driven away. I was in such seclusion I didn't see what was happening. I was really living as a ghost. I can remember trying to engage with services but, at that time, I was being pulled away by John, he was locking me in the house, he was threatening to burn my mum's house down if I got in contact. Obviously, he was scared that I was going to tell the truth and he was going to be outed. He was a big bloke and threatening my family, I felt that I had to stop going and for the safety of staff members, safety of anyone really. So, I eventually just stopped going, I said everything was okay when it wasn't, and I was being horrifically treated but I was too scared. He had already terrified the staff and he had flipped a table over in the drop-in; he wasn't even scared to be violent in front of people, even staff. As long as I kept my mouth shut and didn't make a statement. But he kept me in that house for so long, I wasn't allowed to leave for around four to five months at all. He took my phone, I didn't have access to the outside world, he had unplugged and thrown out my home phone. I continued to try and engage with the support, but I couldn't be 100 per cent honest with my whole story to staff. I was still being controlled and I had to lie about where I was going so I didn't get in trouble. I tried going to Alcoholics Anonymous (AA, 2018) and Cocaine Anonymous (CA, 2017) meetings; my confidence was low but, I pulled myself to meetings ... I had to try.

Initial involvement

I initially started working with Fay around 2011 when I worked in the generic drug and alcohol team. This was a team which worked with anyone with any drug and alcohol problems, whether active in their addiction or in recovery. Fay initially came in having been referred by her GP due to her alcohol use. There was no information regarding her eating disorder at this stage, however, Fay was clearly severely underweight. Often, Fay would come in with her partner John. It was policy that service users were seen on their own, without their partners. Fay wouldn't ever disclose any domestic abuse at this stage but, call it a hunch or intuition, it was obvious that the relationship was not a healthy one. John would always be waiting outside her appointments for her. Fay was given a treatment plan which she rarely stuck to and she was known as someone who didn't engage with services. She was often closed to services due to 'non-engagement'. It was frustrating as, without any information from Fay, there was no evidence.

I remember the incident Fay recalls of John flipping over the table in the drop-in. John had forced his way into our 1:1 appointment and, despite being polite and professional, he was highly agitated and when asked to leave he threw the table across the room which bounced off the reinforced glass wall. Other members of the team came and removed John from the building and the police were called. This was one of two times in my whole career that I have ever been scared. Fay did not seem that phased by the violence but was embarrassed by John's behaviour, apologising on his behalf. I remember feeling helpless as she left the building, stating that she would be going home with him, despite us telling her that if she wanted to leave him we could support her. Bear in mind, Fay was severely underweight, barely able to hold her own body weight, and John was over 6ft tall.

The difficulty, often, in situations like this is in reality, if we approached a women's refuge, they would be unlikely to accept a referral for someone with substance misuse problems. I have had one lady who was six weeks abstinent from all substances, refused for 54 refuges across England due to her history. Moreover, in the case of Fay, she owned her own house and did not want to leave. I believe that, in cases like this, the victim has a right to remain in the area and the risks managed accordingly if they want to separate – many other agencies do not share this view which makes multi-agency working at times difficult.

Over the years, various agencies completed Domestic Abuse, Stalking and 'Honour'-based violence (DASH) risk identification and checklist forms (SafeLives, 2014) with

▶

◄

Fay and referred her to the Multi-Agency Risk Assessment Conference (MARAC) (MARAC, 2017). MARAC is for people believed to be at high risk or at risk of murder from their partners (SafeLives, 2018). The police reports were becoming more and more frequent in terms of call outs to the property. Fay always declined support stating that she loved him and wanted to remain in the relationship.

The first time he was arrested I didn't give a statement, to be honest, I just hit a bottle of vodka. I was bleeding all over, my head was smashed to pieces, I couldn't make a statement. By the time I could start to think more clearly, he'd been let out of custody and he was back at my door. I was drinking more as I was getting beaten more and, the more I drank, the less it hurt. I mean, he fractured a vertebra in my neck when he kicked my head like a football, he punched me, put me up against a wall and he punched me square in the jaw and then he just kicked my head and I woke up three days later in the same place. I remember that staff had offered support but this was before I was caged, before he really locked me in, and staff would say 'Fay, come on let's try and work together' and I was always so scared I just wanted to get out of the office so no one got hurt [by John]. So, I would agree with what staff were suggesting and say 'yes, I'll do it.' I had to hide any paperwork so he wouldn't find it as he'd check me when I got in, he'd check my pockets.

I think one of the first few times he was arrested was when my mum phoned the police and they got me to safety. I'd lost so much weight by that point but I felt like nothing was done about the abuse. I knew whatever agencies did, he'd find me and follow me; everywhere I went he'd watch me. At one point he rented a property opposite me as he had conditions not to be at my house. He's never moved anywhere further than the next road down, and that was how it was for nearly ten years. I thought he was going to kill me. I could never make a statement against him. Police managed to put a restraining order in place, however, he still came to my house. He's broken two or three restraining orders now which is how he ended up in prison. He was in prison for three months. I didn't believe he was in prison, I thought that it was a lie as he had been following and stalking me all these years. I'd become such an alcoholic at that point my world was so distorted that, to be honest, I didn't even really know right from wrong and I was scared. He got six months and served three and in my head I thought, he will get out. He had been saying 'I'm going to burn your mum's house down,' 'I'm going to kill your mum,' 'I'm going to kill you,' 'I'm going to kill your brother.' So, it's not that I didn't want help to get away, I was crying out for help, but I couldn't … I felt like I had been groomed. I didn't have a choice but that's because I couldn't be open and be 110% honest – I couldn't even be ten percent honest. My social worker knew it, I knew she knew it, even through drunk eyes, I was ashamed. I was terribly ashamed from being such a strong women with such a good job and then I became literally a shell of my former self. As soon as I knew for definite that he was in prison, I breathed for the first time in years.

In 2013 I had started a job as a drug and alcohol social worker for a local authority. The team's criteria were the eligibility not only for adult social services either safeguarding or care management (Feldon, 2017), but also for people who were active in their addiction which impacted on their day-to-day functioning.

Since 2013, the drug and alcohol social work team had received numerous police reports due to the domestic violence. We were unable to go to Fay's property due to the level of risk to staff from John. Every attempt we made to make contact with Fay was blocked by John. The only agency that had any contact with Fay was police when they were called out to the property. Fay always declined support.

In June 2017, the drug and alcohol social services team received another referral for Fay. By this time the Care Act 2014 was in place. Therefore, at this stage, the referral was allocated as a safeguarding referral due to the domestic violence, however it was categorised as an 'other safeguarding enquiry' Section 4, as we were unable to establish at initial stages if Fay had care and support needs, which would have ascertained if this would be a Section 42 safeguarding enquiry (Bournemouth and Poole Safeguarding Adults Board (BDPSAB) Policy and Procedures Group, 2016; Feldon, 2017.)

I was aware from police that John was in custody, so did an unannounced visit to Fay's home address. At this stage, Fay was telling me that John was in prison for a different reason and that she didn't need any support from agencies. I had been in contact with police and probation and had confirmation that John was in prison due to breaching the restraining order that was in place. On the second home visit, I told Fay I knew John was in prison due to breach of restraining order and she was still in denial. I had to ask her directly, 'he is in prison because he's hurt you, what do you want to do about it?' and Fay was still saying that she loved him, that she wanted him back, that he protects her and looks after her. Even with John being in prison, she was still terrified. What did come to fruition was that Fay did have care and support needs and she had become reliant on John for basic day-to-day support. After some direct conversation, Fay agreed that social services could look at assessing her to get support in place to make sure her needs were being met so she could be independent without John as he was in prison.

At this stage, as it was believed that Fay had eligible care and support needs, the Section 4 safeguarding enquiry was escalated to a Section 42 enquiry. This involved holding an Enquiry Planning Meeting (EPM), inviting Fay and all relevant agencies

▶

◀

to make sure a robust plan was in place to support Fay with clear actions which Fay was able to engage with and understand, taking initial small steps so as not to overwhelm her. This was in line with the Making Safeguarding Personal (MSP) agenda. Fay was still not trusting of services, still believing what John had told her. Meanwhile, I also opened Fay to social services under care management to assess her in terms of her care and support needs and if she met the eligibility for a package of care and/or any other relevant services. (BDPSAB Policy and Procedures Group, 2016; Feldon, 2017.)

In some cases, the role of the social worker is to coordinate other agencies to make sure tasks and actions are undertaken, compile risk management plans as agreed from the EPM to make sure all agencies and service users are aware of the plan and actions. However, in this case, I had built up a working relationship with Fay since 2011. While she may not have completely trusted me, she knew that I was a consistent worker, who was able to support her step by step. Therefore, my role was more interactive than it would be in some cases.

John was eventually arrested and convicted for numerous violent acts and put in prison. Julia was brilliant; she put all sorts of plans in place for me to try and regain my life and health. I was very hard to work with at first as I was so scared to speak the truth. I had spent years not talking, trusting or sharing. I now had people [agencies] to contact on the phone for support and weekly meetings involving my eating disorder, my alcohol addiction and depression. I stopped being selfish and realised my mum should not have to bury her own child. I'd put her through so much, endless hospital visits and listening to the ramblings of a washed-up broken drunk. As all addicts, I was secretive about lots in my life as a way of protection maybe, anger and humiliation possibly. The problem was that I was a drunk so I couldn't remember what I said anyway … I couldn't even be a good liar.

Before John got out, I had decided I did not want to go back to the relationship. The police sorted me to have 'target hardening'; the police fitted a window alarm, and they brought in one of the panic alarm black boxes. I didn't know when John was coming out of prison and neither did probation or Julia. It was Julia who called to tell me he was coming out the next day. When I found out, I felt like my intestines, my guts, my lungs, my heart had all dropped out my body. Lots of the agencies kept in contact and changed my appointments for that day and a few days after so I didn't have to be going out and about. He didn't come to my house. Since his release, I've seen him twice when I have been out in town, but he didn't see me. I don't know why he hasn't been in contact since his release, that's the thing, I will never know. I will never know if he could turn up, because he could, that's the scariest thing. I've always been tied to my property which I own and, due to my health and everything, I couldn't just sell up and go – it wasn't an option. I saved every penny to buy that flat when it was derelict and every wall that is covered in plaster, I did that. The floors, the ceiling, I did that. But, I still think daily that I should just pick up and go. I know I shouldn't have to, but there's always that threat from him. But, my mum and brother are here, but I still do think every corner I go around, I don't know where he is or if he might turn up. Even if I did move somewhere else in Bournemouth, he would find me. If he turned up I would call 999 straight away.

While John was in prison, all agencies worked tirelessly to make sure support was in place and Fay felt supported so she wouldn't have to return to John when he was released from prison. Probation did request that John complete his full sentence, however, this was declined and he served three months of his six-month sentence. He was released with bail conditions not to have any direct or indirect contact with Fay until 2019. I do not know why John hasn't been in contact with Fay since his release but, the fact that he has left her alone, both myself and Fay believe has saved her life. It was highly likely that Fay would be dead either at John's hands, or due to her health issues from her eating disorder or her alcohol use. The difficulty the police and Crown Prosecution Service (CPS) had was Fay had never made a statement to police, therefore they could only go on third party information and evidence. Fay, to date, has still never made a statement to police regarding the abuse she suffered. There is statutory guidance for agencies on how to proceed with cases of coercion and control; while this statutory guidance is in place, it remains difficult to prosecute without support and engagement from the victim (Home Office, 2015).

When Fay initially engaged, it was difficult to get other agencies to work with her as, on paper, Fay did not seem 'motivated to engage' due to her history of non-engagement and dropping out of services. Mental health services were reluctant to work with Fay for her eating disorder due to her alcohol use. For a period of time we were weighing Fay weekly and giving consideration to an assessment under the Mental Health Act 2007 with a possible option to detain her for force-feeding. Fay was aware of this and, while she was entrenched with her eating disorder, she wanted to make positive changes and work with agencies (NICE, 2017). The GP was convinced the root of all her problems was her alcohol use and stated that everything she said shouldn't be believed as she probably had an underlying personality disorder, which she had not been assessed for or diagnosed with. Fay was being prescribed a vast amount of medication which she was not taking as prescribed due to her chaotic life circumstances and, in fact, could have been making her health problems worse. I highlight this to show the discrimination and judgemental approaches some agencies take when working with addicts.

Through the Section 42 safeguarding process and Fay's extreme health issues, I was able to request support due to her circumstances. Had any agency refused to work

▶

◄

with Fay this would have been recorded in the risk management plan and subject to scrutiny in the worst-case scenario of Fay's death.

Fay has been supported to engage with the generic drug and alcohol team and work towards an inpatient alcohol detox and complete a structured aftercare programme. Fay has been supported to engage with the eating disorders clinic as an outpatient. Fay's medication has been reviewed and put into blister packs, which is far more manageable for her given the amount of medication she takes. Fay has been referred to occupational therapy for adaptations.

Due to her ill health and low weight, Fay requires bed rails, an adapted chair, a walking stick and rollator. Fay has been authorised for a grant to adapt her bathroom so she has a wet room, which is safer for her and able to give her more independence. Fay also has a pressure cushion to sit on to reduce the risks of pressure sores. Fay has received a bus pass and receives transport to NHS appointments. Fay has been assessed under care management and deemed eligible for a package of care. However, as Fay's health improves since she is currently abstinent and gaining weight and strength, she may only need this support temporarily.

Through Julia's help and other agencies, I was allowed to have a proper detox in hospital and the chance of aftercare for six weeks in a residential facility. I was terrified but knew that it was 'do or die'. In detox, I was very ill to start with but, mentally prepared. On the second day of my detox, I had a bad seizure while in the hospital that made me lose my eyesight completely. I was devastated and thought that it was permanent. Luckily, it wasn't permanent. The sickness was bad, but each day I sobered up I realised how wrong I'd got it. It wasn't right that I was now a shell of my former self. I didn't deserve to get beaten and raped and made a prisoner in my own home. How the hell did this get so bad and I hadn't even realised?

What happened next

I am, however, now sober since 4 December 2017 and drinking more tea than I've ever drunk in my life! Looking back, you know it's terrible, I physically couldn't do anything, and John was limiting what I could eat, so I was losing weight, but he'd push more alcohol on me and force me to drink it; he didn't want me sober. He wanted complete control, like a puppet. But he wanted to live in my home, that I built and I bought and I paid for. I never wanted to be an alcoholic, I would never choose this, no one sane would choose this, but I can say that, throughout all this rubbish and the alcohol, I've never harmed anyone, or stolen, or hurt any human being. Well, my mum, I broke my mum's heart. Now my mum is my number one supporter.

I've had old friends come back into my life recently, but I didn't want to tell them what had been happening – I think it was shame. In your head, you're still that strong fighter that you used to be and then you're nothing. Also, now I am someone else that I am trying to get used to. Due to all the beatings and alcohol use, I have seizures and, because of that, I struggle on a day-to-day basis to do things like use computers and other things like someone with epilepsy.

Plans are currently one day at a time. I need to sort out my health problems, especially after a lot of beatings, it did leave me in a very fragile state inside as well as the alcohol use and the eating disorder. My brain is always going to have, unfortunately, a very short memory span due to the damages, so I have no short-term memory which makes everything a lot harder … but I do want to get into criminal psychology, and find a way to make it work as everything is computerised now, so it's a struggle. All my three previous careers, I now can't do any of those jobs, but they're my trades. I must find another way round and try to have a future, I want a career, I want my life back, I want a life, I want to find out who I am and I want to just be a good person. I've always helped people, but I want to be in a positon to help people who have been abused, psychologically, as I can understand, so I want to be able to train and learn and I have to go a different way around it to normal people. But, I'll find a way. Since stopping drinking I have managed to maintain a weight of seven stone. Everything is so new from what I have seen and I am seeing things through different eyes after ten years.

They say the seizures are never going to go away, but they will hopefully improve as I'm not drinking. Everyday life is hard but I am so glad I am on this side of it. What keeps me sober is an appreciation from the staff and all the teams; I never thought I had a way out. I wanted to die so many times. I never thought anyone would believe me if I disclosed the extent of the abuse as I didn't think people were so horrible in this world, as I am not. In a way, you try and find an element of good in people but in the end I was just trying to stay alive not fix him.

My message to social workers

In terms of social workers and what I think are important factors: I think most important is to be honest and real. Some people feel textbook and like they're told what to say. Some days you need blunt, you need to be able to say you're having a bad day and not for the worker to tell you everything is going to be okay, but to say, no it's not going to be okay until we have done x, y and z. Blunt, but in a pleasant and professional manner. I think getting to know the person is important and knowing when things need controlling and handling. Julia could tell when I couldn't handle it and she had a knack, whereas other people don't. With addicts, it's about knowing no one is ever telling you the truth when they first meet you. If they are in a position where they are being threatened or they're scared; they feel ashamed but they don't not deserve the help as their feelings are so off.

I hated that Julia had to see me in such a bad way, but in a way, I am not. I know I may have been seen as a non-engager and it must be hard to pick out of a hundred people who is most motivated to receive the support but, to be honest, I was probably the most desperate person. I needed someone to say, 'Fay, he is going to kill you,' which is what Julia said. I think it is the only thing that got through to me. If it hadn't,I would probably be dead from alcohol poisoning, liver failure or he would have killed me. Throughout this ten-year madness, Julia was my one solid constant. If I didn't know an agency or couldn't remember who to call, I always knew and I always felt safe because I knew I could call Julia and ask 'who do I phone?,' 'what do I do?' and she would always help me. Working with Julia saved my life. Social workers must deal with hundreds of people all day, every day and it's quite selfless and they don't want anything in return, they are just a security blanket for a lot of people.

I was so drunk at the time and I was desperately trying to get my life together and I couldn't have organised all of that [services] I was just managing to feed myself, if I was lucky enough. People need a voice, people are desperate and need support....If people have turned to drink or drugs because of violence, or due to child abuse, being abused or a bereavement, you know, there are so many cases, not everyone is a statistic, everyone is unique and everyone needs just that little bit. Julia took the bits that we could relate to and would engage me, to want to talk to me. I wouldn't have done that if Julia was all textbook, I couldn't handle any more information, she just told me bluntly, as it is. That's what we need.

Social worker's perspective

My tips: be honest – if you don't know the answer to a question tell them that you don't know, but you will try and find out and get back to them. Talk to them with respect and as a human being. These might sound like obvious basics but you would be shocked at some of the ways I have seen addicts treated and spoken to.

It is hard working with addicts – it can be frustrating and sometimes feel like you're not making any positive progress, but sometimes the smallest positive outcome, reminds me why I do this. I continue to shout from the rooftops as an advocate for addicts and their families. Whatever your opinion on addiction, whether that's nurture vs nature, a disease or a lifestyle choice, put yourself in their shoes for a day.

While Fay's story is unique to Fay, it is not unique to all people with drug addictions. Every person I have ever worked with has a story of trauma, abuse, suffering and pain. No one would ever choose to be 'an addict', but they are, and they all have a story to tell. They sometimes do things that, morally, I wouldn't agree with, such as steal or sex work, but they are just trying to survive. They are desperate to be not in their own mind, and their life is, or has been, so bad they are chasing oblivion. They go to extreme lengths to numb the pain, to self-medicate trauma and, in doing so, put themselves at extreme risk. They say you emotionally and behaviourally stop developing when you experience trauma and abuse or when you start using substances. Therefore, arguably, most addicts emotionally and behaviourally are damaged children trying to survive in an adult world, being heavily judged and discriminated against, with no voice to challenge oppression and no one really caring whether they live or die.

As a drug and alcohol social worker, my job is to be a constant presence within the community so, when that day comes that people are willing to make a change, they know where to go and who to contact. My job is to be an advocate on a service user's behalf, to challenge agencies that sometimes treat 'addicts' as less than human. My job is to sit with someone in a waiting room for three hours as, without a worker there, they would have 'kicked off,' walked out and potentially been labelled as a 'non-engager'. My job is to tell people what their rights are, what choices they have and to give them knowledge to empower themselves to make changes. My job is to ask them what they want and to give them a voice. My job is to tell them they are worth it and they deserve support and they deserve to have a happy meaningful life and that it is achievable.

To social workers I would say try and walk a day in their shoes – try and understand why service users might behave the way they do and why, sometimes, they emotionally might react in ways you might not expect. Most addicts have had a lifetime of chaos, they don't have the same concept of a 'normal' life that we do. Therefore, our expectations of them need to be realistic and achievable for them. Don't set them up to fail, or give them tasks that they can't achieve as you are just then perpetuating their belief that they are useless and worthless. For example, ask them the best time to meet you not book a nine a.m. appointment and then wonder why they haven't turned up. But, they do also need boundaries, clear guidelines of what your role is, what you are willing and able to do with them and what you expect of them in return. Many addicts' experiences of social workers is in children's services, either having their children taken away or being taken away themselves. They will need to know clearly what your role within the Care Act 2014 is and that you are going to put them at the centre of all work in line with MSP – it's their life, their decisions.

As I have said before, people with addictions are survivors which means that they are exceptionally good at reading body language and will be able to tell you are lying to them! Never make a promise you can't keep, if you say you are going to do something, make sure you do it. If you let them down once it could break the working relationship.

Reference List

Alcoholics Anonymous (Great Britain) 2018 [online]. York: Alcoholics Anonymous. org.uk. Available at: www.alcoholics-anonymous.org.uk/.

BDPSAB Policy and Procedures Group (2016) *Safeguarding Adults Procedures. Multi-Agency Procedures for the Protection of Adults with Care and Support Needs in Bournemouth, Dorset and Poole.* Available at: bpsafeguardingadultsboard. com/uploads/7/4/8/9/74891967/bpdsab_safeguarding_adults_procedures_-_ v2.4_-_16_december_2016.pdf.

Cocaine Anonymous UK (2017) [online]. Enfield: CAUK. Available at: cocaineanonymous.org.uk.

Feldon, P.(2017) *The Social Worker's Guide to the Care Act 2014.* St Albans: Critical Publishing.

Home Office (2015) *Controlling or Coercive Behaviour in an Intimate or Family Relationship*

MARAC (2017) MARAC (Multi Agency Risk Assessment Conference) [online]. Dorset: Dorset for you. Available at: www.dorsetforyou.gov.uk/marac.

NICE (2017) *Eating Disorders: Recognition and Treatment* [online]. Available at: www.nice.org.uk/guidance/ng69/chapter/ Recommendations#using-the-mental-health-act-and-compulsory-treatment.

SafeLives (2014) *SafeLives Dash Risk Checklist for the Identification of High Risk Cases of Domestic Abuse, Stalking and 'Honour'-Based Violence* [online]. Available at: www.safelives.org.uk/sites/default/files/resources/Dash%20for%20 IDVAs%20FINAL_0.pdf.

SafeLives (2018) *Resources for MARAC Meetings* [online]. Available at: www. safelives.org.uk/practice-support/resources-marac-meetings.

Statute

The Care Act 2014

Suggested reading

Association of Directors of Adult Social Services (2018) *Making Safeguarding Personal* [online]. Available at: www.adass.org.uk/making-safeguarding-personal-publications.

Bennett, S. and Nelson, J. K. (2011) *Adult Attachment in Clinical Social Work. Practice, Research, and Policy*. London: Springer.

Brown, C. (2006) *A Piece of Cake; A Memoir*. London: Transworld publishers.

Galvani, S. – Anything by Sarah Galvani.

Hart, C. (2013) *High Price. Drugs, Neuroscience and Discovering Myself*. London: Penguin Group.

Statutory Guidance Framework [online]. Available at: www.gov.uk/government/uploads/system/uploads/attachment_data/file/482528/Controlling_or_coercive_behaviour_-_statutory_guidance.pdf.

Keegan, K. and Moss, H. B. (2008) *Chasing the High*. Oxford: Oxford University Press.

Little, E. (1998) *Another Day in Paradise*. London: Vintage.

Petersen, T. and McBride, A. (2002) *Working with Substance Misusers. A Guide to Theory and Practice*. London: Routledge.

West, R. and Brown, J. (2013) *Theory of Addiction*. 2nd edition. Chichester: John Wiley & Sons Ltd.

Watch

Drugsland – BBC iPlayer

Three Girls – BBC iPlayer

Britain's Teenage Drug Runners – BBC iPlayer

Attend

Volunteer for drug and alcohol, homeless or sex workers outreach or drop in service.

Attend an OPEN fellowship meeting – must be an OPEN meeting.

12

I was Detained under the Mental Health Act

Zoe Rooney

Rosslyn Dray, *Lecturer in social work*

> **At a glance**
>
> - This chapter focuses on the statutory intervention of detaining a person under the Mental Health Act 1983/2007.
>
> - Zoe has experience of using mental health services including inpatient units and is now a mental health campaigner.
>
> - Beverly is Zoe's mother and, along with Zoe, shares some of her memories and insights throughout the chapter.
>
> - Rosslyn is a social work lecturer, experienced social worker and Approved Mental Health Professional (AMHP). Rosslyn, Zoe and Beverly met during the process of writing this chapter together. Ros provides the formal knowledge underpinning the interventions Zoe experienced in text boxes throughout the chapter.

My name is Zoe. I am a single mum with two teenage boys, two dogs and a cat. I find it hard to tell you who I am, because I describe myself as a bit of a contradiction. My friends say I am supportive and friendly and they would also probably describe me as sociable. I suppose I am, but I don't really socialise.

I am known where I live because of the social media work I do around mental health, and campaigning for local issues. Standing up for myself, and highlighting injustice affecting others is important to me. It is something I have learned to do as an advocate for community issues and mental health. I don't have any filters. If it is in my head, then it is coming out of my mouth.

My life was unremarkable, almost boring. The average 2.4 working-class family. I passed my 11-plus with a high grade and went to the local grammar school for girls. I was an obnoxious teen, but never broke the law. I went on to have supervisory jobs, never wanting a career. I was responsible, intelligent and carefree. I was very opinionated and judgemental. The irony does not escape me. I had no time or sympathy for mental health or addiction. This is something I now instil into my children daily.

I have two boys, one with special needs. My experiences have helped me to support and understand him. Most of all, it has helped me to protect him from the system that 'broke' me. My relationship with their father was acrimonious to say the least and we separated when I was pregnant with my second child. I was about 26 years old. This is when the thyroid issues really came to the fore and the trouble with my mental health started.

I had a thyroid problem, hyperthyroidism, I managed it very poorly. This led to my brain being toxified from my thyroid which caused this mental health behaviour. After several sections (under the Mental Health Act) of a few weeks it was decided that I would be sent to a prison as the mental health unit deemed they could not manage me. They never forwarded any mental health information to the prison. My mother, who had always worked within a similar profession, rang the prison health wing and explained the situation in order that I was kept away from the general prison population and received care for my mental health. This lasted five weeks. They forcibly took me to hospital in handcuffs and put radioactive iodine in me to try and 'cure' me. This medieval treatment was humiliating. It worked for a year and then the doctors made the decision to remove my thyroid altogether. This is when I sank into a deep depression from the hypothyroidism.

Despite several years in the mental health arena, I was not given any effective therapies. I question how there was any conclusion for me, other than suicide. I was already self-harming terribly. Burning being my weapon of choice. Horrific burns through muscle, taking months to heal. My suicide felt the only option open to me. I didn't want to put my family through any more of this and I did not want my children growing up with a mental mother.

> The pain seemed to help her ... the more pain, the better she was ... she felt she needed the pain because she had been such a bad person ... she felt worthless. (Beverley – Zoe's mother)

Being detained under the Mental Health Act

I do not have any recollection of being sectioned. I do not have any memory at all of several weeks. I remember staring at a photo of my sons, tears in my eyes, as I took nearly a pint glass of various pills. My next memory is difficult to describe. It is like waking from a day-dream. Except, this was the moment that I realised my life had changed forever.

As I looked around me, the scene was surreal. I was barricaded in a small bedroom, not anywhere that I had been before, with people shouting through the door for me to open it or they would smash it down. Terrified would be an understatement. I had been sectioned many times before; I had the whole 'collection', if you like. s5.2, s136, s2 and as I later found out this was my s3. With my other sections, I was aware – I knew the reasons and everything had been explained to me.

As I opened the door to allow the staff into my room, I kept asking what had happened. It was several days before a familiar face came and explained that I had been found by the police. I had been rushed by police car to hospital where my family were told I had an hour to live. Somehow, I pulled through and was sectioned. To this day, I still do not know many details – I feel that I need to. Losing weeks of your life is very unsettling. Knowing that I was 'awake' and active during this spell made it worse. What had I been doing?

Mental Health Assessment (MHA)

A Mental Health Act assessment is an assessment of a person's mental state, under-taken by an AMHP, alongside two registered medical practitioners. The difference between this and any other assessment, is that it carries the possible outcome of compulsory powers being used to admit a person experiencing mental distress, or 'disorder', to hospital.

Zoe refers to different powers under the MHA, informally known by their section numbers within the Act, and colloquially known as 'being sectioned'. The powers Zoe describes have the outcome of depriving a person of their liberty, and are predominantly used in either emergency or urgent situations. The fundamental pur-pose of intervention of this nature is to prevent harm, either to the health and safety of the individual or other persons, and to facilitate an assessment of their mental state.

▶

◄

MHA Powers and 'sections' Zoe is describing:

- s5(2) – Doctor's holding power to prevent a patient leaving an inpatient setting until a Mental Health Act assessment is arranged.

- s136 – Police Constable's power to remove a person who appears to be suffering from a mental disorder to a place of safety for the purpose of MHA assessment.

- s2 and s3 – AMHP authority to make an application for compulsory admission to hospital if criteria for detention is met.

What is common to all interventions is the necessity to evidence, or justify, why the power must be used. Intervention of this nature poses a breach of Article 5 rights, the 'right to liberty and security of the person' as set out by the European Convention and enshrined in Human Rights Act 1998. Professionals acting on behalf of a public authority (such as a local authority, police or health) must demonstrate compatibility to human rights law, unless the breach is authorised by a legal mandate, for example, an application to detain a person under the MHA, or through the Deprivation of Liberty Safeguards (DoLS).

Zoe's memory of the experience is limited and her mother's account (below) indicates there was confusion surrounding the assessment process. At the point of assessing Zoe under the Mental Health Act, as she was detained under s3 (admission for treatment,) one would expect the AMHP to identify her nearest relative and consult with that person prior to making an application. It states in s11(4)b MHA that it is only in cases where the professional deems it is 'not reasonably practicable' or would 'involve unreasonable delay' that it can be justified consultation does not take place prior to application.

'I hadn't a clue what was going on…I don't even know if we knew she was being assessed. We knew she was having problems but I got a phone call to say that the unit couldn't handle her so they were sending her to a more secure unit. They told me she was so bad she was virtually in a padded room … it was the most secure unit they had … with one-to-one surveillance … and that's what she needed. When, and if, she became more stable they would transfer her back…'

'We didn't know about which section was which. I don't think I really understood at that stage that she couldn't come home. I just thought she was there because she wanted to stay there … you know … because she was unwell.' (Beverley – Zoe's mother)

My inpatient admission

As I became more coherent and engaging, I was taken back to my local mental health unit, which I knew very well. Why I had been sent to one miles away, I do not know. I do know that I was only returned after

I promised to be a 'good girl'. I felt like a child. I had no dignity. I was 30 years old.

Once back in my acute unit, I was given a single room with a bathroom. I was allowed to self-harm whenever I wanted, I was given medication for everything, from sleeping to toileting. I was not permitted to make one decision about anything. No real treatments were in place. I was just held away from society. Nurses catering for every need, even washing me, as my self-harm had become so bad, both hands were bandaged. A short, weekly review with my psychiatrist where boxes were ticked was the most discussion about my stay.

After six months a new section was applied. This was comforting to me. The system had made me totally reliant on them. I couldn't imagine doing anything for myself any more. I saw many other patients come and go in the 26-bed unit. Impossible to form a bond with anyone as the turnover was so great. The only constant in my life was the staff. They become my 'friends' and we developed unhealthy attachments to each other. The nurses knew me well because of the length of time I had been there. Boundaries became blurred. For example, I was often allowed into the nursing office to play card games. I was bored and needed some connection.

My behaviour became a cross between a vulnerable toddler and a destructive, angry teenager. When society no longer exists and there are no ramifications for any misconduct then this child-like state emerges. Able to do whatever I liked, there were no consequences, except for the injections. If my behaviour was seen as too hyper, destructive or anything deemed not in the best interests of the unit, then I would be pinned to the floor and given an injection of something that rendered me unable to move for several hours.

After 15 months, I knew that I was in an unhealthy relationship with the mental health services. I remember looking around one afternoon and thinking I should not be here, this is making me worse. I applied to change psychiatrist.

It must get to a stage where you are not improving and you are not doing anything else

The length of stay was too long ... instead of getting better, she got worse. She was bored ... she learned more techniques of self-harm. The longer it got, the worse it got ... it was like being out of work. She was without her children all this time and that was an underlying pain for her.

I remember we made a collage of pictures for Zoe. (Beverley – Zoe's mother)

Ongoing detention under the MHA

Here, Zoe is referring to the renewal of her section. The section can be renewed providing the criteria for continued detention is met, in other words, that it continues to be 'necessary' for the patient to receive treatment as an inpatient, and this outcome could not be achieved unless compulsory powers are used. One of the challenges both Zoe and her mother describe is that the admission started to erode her confidence, and created dependency on the unit and the staff. Zoe acknowledges this was not a healthy relationship and it raises questions about the therapeutic purpose of the admission.

In terms of renewing a patient's section, the onus is on the Responsible Clinician (RC*) and the detaining authority (local authority) to evidence why continued detention using powers under the MHA is necessary. In terms of good practice, this should be done through face-to-face review of the patient, and consultation with family. Referral to a Mental Health Review Tribunal (MHRT) may be requested by the patient to explore a decision made to renew a section, or may be an automatic process under some circumstances if the patient is unable to exercise this right. This provides ongoing legal scrutiny over decisions which are made because of the interface with human rights. The tribunal process is a legal recourse for the patient to challenge continued use of compulsory powers under the MHA.

Zoe is also describing treatment being administered without her consent. Being detained under the MHA, can mean the patient is subject to the consent to treatment provisions under Part IV MHA. This is the legal authority to provide treatment for the person's mental disorder without the patient's consent. This is a complex area and further information can be found within Part IV MHA. For some treatments, regulations require a second opinion appointed doctor (SOAD) to authorise the treatment, following their assessment of the recommended treatment plan.

*'The Responsible Clinician is the approved clinician who will have overall responsibility for the patient's case'
(Dept of Health, CoP 36.2, 2015)

Discharge from hospital

My new shrink firmly believed that those with personality disorders should not be inpatients. To this day I am still not sure on my 'official' diagnosis, but know that it has covered most things and I have been given labels which don't really make sense for me and what I experience. He felt long-term stays for anyone were detrimental. I agreed a leave date with him for eight weeks' time. I tried to have spells of home leave but, as soon as I was out of the unit, I felt too anxious to stay away. I was sent out of the unit but within an hour or two I would want to come back.

The nurses told me repeatedly that I shouldn't be released but I kept trying, to no avail. The nurses told me they did not want me to go, they didn't think I'd survive it. My shrink said it would be 'sink or swim'. I wanted out. I knew this was not normal and, one day, a switch just went in my head and I became determined. Two weeks before I was due to leave I made the decision to come off of all medications, cold turkey. How could I be expected to function normally when I had a plethora of pills in me?

Finally, the day came for my release. I was reassured by the nurses that I could return at any time. I looked them in the eye, thanked them for their friendship throughout this time and told them I would never set foot in this unit again. I was 31 years old then and, at 39, this is still the case.

Life was hard. Life still is hard. Once out of the mental health services reach, I struggled to function with basic day-to-day activities. I found myself unable to leave my house alone. Panic attacks at slight changes to my daily routine. Flashbacks regularly. The long 'sentence' had effectively destroyed me as an individual.

It was explained there was another section where she'd have leave, and she went onto that. We were completely in the dark most of the time … .

She was released with a package of care and a community mental health nurse which broke down after the second day because of the medication delivery.

I still don't know what her diagnosis is … started off with bipolar, then could be schizophrenia … personality disorder … she's been everything. (Beverley – Zoe's mother)

NB: Diagnosis is subjective in that it is the formulated opinion of the assessing doctor based on the evidence they perceive objectively, and description of the patient's subjective experience. The diagnosis a patient is given at any point can change and be reviewed.

Diagnosis

Zoe describes being labelled with a diagnosis of personality disorder in her account. Zoe's mother also describes diagnostic labels changing during contact with mental health services which led to confusion about how to best support her daughter.

▶

◀

Personality disorder is a complex term which attracts much debate and controversy (Pilgrim, 2017; Roberts, 2018; Warrener, 2017; Tew, 2011) The consequences of receiving this diagnostic label for Zoe are described in her narrative.

Specific diagnostic criteria and symptomatology can be found in the DSM-5 (American Psychiatric Association 2013) and ICD-10 relating to specific types of personality disorder. The diagnosis is broadly used to describe a collection of symptoms or behaviours which can include emotional instability, acts of self-injury, behavioural impulse control and pervasive identity, self-esteem and relationship issues.

Zoe also refers to leave from hospital as she approached discharge from hospital. She talks about her psychiatrist (in charge of her care) being the person who agrees discharge, and that she tried periods of time at home. Section 17 MHA provides for leave of absence from hospital for patients who are detained. This is authorised by the RC (the doctor overseeing the patient's treatment). Leave can be granted for specified periods of time and may be subject to specific conditions. It can be used to trial a plan for discharge, to phase transition home, and to introduce greater opportunity for occupation in routine activities outside of hospital for the patient. It can be a way of maintaining social contact which can be important for recovery.

My reflections

I understand the need to keep me safe. I totally agree with confinement in emergencies. But what did I do to deserve having my future taken? I will never work again, too afraid of the world outside. I cannot trust anyone for fear of being controlled. I hide many of the mental health difficulties I face in case I am readmitted. I am labelled. Stigma everywhere. I attend A&E with a broken finger or any ailment and it will be due to my mental health. I fear everyone.

I now live with my children in my own home. I have rebuilt my relationship with my family. I am a community leader and mental health advocate, but all this is done behind a computer screen. I cannot attend any gathering, parties, functions, coffee shops. My children having to accompany me everywhere I go.

My life was saved by the police that fateful afternoon but was stolen by the mental health services that I was entrusted to.

Staying sane in a crazy world

Life is difficult. I have to accept my limitations and work around them. For a long time I couldn't own a kettle as the urge to pour the boiling water down myself was too strong. I used a water boiler instead, that didn't reach the same temperatures. Having my boys meant I had to learn to live in a world that terrified me. My youngest son has become my carer. A fine balance between allowing him to be a child yet making the 'caring' as minimal as possible. I never go out alone but have slowly learned to trust and have some amazing friends who accompany me when out and support me. My best friend, Foster makes me feel safe. With him by my side, I have the courage to venture out on long walks, although always to secluded areas. But, it is still an achievement for me.

I forced myself to learn to drive. I now have a sense of freedom for the first time. Very often, I can't get out of the car at my destination and, instead of berating myself, I give myself a virtual pat on the back for just getting there. I am very open with everyone on my mental health. I am not ashamed. I do not cover my scars. I engage mostly on social media, writing articles for newspapers and blogs. Bizarrely, I am well known in my community despite rarely going out. I am a mental health advocate now. I refuse to allow my experience to define me, instead I appreciate it for the understanding it has given me and with that the ability to help others. My life is far from normal but it works. I am just Zoe … a normal girl trying to live in the crazy world around me.

Social worker's perspective

Collaboration: Piecing together memories

A barrier to Zoe sharing her experience has been patchy memories of the formal statutory assessment process; being assessed under the Mental Health Act. What Zoe powerfully recalls, is how the experience felt, and the impact it subsequently had: finding herself in hospital detained under a section of the Mental Health Act'; feeling scared, disorientated; and not aware of the sequence of events leading to that point. Zoe's story is a poignant reminder of the sense of powerlessness, disorientation and lack of dignity no person would wish to experience.

This is presented as significant in itself, because of the trust placed with professionals to follow due process – expectations they will practice in ways which promote the dignity and rights of individuals at all times (Dept of Health, 2015; NICE, 2011). It is an uncomfortable truth to learn how services are experienced, and how the issue of dignity creates a sense of intense vulnerability; cited as a factor which particularly damages self-esteem and recovery (Chambers et al., 2014).

As a practitioner, it places a harsh spotlight on actions, decisions, words and inactions that we are accountable for. Zoe's words attempt to rebalance professional focus on the importance of relationships, communication, and sound ethics and values; alongside the required knowledge, lawful practice, and understanding of practical and resource processes in statutory work (Beckett et al., 2017; Hood, 2018). Zoe's account is accompanied by reflections from her mother, Beverley, who talks about what it was like trying to support Zoe at this point in her life, and her observations within the process.

A key theme within the narrative is balancing risk. A strong focus on the negative connotations of risk can prevent an inclusive process of planning care and hospital discharge with the person and their family (Farrelly et al., 2015). This reduces the possibility of smooth transitioning back to 'normal' life and it becomes problematic and daunting; reflected in Zoe's lived experience. Through exploring the narratives with Zoe and her mother, it became apparent information and genuine partnership working did not always happen. There were gaps in their knowledge, for example, around patient and nearest relative rights. Clear information may have helped promote the role of advocacy, and provided a stronger voice within the decisions made about her continued admission.

Fear of risk can also lead to unintended consequences, for example, decisions or inactions resulting in deskilling the person, creating dependency, delaying decisions and inaction. Zoe describes how staff felt she should not be 'released'. One questions how the emotional component of risk assessment and decision-making influences that situation; where the stakes are perceived as high for both the person and the professionals who are discharging a duty of care, and who would be scrutinised if harm occurred (Kemshall et al., 2013).

The following explains some of the underpinning legislation of this statutory intervention. It is peppered with terminology which is used commonly within the Mental Health Act. Explanations are included where meaning may not be clear-cut. By the nature of law, however, there are ambiguities in language and meaning which are useful for developing practitioners to be aware of. This is where law becomes the framework, with practice encounters and decisions creating a fabric of experience on which learning and professional interpretation is drawn from. Thus demonstrating the importance well-rooted values and ethics underpinning practice decisions.

The Legislation and Code of Practice – Assessing a person using the Mental Health Act 1983/2007

A Mental Health Act Assessment carries with it the possibility of use of compulsory powers and, as such, creates a plethora of ethical, moral and legal tensions.

A Mental Health Act Assessment is not a routine intervention and, as Zoe's account addresses, being 'sectioned' has consequences which extend beyond the scope of that one decision. As such, it is only practitioners who have specialist training and delegated authority to act who can undertake a Mental Health Act Assessment. A person who is authorised to do this is called an AMHP.

What is an Approved Mental Health Professional (AMHP)?

Historically this role was called an Approved Social Worker, however, since the 2007 MHA amendments, an AMHP can be a person who is suitably professionally qualified, and who has also undertaken appropriate specialist training which enables them to be authorised to act by a local authority under delegated authority. This has enabled practitioners of different disciplines to undertake specialist training to become an AMHP.

The MHA and the Code of Practice

The MHA is supported by a Code of Practice (applicable to persons residing in England only). While the Code of Practice supports the primary legislation, it is not a statutory instrument in its own right. It outlines how the law should be applied, and it is intended to guide the decisions of those undertaking duties in relation to the Act. It is to be regarded as statutory guidance by medical practitioners, AMHPs and local authority staff in terms of the importance of its role in underpinning practice decisions and how deviation from the Code would be viewed if a decision was legally challenged in court.

Guiding Principles – MHA Code of Practice (Department of Health, 2015):

1. Least restrictive option and maximising independence.

2. Empowerment and involvement.

3. Respect and dignity.

4. Purpose and effectiveness.

5. Efficiency and equity.

There are key principles which guide the conduct of those exercising powers and functions of the MHA, and these are intended to remain central to the principles of care and decision-making. They are a statement of the values and principles those working within the Act should adhere to. Given the invasive nature and human rights incompatibility of depriving a person of their liberty, there are strong messages within the principles. It suggests it is not merely the technical application of legal knowledge which is important, but the interweaving components of the conduct, values and ethics of those applying it.

The principles apply to not only the direct decision makers, but also the systemic relationships in wider service provision, for example, commissioning and community partners in health, social care and the police. For the AMHP conducting Zoe's assessment, they would be required to evidence their adherence to the guiding principles as part of a written report on the intervention.

Basis of the statutory intervention – Does the Act apply?

The basis of this statutory intervention lies in the application of the Mental Health Act 1983/2007 (MHA). This centres on what is understood to be the definition of mental disorder and whether it applies to the person (patient) who is being assessed. The MHA covers the arrangements for the 'reception, care and treatment' of people who have a mental disorder, and applies in both England and Wales under Section 1(1) MHA.

Purpose of the Mental Health Act Assessment

The purpose of an assessment is to establish whether:

1. The person has a mental disorder (as defined in s1(2) MHA) or not; whether the Act applies.

2. If there is evidence the person has, or appears to have, a mental disorder, what decisions/actions are required to ensure the person receives an appropriate and proportionate response to their presenting circumstances.

3. If there is no evidence of mental disorder, there may be a role for onward referral to services appropriate to the person's need.

S1(2) Mental Health Act

'In this Act – Mental disorder means any disorder or disability of the mind.'

This is asking the question, 'does the person have a mental disorder?' If the answer is no, you cannot use the powers set out in the MHA. It is, however, a broad definition of mental disorder and covers a range of conditions. (Brown, 2016; Dept of Health, 2015)

There are exceptions to whom the Act applies which can be found in s1 MHA. Available from: https://www.legislation.gov.uk

The decision on whether a person has a mental disorder is one where clinical evidence is required, and why the involvement of appropriate registered medical practitioners is necessary.

The question of determining if there is evidence of mental disorder requires the formal opinions of two registered medical practitioners, one of which who must have 'special experience in the diagnosis or treatment of mental disorder' as outlined in s12(2) MHA.

What is a registered medical practitioner?

The term 'registered medical practitioner' is outlined in the Medical Act 1983 (gov) and refers to medical practitioners who hold registration with the General Medical Council.

The MHA goes further in Section 12(2); identifying registered medical practitioners who are approved by the Secretary of State 'as having special experience in the diagnosis or treatment of mental disorder'. This is colloquially known as a 'Section 12' doctor as this is where the definition and duty is set out in the Act. Under Section 12(2) an AMHP is required to involve at least one registered medical practitioner with 'previous acquaintance' and 'or an S12 doctor'. This ensures there is prior knowledge of the patient's circumstances and relevant expertise; creating a balanced assessment and relevant context.

Assessing evidence for the presence, or absence, of mental disorder will also, however, be informed by patient history, meeting with the patient, information from family, information from teams/professionals who may be supporting the patient and the objective assessment of the patient's mental state by the authorised professionals involved in the assessment. The choice of medical practitioner will be influenced by any special expertise that is required, for example, the patient may be a young person, a person with an eating disorder, or a person with a learning disability.

Planning and undertaking the assessment

Before meeting with the patient an AMHP needs to gather relevant information from a number of sources to inform their assessment. This may include health, social care, family and police. This starts to piece together a picture of the patient's circumstances, who they are, and what key issues underpin the need for a Mental Health Act Assessment. The AMHP's role is to consider the patient's circumstances holistically.

Information gathering is an important stage when coordinating the assessment. It enables the AMHP to determine how to approach the assessment in order to meet their s13(2) MHA duty of interviewing the patient in a 'suitable manner'. Planning is key in any social work intervention, however, an AMHP will also need to consider the health and safety of all involved, resources required, risk (historical or present), family relationships and practical considerations of the assessment, for example, any specific communication or cultural needs.

The role and rights of the nearest relative

'Nearest relative' is a legal term in the Mental Health Act which is defined in Section 26 MHA; it is not a person chosen or identified by the patient. Their role is an important one which provides recourse to challenge decisions made under the provisions of the MHA. This could be in terms of objecting to an s3 application, applying for the patient's discharge from hospital under s23, making an application for admission, or making a request for an AMHP to consider the patient circumstances (assessment) with a view to making an application under s13(4) MHA.

The task of identifying a patient's nearest relative can be complex, as it is a subjective judgement based on applying the criteria of s26 MHA. It is an area where there is a wealth of case law outlining historical legal challenges to decisions. The duties the AMHP needs to adhere to are set out in s11 MHA.

We weren't aware. We assumed when she was first sectioned that she would be out in six months, because I knew it was a six-month section. They turned around and said they were re-sectioning her for another six months. We weren't even aware you could do that.

'At no stage did they say you could challenge this, so we had no idea we could do anything about it ... and some of the staff didn't know either because I'd ask the staff questions and they clearly didn't know.'

Beverley explains she was not given sufficient clear information in order for her to understand rights.

The nearest relative of a patient can change, with the evolution of age, the changing nature of relationships and residence. This is where accurate information about a person's background is important. It is a requirement of the AMHP in s11(3) to identify who 'appears' to be the nearest relative. The decision on whether the person identified as nearest relative is suitable to act as such may arise, but it is a separate consideration from the process of identification.

Further information for patients and carers can be found on http://www.NICE.org, https://www.mind.org.uk or the NHS choices website http://www.nhs.uk

Our messages to social workers – Zoe and Beverley Rooney

➤ The impact of an admission has long-term consequences for the person and their family.

Be mindful of the focus and function of admission. The hospital admission may be necessary; to promote the safety and well-being of the person in the short term, but reviewing the therapeutic aims is crucial. Questioning the options and appraising the risks holistically, to enable positive risk taking, provides a better chance of maintaining a sense of fresh perspective about what an intervention is achieving.

➤ Explain the terminology ... explain my rights.

Do not assume the person or their family members understand the terminology used to explain treatments, or arrangements for their relative's care. They may not feel comfortable asking for clarification. Checking understanding and clear language is necessary.

The context of high emotion or stress can add to potential confusion over communication and what is heard and remembered from that interaction. Consider the format information can be provided in and whether information needs to be revisited. Practitioners need to have a working knowledge which enables them to understand what rights service users and carers have, and to be able to signpost to services which provide independent advocacy.

➢ I'm not interested in the lack of staff, annual leave or anything ... I'm concerned about my daughter.

When in communication with the hospital ward, or with involved professionals, a lack of resources was used as a reason for why care was not ideal, why things had not been achieved, or why there had been a lack of information.

It has become a familiar situation for service users and carers to develop low expectations of the service they may receive, and to become accustomed to the narrative of a lack of, or cuts in, resources. This message reminds professionals of the need to consider the service user and carer's priorities at any given point.

➢ Working together should be improved.

Zoe's mother described an incident prior to this admission where Zoe had been arrested by the police following self-harming in a public place. She particularly remembers this as an example where services worked together to help prevent harm to Zoe – 'That was the probably the best night's sleep I ever had because I knew, for once, she was with someone I could trust, and that nothing would happen to her, and she would be safe.' – Beverley.

Due to the nature of the incident, police tried to arrange admission to a local mental health unit. This was not successful, and Zoe was held in custody pending court appearance. They entered a dialogue with Zoe's mother about what approach to take to ensure Zoe remained safe, got the care she needed and that family were aware of what was happening. The actual outcome was not as planned, as Zoe was remanded in custody; however, they were able to access appropriate mental health care for her in prison. Zoe's mother had high praise for the responsiveness of the care Zoe received, and the partnership work between the prison service and police.

The sergeant's actions in following up with a telephone call to acknowledge the outcome was not as expected, and what could happen next, was a key factor in this being viewed as a positive interaction. He had telephoned Zoe's mother to discuss the outcome, had been open about the unintended outcome, had apologised and provided information and dialogue on what would happen next. This is a significant lesson for professionals because of the discomfort in having to deliver bad news, however, it is an important point linking to professional codes around duty of candour and being honest and open (PCF).

Conclusions from a social worker's perspective

While the role of an AMHP requires specialist training, as a social worker, or allied professional, there is a role in the overall care of the person; both informing the MHA Assessment and extending beyond the assessment process.

Linked roles for social workers or allied professionals within the Mental Health Act Assessment process

- Making a referral for an MHA Assessment – as the person's key worker.

- Providing information to an AMHP about the person (history/circumstances/health issues relationships/risks).

- Considering viable options for planning care and support.

- Following up on the outcomes of an MHA assessment (onward referrals and signposting).

- Assisting the AMHP in protection of property (s47 Care Act 2014) or supporting with tasks, for example, ensuring appropriate care for the person's children and/or any pets they may have.

- Discussing the patient's or nearest relative's rights.

- Facilitating hospital discharge.

- Attending an MHRT to present a social circumstances report on behalf of your local authority (following an appeal to the hospital managers).

In social work practice the interface with services is often at the point of crisis; through requesting advice, assessment relating to care or support needs, or through systems where a person may not consent to involvement or intervention. There can be a strong emphasis on core knowledge for intervention, but it is the skilful weave of sound values and ethics, and exercising duty with humanity and professionalism which is crucial for ethical, evidence-based decisions and anti-oppressive practice (Larsen,

2008). It is this element which creates the 'emotional labour' contained within the role (Gregor, 2010; Morris, 2016).

Zoe's story reveals her experience of feeling like she was treated with a lack of dignity; having little involvement in decisions about her life. This presents incongruence with the guiding principles of the MHA, which is significant because the Code of Practice places importance on the way in which intervention is delivered, and legal duties interpreted. The intention is clear in the principles and, despite all the technicalities and minutiae of the Act, the technical and rational do not outweigh the ethics and values behind action; in line with human rights.

The purpose of an assessment is to gather relevant information on which to base a decision. The intersecting elements of an evidence-based decision, however, make this a complex task. It is not only the presence of urgency, and potential for harmful consequences, which can increase both the conscious and unconscious emotional aspects for those involved (Ingram, 2013), but it is also coupled with ensuring legal compliance within the process, ensuring duties are discharged appropriately, facilitating effective partnership working, communication and the logistical challenge of mobilising resources in increasingly constrained services (Gregor, 2010; Morris, 2016).

The concept of recovery is founded on principles of partnership, personalisation, dignity, hope, choice and control (Castillo in Repper and Perkins, 2003; Walker, 2013). Moreover, it is argued that it is vital for the voice of people with lived experience to be embedded with education about mental health to enable students to understand recovery is possible and what aspects make a difference (Dorozenko et al., 2016). While Zoe acknowledges she needed to be admitted at a time when she was not able to make decisions in her best interests, she expresses concern over the length of time before her views were taken into account. This has affected her confidence, self-esteem and long-term recovery.

Zoe argues there needs to be a transition from professionals being custodians of power; decision-making when necessary, but progressing to a point of genuine dialogue, where the person is actively valued for their expertise. Collaboration and the nature of the staff-patient relationship can be a crucial building block for recovery (Gregory and Thomspon, 2013). Utilising supervision to identify and explore potentially harmful relationship dynamics is also vital here; to understand the risks and benefits in the 'therapeutic' helping relationship reflected in Zoe's account (Hood, 2018).

Systems in place to provide the start to that journey of recovery for those experiencing acute mental ill health continue to reinforce stigma (Beresford et al., 2010; Chambers et al., 2014; Farrelly et al., 2015; Henderson et al., 2014).This echoes Zoe's experience of being detained and admitted to hospital under the MHA. Moreover, the sense of powerlessness, loss of control and dignity do not create fertile conditions for cultivating hope and enabling recovery.

Recovery has become an increasingly prominent discourse in mental health practice (Bogg, 2010; Roberts, 2018). It promotes a shift in understanding, from a purely medical model, towards a social model of understanding; whereby recovery is defined by what it means to that individual (Repper and Perkins, 2003; Roberts, 2018). This aligns with duties to work with compatibility to human rights, equalities and mental capacity legislation, and the underlying principles set out in the Care Act 2014. The Care Act 2014, in particular, places a duty on local authorities to promote the well-being of service users in all interventions; considering preventative strategies, acknowledging the expertise of individuals with care and support needs, promoting choice and control and personalising targeted interventions.

Zoe describes her experiences with a level of candour that is a sharp, but humbling, reminder of the impact an intervention can have. Though a professional may be a brief visitor in a person's life what they do, say, and how they behave can have a lasting impact on the way the interaction is experienced. This creates genuine opportunity to influence practice in a positive way and to consider what factors make a tangible difference to service users and carers; particularly in times of intense crisis and vulnerability.

References

American Psychiatric Association (2013) *Diagnostic and Statistical Manual of Mental Disorders.* 5th edition (DSM-5). Arlington: American Psychiatric publishing.

Beckett, C., Maynard, A. and Jordan, P. (2017) *Values and Ethics in Social Work.* 3rd edition. London: Sage.

Beresford, P., Nettle, M. and Perring, R. (2010) Towards a social model of madness or distress? Exploring what service users say. Joseph Rowntree Foundation. Available at: www.jrf.org.uk.

Bogg, D. (2010) *Values and Ethics in Mental Health Practice.* Exeter: Learning Matters.

Brown, R. (2016) *The Approved Mental Health Professional's Guide to Mental Health Law.* 4th edition. London: Sage.

Chambers, M., Gallagher, A., Borschmann, R., Gillard, S., Turner, K. and Kantaris, X. (2014) The experience of detained mental health service users: Issues of dignity in care. *BMC Medical Ethics.* 15: 50.

Department of Health (2015) *Mental Health Act 1983: Code of Practice.* TSO.

Dorozenko, K., Ridley, S., Martin, R. and Mahboub, L. (2016) A journey of embedding mental health lived experience in social work education. *Social Work Education.* 35: 8, 905–917.

Farrelly, S., Lester, H., Rose, D., Birchwood, M., Marshall, M., Waheed, H. C., Szmukler, G. and Thornicroft, G. (2015) Barriers to shared decision making in mental health care: Qualitative study of the joint crisis plan for psychosis. *Health Expectations.* 19, pp. 448–458.

Gregor, C. (2010) Unconscious aspects of statutory mental health social work: Emotional labour and the approved mental health professional. *Journal of Social Work Practice*. 24: 4, 492–443.

Gregory, M. and Thompson, A. (2013) From here to recovery: One service user's journey through a mental health crisis: Some reflections on experience, policy and practice. *Journal of Social Work Practice*. 27: 4, 455–470.

Henderson, R., Corker, E., Hamilton, S., Williams, P., Pinfold, V., Rose, D., Webber, M., Evans-Lacko, S. and Thornicroft, G. (2014) Viewpoint survey of mental health service user's experiences of discrimination in England 2008–2012.

Hood, R. (2018) *Complexity in Social Work*. London: Sage.

Ingram, R. (2013) Emotions, social work practice and supervision: An uneasy alliance? *Journal of Social Work Practice*. 27:1, 5–19.

Kemshall, H., Wilkinson, B. and Baker, K. (2013) *Working with Risk*. Cambridge: Polity Press.

Larsen, G. (2008) Anti-oppressive practice in mental health. *Journal of Progressive Human Services*. 19: 1, pp. 39–54.

Morris, L. (2016) AMHP work: Dirty or prestigious? Dirty work designations and the approved mental health professional. *British Journal of Social Work*. 46: 3, 703–718.

NICE (2011) Improving your experience of mental health services in the NHS.

Pilgrim, D. (2017) *Key Concepts in Mental Health*. 4th edition, London: Sage.

Repper, J. and Perkins, R. (2003) *Social Inclusion and Recovery a Model for Mental Health Practice*. London: Balliere Tindall.

Roberts, M. (2018) *Understanding Mental Health Care Critical Issues in Practice*. London: Sage.

Tew, J. (2011) *Social approaches to mental distress*. Basingstoke: Palgrave Macmillan.

Walker, S. (ed.) (2013) *Modern Mental Health – Critical Perspectives on Psychiatric Practice*. St Albans: Critical Publishing.

Warrener, J. (2017) *Critiquing Personality Disorder – A Social Perspective*. St Albans: Critical Publishing.

Statute

Mental Health Act 1983/2007
Human Rights Act 1998
Care Act 2014
Equality Act 2010
Mental Capacity Act 2005

Recommended Resources

www.mind.org.uk
www.rethink.org
Hood, R. (2018) *Complexity in Social Work* London: Sage.
Roberts, M. (2018) *Understanding Mental Health Care; Critical Issues in Practice* London: Sage.

13

I had a Carer's Assessment

Sue

Emma Spicer, *Social Worker*

At a glance

- This chapter focuses on the statutory intervention of having a carers' assessment under the Care Act 2014.

- Sue is a carer for both her adult son and her mother.

- Emma is a social worker in an adult locality team and was introduced to Sue as part of the process of writing this chapter. Emma provides formal knowledge underpinning this statutory intervention in the text boxes throughout the chapter and, at the end of the chapter, reflects on her learning from Sue.

About myself:

My name is Sue, I am 68 and retired from full-time employment when I was 62. I am a carer. I was born in Hertfordshire and have lived in Dorset for 40 years. My background is administration (PR, Marketing, Fundraising). I am married and have one son aged 41 years who has special needs (microcephaly) and lives in a supported living intentional community nearby. My mum is 91 and has been diagnosed with vascular dementia and Alzheimer's.

Background:

My son went to live in a supported living 'intentional community' when he was 19 years old. He is now 41 years old. We are not parents who have ever wrapped Toby in cotton wool. We have always believed that he has a life to lead and we were intent on him living it to the full, gaining as many skills as possible and enjoying as much independence, with support, that he could manage. Yes, there were risks involved; there are risks for us all in everyday life. However, supported living provided a real community setting within the wider community – a kind of safety network where he has worthwhile work and can contribute whatever skills he has to benefit the environment he calls home. Also, that he has a network of friends who support each other in their everyday lives, have a good varied social life and have the benefit of qualified support staff to help them achieve some of their hopes and dreams.

Supported living settings are designed to provide adults with support needs with a high level of flexibility and control over their support. Supported living schemes may range from single-occupancy flats to shared houses or self-sufficient communities, with tenants having access to registered care providers to help with everyday tasks such as personal care. This may mean that there has been a change in the type of care that Sue provides for her son. The caring role can involve providing support for someone in a variety of different ways, so the fact that Sue's son was in supported accommodation would not have excluded her from being eligible for carer's support.

Although our son is in a supported living environment, he does suffer from bouts of anxiety. This can be over something we would find incredibly minor but, to him, it is a serious and very real problem. Recently, moving to a more spacious room, literally just 25 yards from his previous room, caused a lot of stress and he needed constant encouragement and support from us as well as staff that all would be well and that the larger room meant that he could have the double bed he had been wanting for a while. It was so important to give him this reassurance and comfort but, nevertheless, exhausting, especially alongside dealing with a very difficult time with my mum while she was still living alone in her own home. It was difficult to make my mum realise that Toby had to be our first priority. She kind of resented this and said that Toby was okay where he was with all the others.

Mum has always had a number of health concerns, including some minor mental health issues, even when she was younger, and was very dependent on the support of my dad, who passed away 14 years ago. My relationship with my mum has never been completely 'comfortable'. I had a better connection and bond with my father. When he died, I was at his hospital bedside at the time. He asked me to promise to take care of my mum and, although I knew this would not be easy, I made him that promise. My father had always placed mum on a pedestal and, for as long as I can remember, we all tiptoed around making sure that she was happy.

After Dad's death mum remained on that pedestal and things were not so easy. Mum was not a self-motivated person and relied heavily, mainly on myself rather than my brother. She expected a lot from me and nothing ever seemed to be enough. Mum took a lot of things for granted. My brother, three years younger, had always been aloof and at a distance with both mum and dad and very much a loner who did not connect socially with any of us and always had difficulty in working with people as a team member and he always took jobs whereby he could work alone.

Gendered roles

In 2011, females were notably more likely to be unpaid carers than males; 57.7% of unpaid carers were females and 42.3% were males in England and Wales (2011 Census)

My son, who has special needs was, and still is, my and my husband's priority. At times it was difficult juggling all aspects of our family life and I often felt that we were a dysfunctional family. We moved to Dorset from Kent because mum said she would be able to help with Toby. However, we had only lived here for around 6 months when my parents moved. My mum did not drive and, at the time, I didn't have a vehicle of my own so there was very little help on offer and I felt quite isolated.

I had struggled for a number of years, since my father died, with my mum's need for care and support. This, obviously, became far greater when she was diagnosed with vascular dementia and Alzheimer's. Mum relied heavily on me taking her out for days, shopping, medical appointments etc., even though she could drive herself and had her own vehicle. I sourced all the leisure activities locally and suggested she join in with some of the age-related clubs in order to stimulate and fill her days as she got older. Also, this would encourage her to make new friends as she was always saying that 'all my friends have died, I am so alone'. Unfortunately, Mum would never do anything alone and would only agree to go to centres and clubs if I took her and sometimes even staying to join in. This was not the object of the exercise and I found this really depressing at times. I felt she was wanting too much of me and this became worse when I retired from full-time employment. There was an expectation that I would be there for her every day and when I phoned she would ask 'where are we going off to today?'. If I said I wasn't available she would say 'oh well, another day on my own I suppose'. Mum was a master of the guilt complex.

Impact on carers

Pickard et al. (2018) completed a longitudinal study with carers over a two-year period, looking at the employment status of carers. Findings suggested that carers were more likely to leave work where there was a lack of external services being provided, for example, a day centre, domiciliary care for the 'cared-for' person. This is an area that could require additional research, as a 2016 study by Carers UK found that 49% of carers had given up paid employment due to their caring role.

It became clear some five years ago that Mum needed help and support in her own home. She was forgetting to wash, dress, eat, take medication etc., and her increasing continence needs became very apparent. I sometimes wondered if this was a kind of ploy to get attention as she loved me showering her and washing her hair.

It took several social service assessments to finally get the home care package she needed in place. This struggle was frustrating and exhausting and I felt that the needs of my own family were never considered. However, when we did, this was reasonably adequate, with the addition of myself and my husband being part of the 'care team'. About two years ago it became abundantly clear that the 'package of care' was no longer adequate and Mum was no longer safe in her own home. She needed 24-hour care and there were several near misses with accidents. She also began to fall/stumble frequently and press her care line frequently which activated paramedics and hospital admissions.

The Care Act 2014 states that local authorities have the duty to provide an assessment of a person's needs before determining whether the needs are eligible. In order to have eligible needs, local authorities must consider the following three conditions:

1. Whether a carer is providing necessary care to an adult with support needs.

2. As a result of their caring responsibilities, the carer's physical or mental health is either deteriorating or is at risk of doing so or the carer is unable to achieve any of the following outcomes:

   - Carrying out any caring responsibilities the carer has for a child.

   - Providing care to other persons for whom the carer provides care.

   - Maintaining a habitable home environment in the carer's home, whether or not this is also the home of the adult needing care.

▶

◀

- Managing and maintaining nutrition.

- Developing and maintaining family or other personal relationships.

- Engaging in work, training, education or volunteering.

- Making use of necessary facilities or services in the local community, including recreational facilities or services.

- Engaging in recreational activities.

3. As a consequence of being unable to achieve these outcomes, there is, or there is likely to be, a significant impact on the carer's well-being.

Once eligibility has been determined, a local authority has a duty to work with a person or carer to identify their wishes, and how eligible needs can be met. Local authorities should give consideration to whether services could help to prevent a person or carer from needing additional support in the future.

Once appropriate support has been identified and agreed on with the person, the local authority has a legal duty to provide the person with a copy of their Care and Support plan, showing the agreed ways in which their eligible needs can be met, and whether a 'personal budget' has been agreed for the person (the cost of any services to the local authority).

The Care Act stipulates that a person's care and support plan should be 'kept under review generally'. In order to do this, social workers are often reliant on other professionals who have regular contact with a person, to share information and raise any concerns or changes in need that may warrant an unplanned review of the person's care. Multi-agency working is also a key competency for social workers and is highlighted in the British Association of Social Workers' (BASW) Professional Capabilities Framework (PCF).

Carer's assessment

It was approximately three years ago when we received the official consultant's diagnosis of vascular dementia and Alzheimer's for my mum. It was around two years ago, after a succession of meetings with social workers regarding my mum's very apparent decline in her general health and her deteriorating memory loss, that I agreed to have a carer's assessment. I had previously, on several occasions, thought this would be a waste of time. However, with Mum's increasing needs and dependence on me, I probably naively thought that having a carer's assessment would show that a more comprehensive care package for Mum was needed and that the assessment would flag up that I was finding it difficult to cope. I am sure that on a number of occasions, within various discussions with social services and the care agency, that my increasing inability to cope became a topic of conversation. I also feel that, in suggesting I do a carer's assessment, the social worker had my best interests at heart but I did rather feel cajoled into it.

Legal duty to provide a carer's assessment

Under the Care Act 2014, local authorities have a legal duty to provide a carer's assessment where it appears that a carer may be in need of support. Suggesting that care planning for a carer and the person they care for should be coordinated, in order to ensure that the needs of the carer and cared-for person are both met (Brooks et al., 2017).

The Health and Care Professions Council (HCPC) 'standards of proficiency' states that social workers should be able to work appropriately with other professionals, but that relationships with carers and clients should also be based on respect and honesty.

While local authorities have a legal duty to offer a carers assessment, the decision whether or not to have the assessment should ultimately be made by the carer.

I was informed of all the advantages of this process and that there were incentives I may wish to benefit from. I wasn't at all interested in the 'incentives' on offer (spa days, short breaks, swimming pass etc.) but, nevertheless, agreed to an assessment meeting at my home. I was assured that it was not a long process to complete the form and was very informal. It actually took around two hours. It was in no way an unpleasant experience but rather lengthy and intrusive. I was asked a number of very personal questions about my relationship with my husband which, at the time, I didn't think too much of. They were not 'awkward' just not what I was expecting. However, after the assessor left, I started to think that some of the questions seemed somewhat inappropriate and not conducive to the outcome I was expecting to receive. The outcome I was expecting and hoping for was that the assessment would give a good indication that I was struggling to cope with mum's needs alongside my other commitments and health issues, which both my husband and I were experiencing.

Carer burden

The 2016 *State of Caring* report by 'Carers UK' found that 42% of carers listed being able to take a break as a main factor that could make a difference to their lives. A carer's assessment should be used as a tool to help a carer identify their personal wishes and outcomes.

▶

◀

Carer burden is commonly recognised as 'the physical, psychological or emotional, social and financial problems that can be experienced by family members caring for impaired older adults' (George and Gwyther, 1986). This definition recognises the variety of ways in which being a carer can impact on a person, and this is reflected in the issues that Sue describes. The acknowledgement that caring can impact on a range of factors in a person's life may also explain why Sue's assessment included questions about her relationship with her husband although, in Sue's case as she pointed out, these questions may not have been as relevant.

We were both stressed, having difficulty sleeping and generally tired a lot of the time. There were daily calls from Care Line as Mum had actioned her line – paramedics were called out, GP and district nurses alerted, and all wanting intervention from me. I desperately hoped that the assessment would take on board that I was no longer able to carry on with such a huge load on my shoulders in future. I needed help to cope and the assessment did not in any way bring this to the fore. It was just a box ticking exercise. I was told by the assessor that she would take all the information she had accrued in note form that day and complete the required form. Also, that it needed to be dealt with quickly and processed so that I could benefit from the incentives on offer.

Under the Care Act 2014, a carer's assessment must consider the following:

- Whether a carer is willing and able to provide care.
- The impact of the carers needs on the well-being principles.
- The outcomes that the carer wishes to achieve in day-to-day life.
- Whether provision of support could contribute to the achievement of these outcomes.

The well-being principles cover personal dignity, physical and emotional well-being, protection from abuse and neglect, control over day-to-day life, participation in work, education, training or recreation, social and economic well-being, personal relationships, suitability of living accommodation and the individual's contribution to society.

In Sue's account she has identified how her caring role was impacting on her well-being, however, Sue did not feel that her carers' assessment reflected this. Findings from a 2016 report from the Carer's Trust, *The Care Act for Carers: One Year On*,

▶

◄

suggest that Sue is not alone in feeling like her carers assessment did not reflect her situation. The report found that 34% of carers who had had an assessment since the implementation of the Care Act found it to be 'not helpful', while 31% found the assessment to be 'partly helpful'. Both the findings from this report and Sue's experience would suggest that, although the principles of the Care Act are designed to give carers more support and rights, this continues to be something that is not consistently delivered by social workers.

When the form was sent to me for signature, and approval to go forward, a lot of the information was completely unfamiliar to me:

➤ It stated that I have no family other than my son – this is not true and we had spoken about my brother, his wife and children.

➤ It stated that I was dealing with everything on my own, when I had specifically said that Stewart, my husband, was an absolutely crucial part of our partnership but that we were both suffering because of the 'burden' laid upon us.

➤ It said that Mum had set fire to the kitchen when in fact this was prevented by intervention from me. She had placed the electric kettle on an electric hotplate but I arrived in time to prevent anything further happening.

➤ It stated that I was willing to continue providing help and support for mum. What I, in fact, said was that I was wanting to take more of a back seat for my own health and welfare but this was not mentioned.

This, and the fact that the layout was a mishmash with repetitions in wrong places, made me feel as though the whole exercise was a waste of time. It was as though it had been completed by someone unfamiliar with the layout of the form and that I was giving childlike answers and not at all articulate, which I feel I am. My desired outcomes were certainly not achieved by this process. I did not sign, nor return the form and there was never any follow up as to why. I suppose I should have contacted the assessor to make a complaint and to try to rectify the information. As I was not wholly on board about doing the assessment in the first place, I just didn't bother.

Standard 10 of the HCPC standards of proficiency highlights that social workers need to be able to keep accurate records. In Sue's case the fact that her assessment was not accurate made her feel as if she had not been listened to which may have

►

◀

resulted in the social worker missing an opportunity to provide Sue and her family with appropriate support.

Research in practice for adults (Ripfa, 2018) has worked with a range of carers and social workers to create an online resource page specifically around how best to support carers. This resource includes 'do's and don'ts' for practitioners and includes points similar to those raised by Sue, such as explaining clearly what the carers assessment is for. This resource can be found here: https://carers.ripfa.org.uk/.

After the assessment, and when I didn't get any further with it, I contacted a local voluntary agency who then arranged for a 'befriender' to visit Mum for an hour each week and just have a chat over a cuppa. This carried on for over a year and worked well. It was, in a way, the kind of thing I was hoping the carer's assessment could have recommended or arranged.

It is just a little thing but did a lot for Mum and for me knowing that someone else was visiting Mum. The 'befriender' also kept in contact with me after some visits if there were any concerns or suggestions.

Outcomes and final thoughts

Mum went into a care home recently, initially as a respite break for me to enjoy a special holiday with my husband and son over Christmas. It was as though a huge weight had been lifted from my shoulders. Of course, I felt guilty that I was unable to manage the situation any longer and some of her friends said horrid things like 'oh, my dear they have thrown you into a home have they'? – very hurtful and unnecessary considering all that I had done for many years. However, seeing Mum now as a very different person has made me realise that the right decision was made. She has made friends, enjoys all the crafts and entertainment the care home provide, has her hair and nails done regularly and is smiling when we visit. It wasn't an easy decision and there were difficult meetings and battles with social workers as to whether a care home was in Mum's best interest. There was a huge fallout with my brother who felt this wasn't a necessary step although, over the years, he had done very little towards Mum's care. Unfortunately, I rather feel that he was thinking of his inheritance and that, as Mum would be self-funding, the money from the sale of her bungalow would quickly be consumed in care home fees. My feelings were that it is her money and if the last years of her life could be made comfortable, then this was the way her money should be used.

I also needed to consider my own health issues which had become very apparent: high blood pressure, weight gain, stress levels and mood swings through not coping well.

Respite

Respite can be provided in many different ways, from a short stay in a residential home, to overnight care or day activities for the cared-for person. In a Carers UK 2017 survey, *The State of Caring*, 40% of carers said that they had not had a day off from caring for more than a year. Respite breaks can be invaluable to give carers time to have a break (both physically and mentally). A carer's assessment is a good opportunity to discuss breaks with a carer.

It is suggested that women who care for elderly parents may experience feelings of resentment towards their caring role, particularly if they have also given up other roles or identities to provide care such as giving up work (Murphy et al., 1997). When completing carer's assessments, as a social worker, it is important to be mindful of the emotional impact of caring and the change in roles that carers may experience. For carers such as Sue who support both a parent and an adult child with a learning disability, this change in roles may be particularly complex and difficult to come to terms with.

Under current legislation, local authorities are not required to provide funding support for a person if they have capital or savings over £23,250 – in this case a person would be classed as 'self-funding'. Tanner et al. (2018) identify that older people are the most likely to fund their own care, and although this can mean a wider choice of services to choose from, people who are 'self-funding' may experience difficulties in accessing and managing their own care. The Care Act places a duty to on local authorities to support 'self-funders' with identifying and accessing appropriate support, however, Tanner et al. (ibid.) suggest that this is not always successful.

At the time my husband and I felt that we were being pulled in every direction and considered ourselves very much part of the much talked about 'sandwich generation'. No, we didn't (sadly) have grandchildren and ageing parents, which is the usual description of the sandwich generation, but instead we had a 41-year-old son with learning disabilities and a 91-year-old mother with increasing needs because of her dementia and deteriorating health in general.

Although our son is in a residential supported living situation and, to all intents and purposes, settled, this is not a 'for life' situation and there is no guarantee of 'elder care' provision at present. Several of his contemporaries are experiencing first signs of dementia in their early 50s. This is of great concern to us and will be until the day we die. We can never take our eye off the ball in this case as at any stage in our son's life, if it all goes wrong, the buck stops with us!!!

Future care provision

If Sue and her husband were unable to continue providing support for their son, a review of his care provision would take place to ensure that he has sufficient support. Ryan et al. (2014) highlight the importance of future planning with parental carers of adults with a learning disability and suggest that this should be done as early on as possible.

It is entirely different with my mum's situation. She is settled in a good, care home with wonderful staff. I feel that I have done my best for my mum; that she is being looked after extremely well in her twilight years and I can actually relax with this now. I can even enjoy the odd glass of wine or light the log burner in the knowledge that I will not constantly be called out by paramedics, hospital staff etc. to attend a drama. I just wish it had not been such a struggle to get social workers to see the seriousness of the situation sooner. At the Best Interests meeting to decide whether the care home should be permanent or not, one of the managers of the care agency who provided care for Mum in her own home attended. She said that, although she/they were not allowed to get involved in anything other than the care they were providing for mum, she felt that the move to a care home or 24-hour care should have happened at least six months before it did.

My message for social workers

➢ Make sure you are all on the same wavelength as to what the carer's assessment can offer the client.

➢ Explain fully the purpose of the process.

➢ Ask what the client is expecting in the way of outcomes.

➢ Don't make the process overlong. My experience of two hours was too long.

➢ Make sure the form is completed in an articulate and adult format. No mistakes, spelling or grammar. No repetitions in incorrect columns or boxes. If you expect the client to sign the form it needs to be completed to their satisfaction.

➢ Ensure information is correct and tell the client to contact you if they have any questions or concerns about answers you have put down in writing.

➢ Follow up if the client does not sign and return the form to you for their feedback.

Social worker's reflections

Learning about Sue's story had given me the chance to reflect on the processes and assessments that we use on a day-to-day basis and how these may impact on the clients and carers that we work with. Hearing from Sue and the problems that she had with her carer's assessment has reinforced to me the need to make sure that I continue to have open and transparent conversations with carers and clients, in order to raise any issues with the assessment process as they arise. Carer's assessments are designed to support carers and prevent breakdown in the caring role and hearing Sue's story has highlighted the need to ensure that the assessment provides a genuine opportunity to discuss any issues and provide support.

References

www.ons.gov.uk/census/2011census.

www.carersuk.org/for-professionals/policy/policy-library/state-of-caring-2016.www.carersuk.org/for-professionals/policy/policy-library/state-of-caring-2017.

www.basw.co.uk/pcf/PCF10EntryLevelCapabilities.pdf.

Brooks, J., Mitchell, W. and Glendinning, C. (2017) Personalisation, personal budgets and family carers. Whose Assessment? Whose Budget? *Journal of Social Work.* 17: 2, 147–166.

Carers Trust (2016) The Care Act: One year on. Available at: carers.org/sites/default/files/care_act_one_year_on.pdf.

Carers UK (Nov 2017) 'Make connections, get support' research www.carersuk.org/for-professionals/policy/policy-library/make-connections-get-support.

George, L. K. and Gwyther, L. P. (1986) Caregiver well-being: A multidimensional examination of family caregivers of demented adults. *The Gerontologist.* 26: 3, 253–259.

Murphy, B., Schofield, H., Nankervis, J., Bloch, S., Herrman, H. and Singh, B. (1997) Women with multiple roles: The emotional impact of caring for ageing parents. *Ageing and Society, Cambridge University Press.* 17: 3, 277–291.

Pickard, L., Brimblecombe, N., King, D. and Knapp, M. (2018) Replacement care' for working carers? A longitudinal study in England, 2013–15. *Social Policy & Administration*. 52: 3, 690–709, Business Source Complete, EBSCO*host*, viewed 17 May 2018.

Ripfa (2018) Dos and don'ts for practitioners. Available at: carers.ripfa.org.uk/.

Ryan, A., Taggart, L., Truesdale-Kennedy, M. and Slevin, E. (2014) Issues in caregiving for older people with intellectual disabilities and their ageing family carers: A review and commentary. *International Journal of Older People Nursing*. 9, 217–226.

Tanner, D., Ward, L. and Ray, M. (2018) Paying our own way': Application of the capability approach to explore older people's experiences of self-funding social care. *Critical Social Policy*. 38: 2, 262–282, CINAHL Complete, EBSCO-*host*, viewed 17 May 2018.

Statute

The Care Act 2014

14

Perspectives of People Who May Lack, or Have Limited, Capacity

Margaret Parker, *Social Worker*

At a glance

- This chapter focuses on the perspectives of people with dementia who lack or have limited capacity and how this is underpinned by the Mental Capacity Act 2005.

- Margaret is an experienced social worker in adult services, currently working with people with dementia.

- In this chapter, Margaret considers a range of encounters with people whose communication is affected by their dementia and reflects on her own experiences of interpreting and acting on their needs and wishes.

About myself

I am currently the dementia lead for Tricuro, a Local Authority Trading Company wholly owned by Dorset, Bournemouth and Poole Councils. I am a qualified social worker and practice educator with over 30 years' experience in adult social care, including working for ten years with people who are living with the later stages of dementia within day services settings.

This chapter was always going to be a challenge, as how do you gain someone's voice if they are at the later stages of dementia? Right from the start it raised ethical dilemmas around someone's capacity to comment while heightening the importance of ensuring the person does have a voice. In this chapter, I explore my observations of working with both clients and carers and how, as professionals, we have to delve beneath the surface trying to unravel what the person who is living with dementia is trying to convey. What are their needs and wants? This is an enormous responsibility and it is vital that we use our skills to do the best for the individual; remembering our core principles of upholding good practice within legal frameworks and relevant policies. I shall look at particular situations and behaviours and how these unravel, trying to interpret what the person is conveying. Within the scenarios I will provide my thoughts and the challenges involved.

Informed consent

This, in itself, poses the first ethical challenge: obtaining informed consent from the individual. Where this is not possible due to the complex nature of their dementia, it is necessary to seek permission from someone working in the person's best interests, ideally someone who has power of attorney (health and welfare) or similar legal documentation. It is important to obtain an informed opinion from someone who knows the person well and what their likely preferences would be. Because the clients referred to in this chapter have not been able to give informed consent, it has been necessary to collaborate with family members. I would like to thank all of those people who have helped by sharing their thoughts and feelings, which has then enabled me to write this chapter. I have also used pseudonyms throughout. This is in keeping with ethical practice, however, even this is complex.

When writing the last part of this chapter I had to reflect on my aim of ensuring anonymity. In order to secure this for one person, I had intended to change their nationality from Italian to Spanish, however, I then contemplated as to whether this is what he would want. I knew deep down that he would want to be identified by his true nationality, as I would. This was supported by an observation of him when someone sang to him the Italian national anthem which brought him to tears. I also knew of his love of Italian food from his wife. Both of these instances suggested that his national identity was important to him. It was necessary to clarify this as he wasn't able to express his own opinion. I spoke with his wife who confirmed my thoughts that he would want to be described as Italian. We discussed an appropriate Italian pseudonym and selected one that means something to him, according to his wife. In this chapter, therefore, he is referred to as Mario.

Reflection of self – review of own beliefs

To be able to understand what may be important to a person, it is critical that we reflect on this in relation to ourselves. What would you want from a worker? What would you want them to do on your behalf if you had dementia and may not be able to express your views? What are the dilemmas? It is important to take time out as a worker and think about yourself in this situation. What is important to you?

Consider the following questions:

- How do you identify yourself?
  - what are your interests?
  - who are you?
  - what are your values, beliefs, principles and opinions?
  - what small things are important to you?
- What would you be prepared to compromise on?
  - what are your beliefs from the past?
  - where would you want to live?
  - what impact would you want to have on the people you love?
- Who would you want to speak on your behalf if you did not have capacity to make a specific decision for yourself? (best interest)

In practice, how does the social worker gain the person's voice? How do you ensure that others who contribute provide a voice in the person's best interest?

This part of the chapter is about reflecting on your own personal beliefs and how this could impact on practice. It is essential that I, too, reflect on my own personal beliefs and what dilemmas this would cause me if I had dementia and someone was speaking on my behalf to enable me to understand how it might feel.

My own thoughts and wishes

As a vegetarian for over 30 years and valuing my beliefs and principles, I explored what I would want if I was in a situation where dementia had caused me to be unclear in my beliefs. So, let's say that my dementia caused me to return to an age when I used to eat meat. What would the implications be for me and others around me? Consider the situation that I was attending a service each day where I express at lunch time I want to eat the sausage and not the nut roast which would be the vegetarian choice.

Under the Mental Capacity Act (MCA) 2005, you are required to apply the underpinning statutory principles in relation to people who may lack mental capacity to make decisions for themselves. There are five core principles which underpin the legislation. The intention is to support and enable decision-making and participation for people who may lack capacity in regard to specific decisions, and to guide the actions of those who may be making decisions in the best interest of a person who lacks capacity to do so for themselves.

Mental Capacity Act 2005 – Code of Practice

1. A person must be assumed to have capacity unless it is established that they lack capacity.

2. A person is not to be treated as unable to make a decision unless all practicable steps to help him to do so have been taken without success.

3. A person is not to be treated as unable to make a decision merely because he makes an unwise decision.

4. An act done, or decision made, under this Act for or on behalf of a person who lacks capacity must be done, or made, in his best interests.

Before the act is done, or the decision made, regard must be had as to whether the purpose for which it is needed can be as effectively achieved in a way that is less restrictive of the person's rights and freedom of action.

Using the principle relating to 'the least restrictive' way of achieving an outcome, for example, I might consider an alternative meat free option that resembles a sausage. If this does not work and I start to become distressed each time, what would others around me do? What would I do or want? It is a dilemma of choice and personal beliefs versus potential distress and upset. If every genuine attempt had been tried to uphold my beliefs but I was becoming distressed, I surprised myself by realising that I would eat the meat. This may not be true for others.

An example of this is Lucy who had been attending the day centre for several years and had always adhered to a vegetarian diet. In recent months she began exhibiting signs that she wanted to eat meat sausages, especially when the menu choice for vegetarian option was not the same as the meat eater, such as meat sausages and mash or the vegetarian option of cheese omelette. Lucy often forgot that she was vegetarian and would opt for the sausages. When reminded that she is vegetarian, she remembered and then chose the vegetarian option. However, as her dementia deteriorated, she started to take meat sausages from other people's plates. She was very matter of fact about it, being determined and was not worried about the consequences. At the time it was difficult to stop her.

Questions to consider

What could be the explanations for Lucy's behaviour? Did Lucy just want the same as others as she did not want to look different? Did she not understand the choices? What was her understanding of eating the meat, as she had not rationalised that she had taken food from people's plates? What should be done to uphold her wishes and feelings?

It was agreed to change the vegetarian option on the days there was sausage on the menu, providing a meat free vegetarian sausage. After doing this Lucy was happy to have the vegetarian sausage and she did not repeat taking the meat sausages from other people's plates.

Did this demonstrate that she wanted to be like others? Or, was it because she didn't like the vegetarian option available on that day? If this had not worked then other, less restrictive, options to consider could have been coming back to the dining room, looking at the meal options again or providing her with two vegetarian choices. While I might have views on the potential course of action, I have to be aware of whether my personal beliefs are influencing my practice. I need to make sure it is not about what I want but what the best outcome is for the person, in this case, Lucy.

Learning point – it is important to ensure that you uphold a person's beliefs and views; doing everything that you can to carry this through, while keeping an open mind on what may need to be compromised and how you balance this in your decision-making process or assessment. As a practitioner, it is important to record the rationale for decisions made in a person's best interest, if a person lacks capacity to make the specific decision for themselves. This is to ensure there is a clear understanding of the thought process influencing the decision outcome, and that this can be reviewed as people's wishes, feelings, behaviour and verbal communication can change. Reflect on your own views and principles and consider at what you would be prepared to change and compromise on if faced with dilemmas.

Your legal role

When considering a person's capacity to make decisions, you must ensure you uphold the legal framework and therefore are familiar with both the MCA 2005 and the accompanying Code of Practice. The law states the legal requirements (the 'what' element) and the Code gives direction on how the law should be applied.

The MCA 2005 applies to persons over the age of 16. The law states:

> a person lacks capacity in relation to a matter if at the material time he is unable to make a decision for himself in relation to the matter because of an impairment of, or a disturbance in the functioning of, the mind or brain. MCA 2005 Section 2(1)

The law states the impairment or disturbance may either be permanent or temporary.

Purpose of the MCA 2005

> The MCA 2005 (the Act) provides the legal framework for acting and making decisions on behalf of individuals who lack mental capacity to make particular decisions for themselves. Everyone working with, and caring for, an adult who may lack capacity to make specific decisions must comply with this Act when making decisions or acting for that person, when the person lacks capacity to make a particular decision for themselves. The same rules apply whether the decisions are life-changing events or everyday matters.

Your role as a professional is to weave together a range of legal duties set out in the MCA, the Human Rights Act 1998, the Equality Act 2010 and the Care Act 2014. This is coupled with good person-centred practice. This legislation has the common aim of supporting the ability to make decisions where possible, working in the person's best interest, enabling participation, well-being and keeping interventions focussed on the individual. We should always be working in the person's best interest and to do this it requires us to look further into who the person is.

Section 4 MCA 2005 outlines what factors determine how to interpret the term 'best interests', and the steps a practitioner must take to establish if an intended action, decision or intervention is in the person's best interests and complies with the five statutory principles.

Being aware of legal documents which authorise others to make specific decisions for individuals who may lack capacity is also important. This is vital in terms of involving and consulting other who may know the person's wishes and feelings, or have legal authority to act as a decision maker. This may be a person holding a Lasting Power of Attorney (formerly known as enduring powers of attorney), for welfare or finance, or a deputy appointed by the Court of Protection, for example. More information can be found about the office of the public guardian on http://www.gov.uk.

Professional curiosity: Being a 'reflective detective'

What does that mean? We cannot 'walk in a person shoes' but we can explore what is important to them as an individual. As a professional, it is the ability to uncover what is important in someone's life both in the past and who they are today. It is essential to gather relevant information from all sources which would include family, friends and relevant others. This is to gain a picture of who the person is.

There is a danger that the person at the later stages of dementia can be left out of this process. It is fundamental that we ensure that we gather information from the person themselves. Look at alternative ways of finding this out; becoming the 'reflective detective', means using social work skills such as observation of body language and interaction with others. It is here that you would pick up clues to be able to make an assessment, and then reflect on this assessment when you gather other information such as what the person did as a job and family history. As a 'reflective detective' you are putting together a case where new evidence comes in which helps you to identify what the person may need to meet their care and support needs. This keeps the person at the centre of the assessment and focuses on what outcomes they would want – linking to our legal duty under the Care Act 2014.

Challenges of ensuring someone with limited capacity has a voice

This can be challenging to achieve when working with someone who may not be able to express themselves verbally.

Jane is a woman who attends a day service in her late 50s and who lives at home with her husband John. She has limited verbal communication. Deterioration in her dementia has led to a reduction in her ability to walk, therefore she needs to use a wheelchair to move short distances.

When sitting, Jane can often be seen leaning forward with her hands in front of her. It could be that Jane is wanting to get up due to frustrations of being in a chair. However, when Jane does get up she can still be seen leaning forward looking like she is trying to get something lower down – this can make her unbalanced, increasing the potential risk of falling. It is unclear what she is trying to reach, touch or get to and, when seeing this behaviour, I try to identify with her what she wants. Is she trying to get something off the floor that we cannot see? Does she have visual hallucinations? Jane's response to me is with an expression of disbelief and frustration but she is unable to verbally express what it she is seeing or trying to get. This behaviour can occur at various times throughout the day with different staff trying to establish what she wants to get, seeing her frustrations and not appearing to resolve what she wants to achieve. With this behaviour it can result in staff encouraging Jane to sit down, reducing the risk of falls.

It is essential we try and explore with others where possible what may be causing this behaviour. It was during a chance conversation with Jane's daughter and her husband that we were able to unravel what might be going on. When we looked down at Jane in her wheelchair her daughter said that she keeps telling her dad not to tuck her leggings into her socks. He expressed that 'it was much easier to do that as it keep Jane neat and tidy'. At this point Jane's daughter bent down and said to her mum 'what is Dad like?', pulling her leggings out of her socks. I noted that Jane showed relief in her face. I said to Jane 'what is your husband like?' and she demonstrated an expression of agreement and rolled her eyes up. I took this expression to possibly mean that how her husband had dressed her was not what she would have chosen. After this we checked her leggings and, if John had put them into her socks, we would pull them out, with his permission. This did reduce the behaviour of Jane leaning forward trying to get something. I am sure that prior to Jane's dementia she would not have dreamed of putting her leggings in her socks. The power of clothing and the impact this can have on behaviour can never been underestimated. Often, it can be the simplest of things that has an impact on someone's behaviour. It is important to consult others in exploring what makes people behave in particular ways.

This incident of the husband dressing Jane in ways she would not have dressed herself raised the issues of the complexity of relationship changes when becoming a carer and that of the person being cared for. It can have an impact on the potential changes in a person's identity, relationships and loss of independence, which could include how people dress, spend their money and the secrets they may keep from each other, their 'guilty pleasures'. An example of this is when a male carer talked of how his wife used to love to go shopping with her friends. All he saw was the bill and, at times, noticed she had different things on. He talked of how he has discovered in the wardrobes clothes, handbags and shoes, some still with the labels on and others that he had never seen before. He talked of how she would go out shopping around Christmas and buy lots of sparkly gifts for the grandchildren and items for the house, just pure indulgence. This was something he did not get involved in and left his wife to organise.

This raises the issues of our roles in a relationship, of how the carer has to think for both people, taking on tasks they possibly never anticipated.

It is also about how the cared-for person loses the ability to contribute to their role, with the frustration of seeing someone else taking this on or not fulfilling it at all.

As a professional we have to think how we support both people in being able to navigate the dramatic changes that can occur in their relationship. How we can provide a realistic approach to them being able to continue their lives together, and meet their care and support needs? It is important that we think creatively.

As mentioned earlier it is good to reflect on ourselves and how we may behave if someone made decisions about our clothes or how our money was spent or what the house looked like and the impact this may have on us, especially if we are unable to express this verbally.

'I've got Alz, I've got Alz, Alz': Do we talk dementia?

Should we talk to someone about their dementia? This is always a controversial topic. As this heading opens with 'I've got Alz, I've got Alz, Alz', this was a conversation I had with someone.

Sue is in her early sixties with younger onset Alzheimer's with reduced ability in speaking and word finding. When Sue made the statement I responded with 'Do you mean Alzheimer's?' and she responded with a clear 'Yes.' I stated, 'It must be hard for you.' We talked about how this must affect her and she responded by nodding, dropping her shoulders and audibly sighing. I read this body language as expressing signs of relief that someone had acknowledged her situation.

Although she has limited words her body language and facial communication were very expressive. I cannot categorically say that she understood, but genuinely believed her body language demonstrated she did. I felt that she seemed calmer after this.

Another example is of Jack who has vascular dementia and Parkinson's disease. He lives at home with his wife.

Jack wanted to leave the centre and was becoming verbally aggressive. I went to speak to him and asked if he was okay. He responded back to me 'No, the doctor said I have a contagious disease.' I asked him what that was and he replied 'dementia'. I responded that it must be difficult for him, and he responded that he wanted to kill himself.

I wanted to talk to him about his dementia and how this made him feel. This had to be balanced with his condition and level of understanding. We did talk about his dementia and feelings as it was not appropriate to distract him from his real concern, which he clearly wanted to talk about. When first talking to him he was very angry and it took some time for me to calm him. The difficult part is that I want to resolve problems and make things better. The only way I could support him was to listen; we cannot always make it better but we can make a positive difference.

Learning point – ignoring someone's feelings about dementia does not mean that they then will not worry about it. It is essential that we value the person and are led by them, responding to their needs and being open about their condition. I have been surprised about people's level of understanding.

With Jack, was the anger due to not being able to leave or was it the frustration about how he feels? People's actions may not be what is causing the problem so it is important you look at what may be the cause.

Julie is living with Alzheimer's dementia and is supported in her own home by family; she attends the day service. Julie knocked at my office window, gaining my attention. When she came to the door she appeared worried. On entering the room she asked about going home, stating that she wanted to be with her family. I reassured her that she would be going home.

Usually, after being told that she would be going home later, she would be reassured for a period of time. I could see that there was something else still worrying her. So, I thought it was important to follow this up. I asked if she was okay and stated that she looked worried. She replied by saying 'it is not worth living' and talked about being tensed up and scared. I thought it was important to explore this further as she appeared to want to express her feelings about her dementia.

Using effective communication for someone who has dementia, I encouraged her to try and explain her feelings. She explained that, when she enters a room with lots of people, she is aware that they are all smiling but she does not feel this inside. The pain goes from her stomach to her head. Julie then gestured using her fist which was rotating around her stomach, stating that her 'stomach was knotting up to her head'. She said that she was 'scared out there!' Julie was looking out of the office into the main area of the building, I spent more time with Julie trying to comfort and reassure her. I thought that Julie was showing signs of distress with her dementia and she was trying to express this. This led me to consider how she could be supported with her anxieties. It made me reflect on the impact of her dementia and how this could make her feel. I was conscious that she had expressed very powerful feelings. At that point, I was not able to get to the bottom of what her worries were but she seemed happier having been able to sit and talk with someone.

Julie did not come in for a few days and we were then informed that her absence was due to her having gallstones, which causes sharp pain in the abdomen which goes up to the shoulder.

On reflection, this challenged my assessment of Julie and made me reflect on what she had been describing. Had I jumped in too quickly to the view that Julie was expressing feelings of despair from the impact of her dementia? It made me reassess my practice and the need to remember the person and the importance of reflecting on how the dementia may impact on the person's ability to express themselves, particularly with expressing physical pain.

Learning point – what this example shows is that it is vital to keep an open mind and consider all options, not becoming blinkered in an assessment by your own assumptions.

When can I go home?

This statement may be heard from someone who has dementia. The person may say this when in their own home as they have become disorientated about their age and the ability to recognise self. The home they recognise could be from a different time in their life. This could mean that, if the person living with dementia is at their current home, they may want to leave to get back to their perceived home or those they care for. Alternatively, they may not recognise why they are not at home but in a different setting. The challenge this may bring is when someone wants to leave but does not understand the implications of leaving. This, then, raises the dilemma of someone's capacity to understand the consequences of their actions.

Stella, for example, has Alzheimer's disease and is living at home with her husband. Her speech is disjointed and at times she has difficulties word finding. She attends the service to give her husband some respite to enable him to be a full-time carer.

Stella wanted to go out of the front door of the day services building; as she was going to the door she was saying her husband's name. She was unable to open the door as it is on a keypad to exit and she did not know how to operate this. Stella commented that she could not understand why she could not leave. I talked to her about her husband and that he was probably working or doing odd jobs. She looked at me and said that she still did not know why she could not leave.

When responding to a client I have to think about how to give an explanation that she understands ensuring that it is in clear statements. On this occasion, I had not explicitly stated why there was a keypad. I asked her to join me in my office so I could explain why she was unable to leave the centre. I informed her that the door was like this as some people at the centre may not know what to do if they left; at this point Stella became tearful.

I questioned myself. Was I making her feel like a prisoner or did this highlight that she may not know what to do if she went out? I had to use skills to explore what may be causing her upset without adding to her confusion. It may not be anything to do with leaving the centre, but she was clearly upset.

Stella went on to try to express her feelings but the words that she used were difficult to follow due to her dementia. However, observing Stella's body language and the intonation of her words, it appeared she was describing that she did not think she could do things any more, and she began to cry.

I felt it was important to try and explore this with her but aware this could increase her anxiety. I thought that talking about her work may be positive but was aware this could be a risk as she is no longer able to do this role. I felt she needed the opportunity to be able to express her feelings in a quiet space and time. I did not want to lead her, but could see she wanted support in trying to express herself.

I decided to keep to the positive theme of her role about how skilled she was in the job, asking if it was her job that was making her upset. She then implied with facial expression that it was. The words were out of context but flowed with her body language. She then implied that she tried to do things and it got a bit better. She then stated, 'Can't do it, can't do it.' I checked this was in relation to her work, which she confirmed. I acknowledged how difficult that must have been for her and she again responded with facial and body language that implied that was the case. I continued to talk to her in general terms and we had a drink together. She sat with me for a little longer and then went back into the other room with the others and did not return to the door.

I hope us talking about her feelings helped but I recognise how difficult this can be for someone. The challenge is about someone wanting to leave, their capacity to understand and what could be the underlying reason for wanting to go. We have to be a detective in finding out what may be happening for someone. Was it her feelings of loss, changes in circumstances or is this just my perception of how I see her?

Another situation is where someone comes to see me as I am near the main exit to the centre, wanting to know what time they go home.

Anna has mixed dementia, in her mid 70s, lives at home with her husband and attends the day service five times a week. She has been attending for over two years.

It is common for Anna to come and see me regularly through the day, asking about what time she goes home. This can happen frequently during the day and the person can ask the question and, within a minute, can ask again. When this happens I will tell her the time, which usually reassures her, and she may chat for a bit. She may ask the time again and I confirm the time and that no one stays at the centre overnight. After this, she will go back to what she is doing. However, on this occasion she sat down and went on to state 'I'm frightened.'

It is important to explore the reasons why someone wants to leave; it may not always be the reason we think. My initial thought was it was due to her being kept somewhere she did not want to be, that she may miss the transport to get home or that someone was upsetting her. I have to make sure that I get her view and not my projection of the issue.

I responded back to her 'What are you frightened about?' She went on to say 'Well it is my mum and dad (both her parents are deceased). I worry if they go. I know it is selfish but I just worry. I know I am being silly.'

I was surprised by her statement as I did not think this was her worry. I therefore thought at that point it was important that I acknowledged her worries and reassured her. I did not want to bring her to the current day as this would add another layer of upset that her parents were no longer alive and therefore the potential upset of bereavement and loss.

I responded that she was not silly and I did not think she was being selfish. She expressed that she worries when they may not be around any longer and how she will cope. We were able to talk positively about her parents – I asked what they did for work which she enjoyed talking about. This distracted her and she seemed to relax. She left the room thanking me for listening to her.

There is always a dilemma for me in getting the balance for the person living with dementia; of valuing what they say and supporting them with their reality. Validating someone's comments often enables them to settle.

Learning points from these examples:

➢ Getting to the issue for the person and not what we perceive it to be.

➢ Respond back to the person. Don't correct what they have said but, validate it.

➢ Listen to what is being said as dementia can bring up issues from the past that are unresolved, potentially revealing their deepest thoughts. The initial reasons for wanting to know what time she is going home may be more complex.

Applying law in practice

The social work role requires practitioners to be aware of when a legal process should be followed to underpin a decision or action. The example discusses the issue of preventing a person leaving a day centre. At face value this presents an ethical dilemma as the member of staff may be effectively depriving the individual of their liberty without their consent. This is where a good understanding of how to apply the MCA 2005 is vital and should underpin any decision made.

In terms of the lawful practice, Human Rights Act (HRA) 1998 Schedule 1, Article 5 (the right to liberty and security of person), it is not lawful to deprive a person of their liberty, unless it is done within a 'procedure prescribed by law'. This means a legal process must be followed. This presents a dilemma to those providing care to a person who may lack the capacity to make a decision to leave, as in this example. This means that, if the person lacks capacity to make this decision, then a decision may be made in their best interests and this would fall under the scope of Section 5 MCA 2005; demonstrating following a procedure set out in law.

It may be a valid decision to prevent a person leaving the day centre in terms of the person's safety, orientation and understanding of risk to themselves. To be lawful, however, this must be assessed through applying the MCA 2005 – a 'procedure prescribed by law'(HRA, 1998). If the person lacks capacity to make a decision to leave, then the assessment of their capacity should be documented and a best interest decision recorded to document the reasons for this. This is to demonstrate how the law has been applied in regard to this decision. In linking with the examples, this is where knowledge about the context of the person's behaviour, their relationship to the environment, their understanding and information from those who know the person is vital.

Section 5 of the MCA 2005 outlines the duties around acts done in connection with care or treatment. It is vital practitioners understand the law around this as this provides the legal basis on which decisions are made on behalf of a person lacking capacity to do this for themselves. For social workers, it is important to check these procedures are followed in order to protect and uphold the rights of individuals, and to ensure those who are providing care for people who may lack capacity to make specific decisions for themselves are applying the law in the spirit it was intended.

Amendments to the MCA 2005 under the Deprivation of Liberty Safeguards were introduced in 2007. This addressed a specific gap in the legislation affecting people who were subject to arrangements for their care which effectively deprived them of their liberty, and who were unable to provide valid consent, This applies to Registered Care Homes and hospital settings, and applies to persons over the age of 18.

Capacity to make decisions

When considering someone's capacity to make decisions, we often think these to be big life decisions, such as where to live. What can often be forgotten are the simple decisions we make on a day-to-day basis. These could have a great impact on a person's behaviour when living with dementia. It is vital that we ensure we get to know the person, enable them to make choices and what could have an impact on them. Some examples could be as follows:

➢ what music they listen to.

➢ how they like their drink made, e.g. little milk, strong, a particular mug or cup.

➢ someone going with them to the toilet.

➢ who they sit with.

➢ being in a group or sitting on their own.

The list is endless but the impact of getting this wrong can lead to the demonstration of behaviour that could otherwise be prevented. It is, therefore, important as a social worker that we record and pass on this information to relevant others to prevent the simple decisions being missed and becoming big issues. For this very reason, our statutory responsibility is to ensure that this is included in our assessment process.

What is involved in assessing a person's capacity to make a decision?

Assessing a person's capacity to make a decision is decision-specific and must take account of the five principles outlined earlier in the chapter. This is particularly important in terms of evidencing that the person has been given all appropriate support to make the decision for themselves in line with the statutory principles.

It is important to be able to apply the law, however, a good starting point could be to apply it to every day decision-making – a process we often do automatically. Start by thinking of a decision you may have made today and questioning what process is involved in making a decision?

You need to know:

• What information might I need to make the decision?

• Is it provided in a format I can understand?

• Do I need some support to make the decision?

• Does a decision need to be made right now?

▶

◄

- Is now the best time?

- What factors might I need to weigh up in making this decision?

- Am I aware of the potential consequences of the decision? (the risks and benefits)

Section 3 MCA 2005 states that a person is unable to make a decision for themselves if:

1. They are not able to understand information relevant to the decision to be made.

2. They are unable to retain that information.

3. They are unable to use of weigh the information as part of the decision-making process.

4. They are unable to communicate their decision (by talking, or using any other means of communication)

When speaking with one client who was getting verbally upset, I asked her if she did not like the music, which was contemporary. Her response back was: 'It is not the music I don't like, but the silly skipping dancing.'

I had presumed that as a woman in her nineties she would not like this type of music when, in fact, it was the behaviour of someone dancing. It is not to say that you can know what everyone likes or dislikes but it is important to try and find out what may give a strong reaction which could be prevented and not presuming it is the person's dementia, but their personality.

With this in mind, it is again important to look at ourselves and what would have an impact on our behaviour if we were living with dementia.

Why bother? – Message to social workers

We owe due regard to those we work with. When providing an assessment and ultimately a package of care we need to be confident that we have considered all relevant options with the person at the core. This is paramount when the person may not be able to verbally express their preferences. We need to access the fundamental tools of positive social work practice in line with the Professional Capabilities Framework for social work. When the psychiatrist Alois Alzheimer worked with Auguste D back in 1901, he recorded her comments about her condition when she repeatedly stated, 'I have lost myself.' Over 100 years on we are still unravelling the impact of Alzheimer's and dementia on a person and how we can improve the person's life, together with those around them (Ryan et al., 2015). My advice is, do not give up in exploring the best outcome for the person.

In my experience as a social worker, I consider it essential that we include the following in our practice:

➤ effective communication.

➤ being a 'reflective detective'.

➤ looking at solutions creatively.

➤ balancing being person-centred with a holistic approach.

➤ focusing on prevention.

➤ incorporating carers views and support.

➤ working with relevant others.

➤ giving consideration to what the person with lived experience has to say.

Finally, as this chapter is about the voice of the person with the lived experience, coupled with the complexities of meeting their needs, I thought it was powerful to end on a heart-warming example which exemplifies why we all do this job.

Mario is Italian and has lived in England for 50 years; he is 80, married and once owned his own business. Mario used to speak fluent English. With his dementia deteriorating his use of English has reduced dramatically, with him mainly speaking in Italian.

I was working in my office alone on the computer when Mario came in and sat down. He pulled the chair, coming closer towards the desk where I was sitting. He initially just looked at me with a slight sigh. I greeted him, smiling, and asked if he was okay; he patted me on the arm and said, 'It is very good, you all do good, it is not easy but it is good, you do the best.'

I said, 'oh, thank you Mario, it is good to have you here with us.' He smiled and said earnestly 'you all do good, I am thanking you, it is not easy'.

He then got up from the chair touched the top of my arm and pointed at the computer and said something in Italian which I could not understand but assumed he may be indicating he would leave now so I could finish my work. I smiled at him again and said, 'see you soon' and he nodded towards me as he left the room.

This was so powerful. His comments were verbally clear in English and with true conviction. It highlighted how people with dementia have insight and want to voice their thanks.

Later on in the day, Mario went up to a student and sat with her at the table with one other person. This time the words he spoke took a little longer to say as it appeared he was thinking in Italian and then translating it in English. He initially started the conversation in English talking about his wife being at home. He again expressed that he felt that everyone was trying their best for him and then thanking us. When saying this statement, he touched the student on her arm, with an expression of warmth and kindness. He then said to the student 'you need to be safe with money and who you give it to'.

It could be that we were seeing the person how they were prior to their dementia, providing thanks and guidance to someone younger than him. It struck me that we must also allow others to express their thanks, valuing them and what they say and remembering who they are, the whole person and not just the person with dementia.

It makes me never underestimate the power of humans, their insight and the importance of what they can contribute.

My final message is: make sure you see the person first.

References

(2005) Mental Capacity Act: Code of Practice: Crown Copyright Third Impression 2007. London: TSO. Available at: assets.publishing.service.gov.uk/government/uploads/system/uploads/attachment_data/file/497253/Mental-capacity-act-code-of-practice.pdf.

Ryan, N. S., Rossor, M. N. and Fox, N. C. (2015) Alzheimer's disease in the 100 years since Alzheimer's death. *BRAIN: A Journal of Neurology*. 138: 12, 1 December 2015, 3816–3821. Available at: doi.org/10.1093/brain/awv316.

SCIE 2016 Guide to the Mental Capacity Act. Available at: www.scie.org.uk/files/mca/directory/guide-to-the-mental-capacity-act-for-people-caring-for-someone-with-dementia-sitra-2016.pdf?res=true.

Statute

Care Act 2014
Equality Act 2010
Human Rights Act 1998
Mental Capacity Act 2005

15

Incorporating the Lived Experience into Our Everyday Practice

Mel Hughes

The aim of this chapter is to build on the learning achieved by reading the chapters so far and to explore how, and why, you might seek to incorporate learning from people with lived experience into your social work practice. Students often identify that they understand the importance of collaborating with people with lived experience, but are not always sure how to do this, particularly within the constraints of statutory social work where power imbalances are particularly evident. This chapter will draw on evidence within the wider literature of service user participation and involvement in social work practice as well as the experiences of those shared in this book. We explore what involvement and participation in practice looks like; the challenges you may encounter; and suggestions and recommendations from student social workers.

Understanding the complexities of involvement

In the Introduction to this book and in Chapter 1, we identified the requirements and evidence for involving service users and carers in your learning and personal and professional development as a social work student. Involving people with lived experience is now well established in social work education due to increasing recognition of people with lived experience as experts. Service user and carer expertise is clearly demonstrated in Chapters 3–14 of this book. Those with lived experience have shared significant insights and knowledge of statutory interventions from their perspective. Reading about these insights and experiences can enhance our own knowledge and understanding. It can act as a catalyst for our own learning and reflections and as a basis from which to explore and critique wider research, policy and practice.

In addition to social work education, expectations and requirements for service user and carer involvement and participation have

223

also increased in social work practice. The British Association of Social Workers (BASW) Code of Ethics for social workers, for example, specifically identifies the right to participation as one of five ethical principles within the codes. They state that 'social workers should respect, promote and support the full involvement and participation of people using their services in ways that enable them to be empowered in all aspects of decisions and actions affecting their lives' (BASW, 2012). The United Nations Convention on the Rights of the Child, Article 12, identifies the right of the child to have their views respected; to say what they think should happen and to have their opinions taken into account. Similar statements are reflected across government strategy documents informing social care with a range of groups. In the Professional Capabilities Framework (PCF) at the Assessed and Supported Year in Employment (ASYE) level, under the values and ethics domain, you are required to 'demonstrate respectful partnership work with service users and carers, eliciting and respecting their needs and views, and promoting their participation in decision making wherever possible' (ibid.).

The benefits of user participation in social work practice have been explored in a number of research studies. In Australia, Head (2011) identified three main rationales for involving young people in the development and delivery of children's services. First, because they have a right to be involved and consulted; second, that services can only improve when young people's views and interests are well represented and third, the benefits resulting from involvement to the individuals themselves and society as a whole. Whiteford (2011) in a study exploring the involvement of rough sleepers in the development of policies and service provision, drew similar conclusions. In addition to users' right to create their own solutions to homelessness, the study identified how practitioners and services benefitted from their expertise and perspectives when homeless people were involved in shaping services. Whiteford concluded that increasing involvement challenged paternalistic views of homelessness where rough sleepers in particular were seen as irresponsible and anti-social. He argues that this creates opportunities for us to 'reactivate the interpersonal aspects of social work in order to support homeless people' (Whiteford, 2011, p. 55). Evident across these studies is that effective user involvement improves the quality of the professional relationship and the potential for improving outcomes for the individual and others.

Despite this strong evidence base and policy requirements to involve service users and carers in decisions about their lives and in reshaping services, there is concern that it remains at a tokenistic level. It is important in this chapter for us to give some thought as to why this might be so we can identify best practice in overcoming these challenges in our own practice.

Consideration of the context

Requirements for user involvement in social work practice are as a result of shifts in thinking about the role of social work more broadly. McLaughlin (2009) suggests that shifts in terminology since the 1970s reflect the changing relationship between commissioners and providers of services and the recipients of those services. He argues that changes in terminology reflect the perceived shifts in power from 'client' which was perceived as a passive role, to customer or consumer where welfare was viewed as a commodity with the need for services to be more 'customer focused' with 'consumers' able to 'exercise choice' (ibid., p. 1104). This led to requirements for the 'consumer' to have a say about the service(s) they received and have opportunities for influencing broader service design and delivery at a strategic level. Increased emphasis was placed on the need for service users and carers to be listened to.

Activity

Have you had the opportunity to receive feedback from service users and carers while on placement or in a work setting? What was your reaction? Have you been able to learn from the feedback or did you find yourself becoming defensive? While on placement, it is important be proactive in seeking feedback and encouraging people who use services to feel confident that that this will be listened to. You can also seek out the opinions of people on their experience of social workers. If on placement, try identifying five people with lived experience who would be interested in meeting with you to discuss their experience of social workers and what, as a student, you can learn from them.

There are concerns that involvement has had limited impact on service delivery. In some instances, involving service users and carers in practice decisions can be viewed by practitioners as a threat. In a study into the impact of service user involvement in social work education on subsequent practice (Hughes, 2017), a newly qualified social worker (NQSW) identified that she had viewed the process of seeking feedback as a way of service users and supervisors criticising her. Since actively engaging in different approaches to involvement and participation, she was able to challenge her misconceptions and recognise the expertise of those with lived experience and the value of using this to inform her developing practice and improve outcomes for those she was working with.

The example of the student feeling fearful of seeking feedback is not an isolated example. Davies et al. (2014) argue that a move to a consumerist model of social work led to consumerist notions of participation. Involvement is viewed as the right for service users to exercise choice over services received; and to provide feedback or to make complaints about the standard of care. Davies et al. (ibid.) argue that such approaches have little impact on participation at a structural level or in reshaping services. Consumer engagement of this kind may be of benefit to those with the confidence and resources to engage but can marginalise those who are at their most vulnerable and don't currently have the means to 'actively consume' (ibid., p. 126). They advocate for a shift to a more collective social justice model of participation which seeks to highlight ways in which people are 'prevented from taking part in the full spectrum of opportunities available to members of mainstream society' (ibid., p. 125) and refer to Fraser's (2008a) model of 'parity of participation' where participation is extended to issues of 'access to economic, social, cultural and political opportunities'. All service users have a right to participate and gain full citizenship status and should be supported to do so.

A common form of involvement at a strategic level is through service user or carer representatives on committees or decision-making panels. In your practice setting, you may be aware of user representatives or ambassadors. Davies et al. (2014) however, are critical of individuals representing their 'peers' as this assumes a shared identity, for example, as a mental health service user. They argue that this minimises multiple identities and complex experiences and the diversity within a community of people. Participants in their study said that a simplified and imposed identity led to misunderstandings of their skills, capacities, interests and preferences. Participants identified that they wanted 'a more tangible role in the problem-solving process' (ibid., p. 126). Whiteford (2011) considers the involvement of marginalised and socially excluded service users (in his case, rough sleepers) and the need to be creative with how we enable people to influence decisions which directly affect them. He argues that this involves creating 'the conditions in which a new sense of personal worth, solidarity and belonging can begin to flourish' (ibid., p. 52).

In relation to your own practice, it involves recognising that genuine and meaningful service user and carer involvement goes beyond seeking feedback on your own practice and involves engaging and supporting people to influence service design and delivery. Involving service users and carers and drawing on their expertise in ways which lead to improved outcomes for all, involves adopting a range of approaches to engaging people at different levels. In particular, meaningful involvement requires a mindset which views people with lived experience as experts from which practitioners and service providers can learn.

Gallagher et al. (2012) explain that involvement in social work practice needs to be at whatever level of involvement the individual can achieve. To use this book as an example, the process of writing each chapter was adapted for each contributor. Some took the lead for writing their chapter and advising on content; others were audio recorded to provide their narrative or interviewed over a number of sessions. In the case of Chapter 14, where participants lacked capacity, Margaret Parker reflected on the meaning of interactions and different ways of communicating and discussed these with colleagues and each person's family. They participated in different ways but their contributions are of equal value.

There remains a disparity between the policy requirements for involvement to be embedded and how it is experienced by service users and carers. Looking back to the narratives shared in this book, many of the contributors described experiences where they had not felt listened to and had not had the opportunity to be fully involved in decisions about their lives. This is despite numerous policies requiring this to happen.

Gallagher et al. (ibid.) review the literature on children's and parents' involvement in social work decision-making and found similar results. Despite clear policy requirements to work in partnership, they found that, in practice, participation 'tends to be more messy, difficult and compromised than the policy rhetoric tends to suggest' (ibid., p. 75). The situation is not unique to UK based social work. Darlington et al. (2010) who interviewed 28 child and family welfare practitioners in Australia identified the complex nature of involving parents where children's safety and well-being was at risk and where there may be conflicts between the goal of participation and the duty to protect. Social workers valued participatory practices and recognised this as central to achieving positive outcomes for children but identified parent-related factors such as limited cooperation and insight as barriers. A study in South Estonia, however, identified differing perspectives from parents, children and practitioners in children's services with practitioners identifying reluctance and self-defence from the parents as a barrier and parents identifying deficit-based, dismissive, hostile and distrustful attitudes from the practitioners (Arbeiter and Toros, 2017). This exemplifies the importance of a trusting relationship for any meaningful involvement to occur.

Involvement and participation, whether at an individual or strategic level, needs to have an impact and lead to tangible changes and improved outcomes to avoid being viewed by participants as tokenistic. Leung (2011) found that 'both a service providers' genuine belief in the primacy of the user's voice and a user's legitimate claim of experiential knowledge are imperative to realising the potential of client participation' (ibid., p. 43). In his study in Hong Kong, he identified that social workers gave more legitimacy to the contributions made by older and disabled people who were viewed as 'deserving' than they did to users of family centres, ex-offenders and children in care. This may have been a factor in the findings reported above by Darlington et al. (2010) where social workers identified limited parental cooperation as a barrier to meaningful involvement. Smith et al. (2012), for example, argue that with involuntary service users, meaningful involvement is best achieved through effective communication, relevant information and more direct, relational social work with time to develop trust. These were all factors in the positive experiences identified by contributors to this book. Smith et al. (ibid.) argue that this is challenged by limited time and resources social workers have access to and by the influence of managerial processes which focus more on performance management and accountability, than on supporting relationship building.

In terms of involvement at a strategic level, Goodwin and Young (2013) advocate the need for 'bottom-up' community development initiatives to be used. They recommend this as a way of seeking out the perspectives of children, young people and other marginalised groups and of empowering community members. These are congruent with the social justice models of participation and involvement previously mentioned by Davies et al. (2014) and Whiteford (2011). Users have a right to inform decisions which affect them and achieving this involves placing users at the heart of service design and delivery.

What these approaches demonstrate is the significant influence we have as social workers in our commitment to finding meaningful approaches to involvement and in ensuring that we find ways of acting on what we learn. What many of the contributors in this book identified was that it wasn't always about *what* the social worker did, but *how* they did it. Particularly evident was the impact of social work involvement on people's lives and the significant and positive impact social workers and others can have even in the short term. As Jennifer Bigmore mentions in Chapter 3, even when our involvement is brief, we become part of that person's history. This highlights the responsibility we have as practitioners to manage this impact well.

One way of ensuring that people are involved in decisions about their lives and in reshaping services, is to manage expectations about what this means. There can be different perceptions of what involvement and participation is and what impact it should have. Gallagher et al. (2012) highlight a study by McLeod (2006) which showed that despite the best efforts of social workers to listen to children and enable their participation, few young people felt their views had been heard. The social workers viewed listening to enable participation as 'a receptive attitude involving respect, openness and attentiveness' (ibid., p. 75) whereas the young people in the study wanted what they had said to influence actions. McLeod concluded that the young people sought autonomy, self-determination and empowerment, whereas the social workers emphasised respect and empathy. Research into this field has identified a distinction between seeking involvement and actually acting on it (Leung et al., 2011; Smith et al., 2012). Consultation in itself is not enough (Gallagher et al., 2012).

Meaningful involvement requires an openness to making changes and acting on the expertise of those with lived experience. In your own practice, it is important to engage with service users and carers not only to learn about their experience and views but also to being open to listening to; learning from; and acting on what they have to say. You will only do this if you value their expertise.

Activity

As you reflect on your learning from reading the chapters in this book, it is essential that you give thought to how you might learn from the contributors' experiences to improve your own practice. How will you act on what you have learnt? Before moving on with this chapter, are you able to identify:

- What you have learnt from the experiences you have read about in this book.

- What messages you will take away.

- What you will do differently as a result.

- What steps you can take to ensure that what you have heard or read makes a difference at a service delivery level.

Take a moment to write these down or to look back on any notes that you made while reading the book.

Incorporating involvement into our everyday practice

In terms of how we go about involving service users and carers in social work practice and valuing and acting on their expertise, Smith et al. (2012), Gallagher et al. (2012) and Whiteford (2011) emphasise the importance of everyday encounters, particularly for involving involuntary service users or seldom heard users such as disabled children and marginalised groups such as rough sleepers. Gallagher et al. (ibid.) suggest three key areas where meaningful involvement can be achieved:

➢ good relationships;

➢ information and communication; and

➢ support to participate.

The remainder of this chapter will focus on suggestions from the contributors and our own experiences for creating these opportunities and embedding these into your everyday practice.

Ways of incorporating the lived experience into your everyday practice:

Meet with community groups and organisations

How?:   Explain who you are (student social worker, NQSW, local social worker) and that you are keen to learn more about your local community. Engage in dialogue and discussion – show curiosity, ask them to identify any specific issues affecting their community and check out opinions and experiences of social work and social care.

Why?:   The aim is to broaden your awareness and understanding and to recognise the diversity of experiences and views. It can help to break down barriers – lead you to develop networks and contacts and ultimately to develop knowledge that will better inform your assessments. Significantly, it will create opportunities for people to have a voice and inform social work practice. What is important is that you go to them.

Familiarise yourself with online resources relevant to the community and population your team serves

How?:   Go online and read contributions to different websites such as discussion forums, charitable organisations and campaign groups.

Why?:   Accessing different forums and websites will introduce you to perspectives you may not be aware of. Doing so can enable you to challenge your taken-for-granted beliefs or cultural norms and to deepen your understanding and expertise.

Discuss with family and friends

How?:   Ask a range of people what their views and experiences are of the service user group you are working with.

Why?:   You may find that you can learn from their experience and expertise. In some cases, it may be that they have lived experience from which you can learn. It can also enable you to recognise generalisations, preconceptions, judgements and stereotypes which may exist which you can then reflect on and challenge. As part of this process, you can reflect on your own beliefs and of how those of your friends and family have influenced these.

Draw on your own lived experience

How?:   Consider your own life experiences and multiple and complex identities. What makes you, you?

Why?:   When discussing the service user–social work relationship, we can unintentionally create a 'them and us' dichotomy. There is a risk that we oversimplify our identities by viewing a person only as a social worker or service user. Identity and life experience is more complex than this. It may be that you have a mental health issue, a disability, are a carer or have had social work involvement in your life as well as being a social worker or social work student. It is important to recognise how your personal experiences affect your professional role. For example, how your own life experiences inform your values and view of the world. Our own life experiences can both help and hinder our social work practice.

Read widely to gain insights into personal experiences and perspectives

How?:   Try reading autobiographies written by people with complex experiences of mental health, substance use, dementia or long-term health conditions; or fictional texts where these themes form the basis of the story.

Why?:   We rarely have the opportunity to gain a rich and detailed insight into a person's long and complex history. Reading an autobiography or well-researched story enables us to reflect on a person's experiences and perceptions and gain insight into the lived experience over a long period of time. As with this book, it should not be seen as a representation of any experience other than their own, written from their particular standpoint, but it can provide rich insights into lived experience from which to reflect.

Make time to learn about the service user or carer you are working with

How?:   When you meet with individuals, families and groups as part of an assessment or meeting incorporate questions which enable you to seek a better understanding and appreciation of who the person is and what is important to them beyond the questions required on the form. If they mention a particular religious or cultural identity or heritage, ask them about it. 'Tell me about that, what does that mean for you?' If they have a particular diagnosis – ask them how that affects them. If they refer to family, friends or a local community, hobbies or interests – show curiosity and ask about it.

Why?:   A key theme throughout this book and chapter has been on establishing a relationship and building trust and rapport. Enabling someone to open up and share their thoughts and feelings with you will enable you to gain a better understanding. It will lead to a more accurate assessment of their needs and will actively involve them in identifying responses and solutions to those needs.

Give people space to talk

How?:   When engaging with service users and carers, whether in a one-to-one, group, formal or informal setting, if you can see that they are thinking, be silent. Listen and respond to what they have said. Put your paperwork down and engage in a conversation.

Why?:   In contemporary social work practice, we can often feel rushed and restricted by heavy workloads, deadlines and the demands of a particular form or assessment framework. There are different models and approaches, however, that you can draw on to ensure that you intervene more effectively, even in limited time frames. It might take a little longer but can be a more productive use of time if it improves the likelihood of achieving better outcomes. The exchange model of assessment, person-centred practice, relationship-based social work are all effective models for engaging in dialogue and developing a more equal relationship.

Discuss with your supervisors what mechanisms are in place to support people to influence service development and delivery

How?:   Speak to your supervisors or manager on placement; identify good practice; visit forums or meet with service user representatives or ambassadors, if they exist, in your organisation; speak to as wide a range of people as possible so as to identify different views and perspectives; create opportunities for service users and carers to be involved in strategic decision-making.

Why?:   As explained in this chapter, people have a right to be involved in shaping services and both the service and the service user will benefit from doing so, if adequately supported. Sometimes you need to influence the culture of a team if this is not part of their day to day practice.

Suggestions from social work students

The following examples have been provided by four social work students undertaking a 100-day final substantive placement in local authority social work teams:

Lauren Phillips: Local authority leaving care team

In my opinion, it is important to understand that learning from service users' lived experiences is not achieved through formal assessments, however informative you may think you find these. Even when we think we are learning in an informal way, if we are searching for specific answers and have an agenda, we are at risk of creating a power imbalance that fails to recognise service users as the experts of their experiences. My placement helped me develop an understanding that young people in care are so often asked to talk about their experiences, lives and feelings that it can become meaningless to them – one young person expressed to me that 'social workers are paid to care'. I have been able to consciously question why a young person would want to share deeply personal experiences with someone they feel has no genuine interest in, or regard for, them. For this reason, I have taken the opportunity to adopt a creative approach to the direct work opportunities I have had with young people and ensure I tailor this towards their needs and interests. I have prioritised building rapport with young people and this progressive relationship-based approach has created natural opportunities for them to share their experiences.

One young person I worked with had a creative, artistic flair – she studied art and design at college and enjoyed creative writing courses. In direct work, I recognised this as a meaningful way for her to express herself. I attended a local exhibition of her artwork and enjoyed looking through her coursework with her. When talking about sensitive issues, such as her disclosure that her stepfather had sexually abused her, I asked her to write or draw how she was feeling. One engagement that was particularly poignant in learning from her experiences followed my introduction to a poem template that centred around the writer expressing what makes them the person they are today; with each line beginning with the phrase: 'I come from.' Presenting this as an activity to the young person appealed to her preferred means of self-expression and reading her poem gave me a unique and powerful insight into her experiences.

It is not only important to learn from service users' lived experiences but also to act on this for it to be truly meaningful. Through direct work with another young person, I gained an understanding of the difficulties she faced as a young mother who felt that she was not welcomed by others in services designed to support mothers and babies due to the fact she was a care leaver and comes from a travelling community. In response to this, I encouraged her to consider her capability, with support, to organise her own mother and baby group specifically aimed at care leavers with children to counteract the exclusion she, and likely others in the same position, felt. We then worked together to plan it.

Lisa Wilms: Children's social services

For me, attending a 'participation people day' for looked after children was a fantastic experience. I was able to listen to a lot of feedback from the children who are looked after by the local authority. One really important piece of information I took away from the day was that, while we as professionals may feel we have found stability for a child in a fostering placement, it is crucial we know their feelings, and regularly check in with them. A child fed back to me she had spent two years in a placement dreadfully unhappy, continually treated differently from the foster carers birth children, and never asked her feelings or wishes. All the children expressed that they really wanted to be listened to. Because of this, after researching direct work, I introduced an interactive app I have found, called *My Three Houses* to the 0–12 Care and Support team (working with looked after children aged 0–12). The app explicitly gains the current views, feelings and wishes of the child; the app is very current, engaging, easy to use; and, best of all, free. This has now been approved to be integrated and used within the local authority as a direct work tool with children. I have used the tool successfully several times, and have disseminated my learning of the *My Three Houses* app by delivering a short presentation to the team where I am completing my placement as well as to another children's team and the corporal parenting officer.

Laura Budden: Adult locality long-term conditions team

One of the key areas that I had identified as a potential learning opportunity was through accessing external settings, one of which included attending support and carer groups. Having spent time speaking with carers and service users, I have had the chance to discuss with them some of the views they have on what makes a good social worker. I have learnt that honesty, transparency and open communication is extremely valuable to them.

Through building a rapport with some of the carers at the group, I have been able to gain a real insight into their perspectives and experiences. By attending carer groups I have been able to further develop my empathy, which has helped me massively. By having this understanding, I have been able to put myself in their shoes, which has enabled me to really hear what I am being told when completing carer assessments.

In addition, I found that through my role as a student I have been able to spend more time with service users than some of the other practitioners in my team. I found that while no two referrals were the same there have been shared experiences; such as the fact that for those carers whose loved ones have dementia or adults who received a dementia diagnosis there was a shared sense of grief for the loss of the relationship they once had or for the loss of the person they once were.

When considering the perspectives provided to me through assessments compared to the more candid responses offered within service user forums and carer groups, I have found that this perception has provided me with awareness that sometimes the picture of the lives painted during an assessment environment is not always a true reflection. This has been one of the biggest barriers that I have come across in my learning and so I have had to rely heavily on my ability to read body language as well as the need to utilise my informal knowledge and skills to gain a sense of what is really being said.

Jennifer Ross: Children's social services

My biggest challenge has been to recognise how easily I can be drawn into decisions that benefit the needs of the service, instead of the needs of the young person. A good example of this was the time I was tasked to complete life-story work, using case notes on a young person I had not met, within two weeks. The objective of life-story work is to create a visual base for children and young people to explore their past, present and future. The work should be completed with the service user, enabling them to integrate their previous experiences into their present day lives.

While I acknowledge structural restrictions such as funding and time, I do not believe these should influence the quality of work completed with a young person. Any intervention should benefit the service user and should not be completed simply to benefit the agency statistics.

This is inextricably linked to the social work values (set out in the Code of Ethics), as well as my own.

As a student I felt significantly apprehensive to challenge this decision. However, by utilising services such as Action for Children, Children and Adolescent Mental Health Services (CAMHS), and using the local authority's guidance on life-story work, I was able to successfully challenge this decision and ascertain management agreement that the work would be commissioned out to a specialist therapeutic worker.

In various other situations, I have found that by working in partnership with young people, we have been able to explore alternative responses to disempowering situations. Often this involves advocating the views of the person during every meeting and assessment procedure. To add weight to this approach, I have often included the views of other professionals when appropriate. I have learned that by consistently involving the person (e.g. sending a text) in all my work, this empowers them to assume a more participatory role in decisions.

I recently had the privilege to help develop activity days for young people in care. This provided young people with the opportunity to engage with others who are experiencing similar challenges. This also allowed the opportunity for informal conversations about their views of being a child in care and what qualities they would like in a social worker. The overwhelming majority agreed they would like to be listened to and for their views to make a difference to their lives.

Conclusion

Throughout this chapter we have considered the requirements for promoting and supporting the involvement and participation of people with lived experience in social work design and delivery at a personal and strategic level. Considering some of the challenges involved has enabled us to recognise that in practice, this can be messy and challenging. There are some key themes however which are evident in the wider literature and the suggestions made from social work students; that is the need to develop relationships which are based on mutual respect. This is particularly the case when seeking to engage unwilling service users who have as much of a right as anyone to be involved in shaping services and informing decisions which directly affect them, but often less opportunity, to have their voice heard. Finding the time to develop relationships is a challenge within the constraints of statutory social work practice but as the suggestions make clear; doing so, can significantly improve the quality of the assessment and the outcomes for all involved.

References

Arbeiter, E. and Toros, K. (2017) Participatory discourse: Engagement in the context of child protection assessment practises from the perspective of child protection workers, parents and children. *Children and Youth Services Review.* 74, pp. 17–27.

British Association of Social Work (BASW) (2012) The Code of Ethics for Social Work. Available at: www.basw.co.uk/codeofethics.

Darlington, Y., Healy, K. and Feeney, A. (2010) Challenges in implementing participatory practice in child protection: A contingency approach. *Children and Youth Services Review.* 32, 1020–1027.

Davies, K., Gray, M. and Webb, S. A. (2014) Putting parity into service user participation: An integrated model of social justice. *International Journal of Social Welfare.* 23, 119–127.

Gallagher, M., Smith, M., Hardy, M. and Wilkinson, H. (2012) Children and families' involvement in social work decision making. *Children and Society.* 26, 74–85.

Goodwin, S. and Young, A. (2013) Ensuring children and young people have a voice in neighbourhood community development. *Australian Social Work.* 66: 3, 344–357.

Head, B. W. (2011) Why not ask them? Mapping and promoting youth participation. *Children and Youth Services Review.* 33, 541–547.

Hughes, M. (2016) What Difference Does it Make? Findings of an impact study of service user and carer involvement in social work students' subsequent practice. *Journal of Social Work Education.* Available at: www.tandfonline.com/eprint/qeHqywW5IgE6IFsfMred/full.

Leung, T. T. F. (2011) Client participation in managing social work service: An unfinished quest. *Social Work.* 36: 1, 43–52.

McLaughlin, H (2009) What's in a Name: 'Client', 'Patient', 'Customer', 'Consumer', 'Expert by Experience', 'Service User'—What's Next? *The British Journal of Social Work,* 39: 6, 1 September 2009, 1101–1117. Available at: doi.org/10.1093/bjsw/bcm155.

Smith, M., Gallagher, M., Wosu, J. S., Cree, V., Hunter, S., Evans, S., Montgomery, C., Holiday, S. and Wilkinson, H. (2012) Engaging with involuntary service users in social work: The findings from a knowledge exchange project. *British Journal of Social Work.* 42, 1460–1477.

Whiteford, M. (2011) Square pegs, round holes: Rough sleeping and service user involvement? *Practice.* 23: 1, 45–58.

CONCLUSION

Mel Hughes

Overview of the book

Throughout the book we have sought to give a voice to people with lived experience of statutory social work interventions. The purpose has been to acknowledge the expertise that people with first-hand experience have in contributing knowledge which can help improve our practice; inform decisions about their lives; reshape and develop services; and improve outcomes for others. While there has been a strong ethical and value base to the contributions, the purpose goes beyond involvement just feeling like the right thing to do. Service users and carers are experts by experience and, to deny them a voice in contributing to our understanding and in deciding outcomes, fails to fully understand their needs and expertise. In Chapter 15, I refer to Head's (2011) rationale regarding the benefits of involving young people in social work practice. We can apply these three principles to consideration of involvement for all. Service users and carers have a right to be involved and consulted – services can only improve when people's views and interests are well represented and involvement has significant benefits for individuals themselves and society as a whole.

In Chapter 1, the principles of involvement were applied to your learning in your social work education. Learning from the expertise of service users and carers and engaging in dialogue with people with experience of social work is an essential part of your education and we explored evidence of how it can benefit you in a wide range of ways. Service user involvement can challenge your views of the world; develop your knowledge; improve your practice and the outcomes for others; and provide opportunities for you to develop your emotional resilience.

In Chapter 2, Richard Murphy introduced the legal framework for statutory social work interventions, many of which were then explored in the subsequent chapters. Students often perceive legislation to be clear cut and set in stone but Richard's chapter explains how law can be interpreted in different ways. He stresses the importance of case law in determining how this should be enacted in practice. Enacting legislation can be messy and having a good understanding of the legal framework in which we operate is an important part of social work practice so you can identify what your own roles and responsibilities are.

In Chapters 3–14, you were given the opportunity to immerse yourself in someone's lived experience. The stories are powerful reminders of the impact we, as social workers, can have on a person's life and the risks and complexities involved. There are examples of social work involvement being perceived as both positive and negative. There are no clear-cut solutions in social work, despite the range of policies and procedures seeking to make it so. Social work is based on our ability to reach an informed, evidenced based judgement; the need for which is made clear by both Munro (2011) and Laming (2003, 2009) in the inquiries following the deaths of Victoria Climbie and Peter Connolly (Baby P). As you read these chapters, you will be struck by different aspects. The aim is for these diverse and unique experiences to serve as a catalyst from which to critically reflect and evaluate your own practice and to consider how these might be experienced differently by others.

Despite the uniqueness of the narratives shared in this book, there are also a number of themes from which we can learn and which we can consider in relation to our own practice.

Trusting relationships

Without exception, all the contributors identified the importance of a trusting relationship with the social worker. A number of the contributors had experienced this first hand. Fay with Julia Armstrong (Chapter 11) and the young carers with Maggie Harris, young carers officer (Chapter 6), for example, whose roles had enabled them to build trust over a number of years; and Zoe and Jenny (Chapter 5) who met years later and were able to reflect back on their shared experience. Longevity in social work relationships is rare but the narratives in this book show that short-term involvement can have equally as significant an impact. There are varying examples of this in the stories such as the immediate connection and trust that Sarah felt with the respite carer in her account of caring for her son (Chapter 4); or the warmth that Mike felt as a child meeting his respite foster family for the first time (Chapter 3).

Conversely, there were examples of brief involvement that had a negative and long-lasting effect such as the social worker (Chapter 6) who met with one of the young carers in school and didn't share her name or explain what the meeting was for; or the social worker conducting Sue's carer's assessment (Chapter 13) who recorded information incorrectly and then didn't follow it up. The nature of social work is that we intervene at a point in people's lives when they are at their most vulnerable. First impressions count if people, who have little reason to trust others, are to trust you.

Persistence when working within the constraints of the system

Persistence isn't a skill or quality we often see identified in social work literature but was identified by several contributors in this book as a valued and necessary quality. It is particularly evident in the student testimonies in Chapter 15; the need to keep the service user central to your practice and to be persistent in seeking what is best for them, even if this requires challenging existing processes and structures. Rachel, in Chapter 10 (being assessed under the Care Act 2014) had experience of being allocated a social worker and then reallocated without her ever meeting or having direct contact from them. It is easy to judge but constraints of resource limitations, bureaucracy and heavy caseloads make it difficult to provide the level and type of care and support we would want to. This creates a system and a culture which can only respond to those with the highest levels of need, risk or crisis. However, as Rachel in Chapter 10 says, it is not really her problem that we are short staffed. Tim, the social worker contributor in Chapter 4, reflects on the drive for efficiency and the need to recognise that sometimes, the need for face-to-face contact and taking time to explain provision carefully, can save time, reduce worry and improve outcomes in the long run.

Power and anti-oppressive practice

A significant theme throughout the book has been that of power and the balance of power within the social worker–service user relationship. The nature of the statutory interventions being discussed is that there is often a significant power imbalance due to decisions being made and the influence a person can have on the outcome. This can be especially so for people who have already experienced significant oppression and discrimination in their lives as a result of their life experiences and identity. This is at its most significant in the chapters focusing on interventions which limit a person's choices such as in Chapter 12 being detained under the Mental Health Act and Chapter 14 where people lack, or have limited, capacity to make decisions about their lives or to communicate their wishes. It is in these areas that the need for anti-oppressive practice is at its most stark. While deprivation of someone's liberty may be in someone's best interest, this does not remove the need for the social workers to seek ways to involve someone in this process through clear communication and transparency.

Communication – clarity of information and transparency

This leads us on to another key theme within the chapters, that of communication and the clarity of information and transparency. Often, as social workers, we are engaging in processes which are familiar to us. Many students report feeling overwhelmed when first entering placement due to the daunting range of processes they need to learn and the jargon and terminology surrounding this. Imagine how it must feel for service users and carers. For them, there is already a significant power imbalance and this is heightened if they don't know what is going to happen. Gareth, in Chapter 8 when going through the adoption process, highlighted how important good communication and information was when navigating such a complex system. Sophie, in Chapter 9, stresses the importance of respecting her right to then make informed choices such as moving into residential care. All the chapters involving statutory interventions with children, highlighted the need to provide clear explanations and updates at regular intervals and to adapt these as the child grows older and can understand more. We can't predict outcomes and shouldn't make false promises, but we can provide regular updates on what the processes, options, outcomes and likely timescales are.

Accountability

Finally, personal and professional responsibility and accountability are key themes throughout the book. The importance of understanding your responsibilities and statutory duties are outlined in Chapter 2 when discussing the legal framework. Accounts shared in subsequent chapters show that this can be messy, open to interpretation and difficult to manage given the many constraints in practice. It is our duty as social workers, as outlined in the professionalism domain of the Professional Capabilities Framework, to 'take responsibility for our conduct, practice, self-care and development' (BASW, 2018, p. 27). Specifically, this involves working in partnership with people who use our services; promoting excellent practice; and challenging circumstances which compromise this (ibid., p. 26).

Activity

As a final activity, look back at the book and identify one chapter which has had the biggest impact on you. This could be because it has personal resonance; because of the emotional impact; because it challenged or developed your thinking; or because it relates most closely to your area of interest or practice setting.

Are you able to reflect on why it had such an impact?

What was it that was so significant?

How has it changed or informed your thinking?

In what ways will this inform your own interactions with service users or carers?

Aim of the book

The aim of this book has been to highlight the uniqueness of each person's story and enable you, as the reader, to gain insight into the lived experience. As a textbook on statutory interventions, the aim has been for you to develop your knowledge and understanding of the social work legal framework from the perspective of those who have experienced them first hand. This enables you to understand the law within the context of how it is experienced in practice. Contributors to this book are experts by experience and are valued for the contribution they make to developing and shaping social work provision and practice. While the focus of the book has been on legal interventions, the learning is transferrable to the much broader context of practice we engage in as social workers in local authority, independent, voluntary or private sector organisations – whether undertaking statutory and legal interventions or not. As mentioned throughout, the aim is not for the experiences shared in this book to be representative. You should not assume that this is, or will be, the experience of anyone else. What their experiences can do is give you insight – a window into the lived experience from which to challenge your own thinking, develop empathy and seek to understand.

The next step is for you to explore how you can gain this level of insight from the people you encounter in practice and how you can support and enable them to shape the direction and nature of social work provision in the future.

References

British Association of Social Work (BASW) (2018) Professional Capabilities Framework for Social Workers. Available at www.basw.co.uk/ professional-development/professional-capabilities-framework-pcf.

Head, B. W. (2011) Why not ask them? Mapping and promoting youth participation. *Children and Youth Services Review.* 33, 541–547.

Laming, H. (2003) The Victoria Climbie Inquiry. Available at: assets.publishing. service.gov.uk/government/uploads/system/uploads/attachment_data/ file/273183/5730.pdf.

Laming, H. (2009) The Protection of Children in England: A Progress Report. Available at: dera.ioe.ac.uk/8646/1/12_03_09_children.pdf.

Munro, E. (2011) *The Munro Review of Child Protection: Final Report – A Child-Centred System*.assets.publishing.service.gov.uk/government/uploads/system/ uploads/attachment_data/file/175391/Munro-Review.pdf.

INDEX

Printed by Printforce, the Netherlands